# Culturally Responsive Pedagogy

Fatima Pirbhai-Illich • Shauneen Pete • Fran Martin
Editors

# Culturally Responsive Pedagogy

Working towards Decolonization, Indigeneity
and Interculturalism

*Editors*
Fatima Pirbhai-Illich
University of Regina
Regina, Saskatchewan
Canada

Shauneen Pete
University of Regina
Regina, Saskatchewan
Canada

Fran Martin
University of Exeter
Exeter, United Kingdom

ISBN 978-3-319-46327-8          ISBN 978-3-319-46328-5 (eBook)
DOI 10.1007/978-3-319-46328-5

Library of Congress Control Number: 2017930194

Cover illustration: YAY Media AS / Alamy Stock Photo

Printed on acid-free paper

This Palgrave Macmillan imprint is published by Springer Nature
The registered company is Springer International Publishing AG
The registered company address is: Gewerbestrasse 11, 6330 Cham, Switzerland

*This book is dedicated to the children of Ranch Ehrlo Society, and to all the teachers who take on the challenge of disrupting hegemonic practices in education, and to the marginalized and minoritized students whose voices are not being heard and whose needs not being met.*

# FOREWORD

Decades ago a culturally responsive pedagogical movement emerged with researchers who offered multiple examples of research and experimentation with cultural inclusion in content and pedagogies to illustrate how it made a difference to some culturally marginalized students. This research movement came as a welcome relief for many of these students and for teachers searching for ways to transform conventional exclusive curricula and normalized cognitive assimilation. The movement has continued with much literature experimenting with teaching methods while asking: what curricula and pedagogical change can provide better educational outcomes for historically marginalized youth? To what extent does cultural inclusion of languages, cultural content, perspectives and histories of Indigenous, Black, Hispanic, Maori, Aborigines, etc. to the conventional curricula and structures of education make a difference to the educational outcomes of these students?

More important to me, a Mi'kmaw educator focussed on decolonizing education is – can cultural inclusion be achieved without a consideration, if not a wholesale radical change and transformation to the structures and conventions of schooling? Or, as one Indigenous professor aptly pointed out at a recent conference: Is this cultural inclusion just another form of lulling Indigenous peoples into assimilation and further colonialism? Will Indigenous students be the agents of their own self-determination or unreflective power agents to the neocolonial structures that continue to exist?

With the advantages of experience with culturally appropriate pedagogy and current theoretical lenses and narratives, the educational researchers in this book address some of these important questions. These academic researchers coming from Commonwealth countries (UK, Canada, Australia, New Zealand) as well as from Africa and Brazil share their educational research and narratives for addressing educational outcomes. These researchers build within critical theory more methods to provide some insight to the issue of inequities in society to specific groups of marginalized youth, revealing at the same time the educational complexities of diverse situations involving cultural diversity. They provide cross-cultural methodologies for teaching marginalized groups, including a critique of the teaching profession and its sense of goodness about itself that they point out needs to be unpacked, including the situations of unseen power and unwelcomed dominance of their cultural assets. They also seek to address the reason behind a disjuncture of learning outcomes among some groups of students within educational systems. Each of the researchers poses questions and provides examples across cultures to discover the methodological solutions under the rubric of culturally responsive pedagogy.

The editors have compiled this book of methodological insights not just to add research and more experiments and assessments of them to culturally responsive theory and pedagogy, but also to engage and critique what continues to be possible by them. These essays extend the reach for teachers to what can be done at their level of education and experience, although the editors point out rightly that the theoretical conversation about the merits and the struggles of pedagogy involving inclusion and diversity cannot be had without a fuller discussion of the power dynamics of colonialism and cognitive imperialism. What the essays reveal is that while teachers have some control in their classrooms to some aspects of learning, it is not all there is. The prevailing Eurocentric structures of education continue to yield to, if not perpetuate, systems of privilege, dominance, and power that will continue to marginalize some students and ultimately impoverish them all. These widespread structures are tied to and embedded in the historical colonial languages, discourses, and practices of education, economics and politics.

Decolonization is posed by the editors as a needed process for unpacking and revealing what has happened to create the inequities and how diverse groups have both been victimized by and challenged by educational developments that do not include their own knowledge systems, perspectives and assets. The concept of decolonization connotes a transformational change that has yet to be fully understood and realized by educators. Consider how the Canadian Council of Ministers of Education in Canada have spent more than the last decade with escalating mandates about improving successes of Aboriginal students in Canada, urging various curricula and pedagogical changes in culturally responsive form. Yet, the variances in educational outcomes continue with these same students, which acknowledges the need for something else, and it may not be or should be totally on the backs of teachers or culturally responsive researchers to find.

Similarly situated are students from other colonial countries, and this book reveals such details from the data generated by researchers in Africa, New Zealand, Australia and other countries, where historically marginalized groups are found. Culturally responsive pedagogy has generated some positively welcomed changes in some classrooms as a better fit with one's lived experience. But it is all too apparent that method alone will not change the success equation for these students or the macro-dynamics through culturally responsive pedagogy. One critique of culturally responsive pedagogies is its focus on supporting culturally distinct minorities with pedagogical inclusive curricula that often infers, however, is that the 'other' requires something to learn, a shift in their view or their skills rather than macro-structures in the whole educational system itself that needs to be changed. Without a fuller examination and change of the structural and macro-colonial effects of Eurocentric education system and a deeper comprehension of the psychological and sociological harm done to the continuing realities of culturally marginalized students, a pedagogical method that does not balance or exclude their knowledges, perspectives, histories and experience will not change the existing structural inequities. A structural deconstruction of the material and cognitive effects is necessary that involves having an evaluation of the long-lasting and continuing relationship of the students with colonialism, cognitive assimilation and imperialism, and conventionality of privileging and "othering" of the students that need to be interrogated and addressed. Perhaps more importantly, each educator must come to the awareness of their own nature of existence that is tied to the racialized, colonial enterprise, the colonizer and the colonized within our minds and hearts and normalized discourses. It is crucial to comprehend how the enterprise has privileged certain groups, their languages and their conventionalities as problematic assets that continue to marginalize other groups.

Education is not just in a state of a crisis for Indigenous peoples, but in a state of crisis for all Canadians and within other countries as well, as noted in this collection. The struggle to unravel colonial education will require multiple responses in multiple sites and not at the pedagogical level alone. More importantly, reform and change will require everyone involved in policy, leadership and educational practice to acknowledge and re-examine the foundations of their cognitive dependencies on and normalization of Eurocentric ideologies and discourses, opening themselves to the best of a wide range of knowledge systems and perspectives drawn from diverse experiences and cultures and from other theoretical critiques. Indeed, the balancing and cocreation of knowledge system for education for all will need to be achieved if we are to reconcile with the Indigenous peoples in Canada as the Truth and Reconciliation Commission in Canada has urged.

Decolonization is an important foundation for addressing the crisis in education although the process of deconstructing the conventional privileges and dominance of Eurocentric structures and reconstructing a cognitive just curriculum must be more fully understood and addressed (Battiste. *Decolonizing education: Nourishing the learning spirit*, 2013). The systemic problem is not in the student(s), in their language, culture, community, in the acquisition of basic skills, but in the existing asymmetrical power relations among cultural groups in the Canadian society. Indigenous peoples are oppressed peoples because of persistent historical systemic racism and prejudice. By focussing on methods and strategies educators make invisible the historical role that schools have played and continue to play, not only in discriminating against many culturally different groups, but also in denying their humanity. The inequities within education and employment, physical and mental health services, the high levels of incarceration of Indigenous peoples, the variances in life and death indicators, and much more must be seen as not the issue of minor adjustments of methods or practices or programmes, but rather an overarching macro-problem of cultural and cognitive imperialism, systemic racism, colonialism, privileging and colonized training of the mind, bodies and spirit of all peoples which requires a more critical reflexive examination of our systems, ourselves and our future plans to affect transformational change. The macro-privileging process of certain groups, heritages and languages has ignored the inherent constitutional and legislative rights of Indigenous students and knowledge systems, without which continue to affect their well-being, their sense of themselves and their belonging to the local, national and global enterprise. The constitutional framework that recognizes aboriginal and treaty rights in Canada generates an emerging reconciliation of indigenous knowledge and culture in learning and pedagogy that must be translated into policy and practice in all public forms of education. It thus creates a context for systemic educational reform and cognitive justice to include indigenous science, indigenous humanities and Aboriginal languages, as well as changes to existing educational philosophy, pedagogy and teacher education, not an add and stir approach but a systemic change.

Saskatoon, Canada                                                    Marie Battiste

# Acknowledgements

We would like to thank and acknowledge the support of our colleagues, students, families and friends all of whom have given inspiration in their own ways.

We would especially like to thank the authors of the chapters who, despite challenges, have carried forward a radical change in instructional practice for those students who have consistently been failed by the hegemonic education systems.

I, Fatima Pirbhai-Illich would like to thank the education board of the Ranch Ehrlo Society, and in particular Hayley Maurer, Director of Education, for the generosity they showed over the years in opening up spaces for collaborative teaching and research that led to the concept of this book. I would also like to thank the University of Regina, Faculty of Education, Dean's Office, for providing financial support and the space for the research to be carried out. Finally, for their financial support, I thank the Saskatchewan Instructional and Development Research Unit and the University of Regina President's Social Sciences and Humanities Research Council.

Finally, we would like to acknowledge and thank Cynthia Schultz for her unwavering trust and commitment to helping us bring this project to fruition.

### Reference

Battiste, M. (2013). *Decolonizing education: Nourishing the learning spirit*. Saskatoon and Vancouver: Purich Press and University of British Columbia Press.

# CONTENTS

# LIST OF FIGURES

# List of Tables

# PART I

# CHAPTER 1

# Culturally Responsive Pedagogies: Decolonization, Indigeneity and Interculturalism

*Fatima Pirbhai-Illich, Shauneen Pete and Fran Martin*

## INTRODUCTION

In this opening chapter we provide a rationale for the book, centring on a critique of what Grosfoguel (2011) calls a "global colonial power matrix" which is a modern/colonial, capitalist/patriarchal world-system of intersecting global hierarchies "produced by thinkers from the North" (p. 10).

[T]he history of Western civilization articulated in what I have called the "modern/colonial capitalist/patriarchal western-centric/Christian-centric world- system" has privileged the culture, knowledge, and epistemology produced by the West inferiorizing the rest. No culture in the world remained untouched by European modernity. There is no absolute outside to this system. The monologism and monotopic global design of the West relates to other cultures and peoples from a

F. Pirbhai-Illich (✉) · S. Pete
University of Regina, Regina, Saskatchewan, Canada
e-mail: Fatima.Pirbhai-Illich@uregina.ca; Shauneen.Pete@uregina.ca

F. Martin
University of Exeter, Exeter, United Kingdom
e-mail: Fran.Martin@exeter.ac.uk

© The Author(s) 2017
F. Pirbhai-Illich et al. (eds.), *Culturally Responsive Pedagogy*,
DOI 10.1007/978-3-319-46328-5_1

position of superiority and is deaf toward the cosmologies and epistemologies of the non-Western world. (Grosfoguel 2011, p. 24)

We use critical theory as an overarching framework, putting philosophical thinking to work on the real world issues that are the subject of each chapter, in order "to make positive transformation possible" (Martínez-Alemán 2015, p. 8). Since its inception in the 1920s, "social sciences have employed critical theory to de-center grand narratives of social and political subjugation" (Martínez-Alemán 2015, p. 8), in this case those of colonialism and race, with the goal of emancipating people from the structures that support white privilege and marginalize all those who are culturally different. The structure that supports white privilege here is the global power matrix which Grosfoguel identifies as an *ongoing* colonial project that influences all aspects of life including education. We then focus on culturally responsive pedagogy (CRP) and how its inception grew out of the civil rights movement in the USA, when there were concerns about the educational achievement of African American students (Ladson-Billings 1995). At the time, CRP was developed to address the deficit theorizing (Berryman et al. 2013) about African Americans that was characteristic of White American teachers. It is our contention that this has been and continues to be insufficient to address the global colonial power matrix, and drawing on our own work in teacher education contexts, we set out the core ideas and arguments that form the foundation of the book, followed by a brief summary of the ways in which each chapter addresses these ideas.

First of all, in keeping with our positioning of this book as a decolonizing project, we talk about our own identities and subjectivities. Our purpose is to make visible the sociocultural and political-historic contexts that have influenced our "selves", our biases and the standpoints (Harding 2009) we inhabit in relation to each other, our work and this book. In doing so we recognize that all attempts to know, and to cocreate new knowledge, are socially situated – as individuals our standpoints will necessarily limit what can be known and what we are permitted to know. It is through solidarity and critical intercultural dialogue that we are able to begin to imagine human relations differently, as in the way Chandra Mohanty (2003) re-envisions feminist solidarity as constituting "the most principled way to cross borders – to decolonize knowledge and practice anticapitalist critique" (p. 7). We are also cognizant of Bowell's (2016) assertion that, while both the dominant and the dominated occupy perspectives, the dominated are much more successfully placed to achieve a standpoint. Nevertheless, it is not impossible for those who occupy non-marginalized perspectives to become part of the process of helping reach a shared critical consciousness with respect to the effects of power structures on epistemic production (n.p.).

## IDENTITY, SUBJECTIVITY AND SELF

As teacher educators, we are actively engaged in reforming teacher education and school-based practices that are often shaped by white dominance. We posit that white dominance in all its forms (racism, colonialism,...) has had a detrimental effect on racialized peoples, but we recognize that it has also had a negative effect on members of the dominant group. As we work to reform education we must by necessity engage in complex, power-laden relationships with one another.

Our professional identities have been shaped by emerging theory and practices associated with multicultural education, critical race theory and culturally relevant pedagogies; yet, at the same time, we have often witnessed (and participated in) practices which re-inscribed white dominance in our teaching. These pedagogical practices are rarely tailored to the needs of minoritized (Gillborn 2010), marginalized, linguistically and culturally diverse students. Thus, we witness a large percentage of minoritized students engaging in school practices that are constructed to suit students and teachers from the dominant culture. To disrupt this tendency in teacher education we are naming dominance and engaging predominantly white, middle-class teacher candidates in critical discussions and analyses of white privilege (Ladson-Billings 1994), colour blindness (Ladson-Billings and Tate 1995; Bonilla-Silva 2014), institutional discrimination and hegemonic practices perpetrated towards minoritized and marginalized students. Decolonizing pedagogical practices and the curriculum become a necessary part of such a project, as does locating ourselves with regard to these issues.

Fatima Pirbhai-Illich. I am a female, Canadian citizen who was born in Tanganyika (Tanzania after independence) to African parents of Indian descent. I immigrated to Canada as a teenager and was educated in Tanzania, Kenya, Canada and England. I have worked in tertiary level teacher education for over 20 years and have lived in many parts of the world including Australia, New Zealand, Tajikistan, China, Singapore and

Saudi Arabia. Presently, I am an associate professor and the chair in Language and Literacy Education at the University of Regina, which is situated on the ancestral lands of the First Nations peoples and in particular the Treaty 4 people. I acknowledge First Nations peoples as the traditional custodians of this land and extend my respect and gratitude to the descendants of this land. As a racialized, minoritized, marginalized and visible scholar of colour, I consider myself an ally to those who have been categorized into similar group memberships. I am interested in postcolonial issues of race and injustice in schools and my community-based research focusses on issues of social justice and in particular, critical multicultural literacy education for marginalized and disenfranchised youth.

Tansi, Dr. Shauneen Pete nitisiyihkson. I am Cree from Little Pine First Nation in Treaty 6 territory, Saskatchewan, Canada. As a teen parent I wanted to offer my daughter a more culturally affirming education than I had received as an urban First Nations person. I registered in the Indian Teacher Education Program (ITEP) at the University of Saskatchewan and began my career as an urban high school teacher, later serving as an Aboriginal Educational Consultant in the school division. In these roles I modelled CRP, expanded the Elders in Schools program and advocated for First Nations Language program development. As an associate professor I model indigenous and decolonizing pedagogies with pre-service teachers in the Faculty of Education. I am completing my term as the Executive Lead of Indigenization at the University of Regina.

Fran Martin. I am a twin, a farmer's daughter, born and raised in the South East of England. My formal education was almost entirely in fee-paying, independent schools. I have seven brothers and sisters and numerous nieces and nephews, great-nieces and great-nephews. My maternal grandmother was born in India and moved with the family back to the UK when she was 3 years old. I have relatives in Australia and New Zealand, and strong family connections with Canada, Scotland and South Africa. I have come to recognize that these are not accidental global connections, but are rooted in the history of British Imperialism and the subsequent formation of the Commonwealth Nations. I am complicit in the ongoing project of global colonization through my birth into White European society, through my White British national identity and through the privileges systematically afforded to people of my race. I work as an ally with these issues through my teaching with pre-service teachers, and research in critical interculturality.

It was Fatima who, having worked with CRP in her Language and Literacy Education course for pre-service teachers since 2007, realized that it was not having the desired effect in its current form. Over the years a number of iterations of the course were developed (Pirbhai-Illich 2010, 2013) to incorporate a relational dimension (Berryman et al. 2013) and a critical service-learning component (Pirbhai-Illich 2013). Fran started working with Fatima as an ally to the cause of social justice, and because both of their works focussed on the ways in which the intercultural spaces afforded by service-learning activities are profoundly affected by colonialism (Martin and Pirbhai-Illich 2015). As the concept of the book began to take shape, some of the contributions were from Aboriginal scholars and it was at this point that Shauneen, Fatima's colleague at the University of Regina, joined the editorial team.

As our positioning pieces mentioned earlier, we come from very different locations in time and space. We each have our own experiences and histories of colonialism, although we all work in education our fields are different (Fatima, Language and Literacy Education; Shauneen, Indigenization; and Fran, Geographical and Global Education), and we have each taken different approaches to the study and practice of intercultural learning. The intersectionalities of ourselves have provided a rich intercultural, third space (Bhabha 1994; Soja 2009) to explore together, paying attention to: the language and discourses evident in our conversations; how we consciously or unconsciously positioned ourselves and each other; and how we negotiated our differences as, for example, when we gave different "readings" of the chapters and had to come to an agreement over what changes to suggest to the authors. To assist us in this task, we audio-recorded some of our meetings, and used these as an example (see Chapter 11) of what it means to live with and learn from differences, in ways that are productive and do not close down those differences. "Such a dialogic encounter of...cultures does not result in merging or mixing. Each retains its own unity and *open* totality, but they are mutually enriched" (Bakhtin 1986, p. 7). This requires an open history, and an ethics of responsibility (Phipps 2013) towards each other for our choices and the consequences of our actions.

> [I]ntercultural ethics can commit to methods which may enable the seeking of justice and equality in relationships. This would take the field beyond the "dirtiest of words", research, and towards an embrace of complexity and open-endedness; engagement with what is known or believed to be

restorative, collaborative, participatory, sensory, even healing; to allowing for methodological creativity and artistry, which moves towards shaping an intercultural poetics (Phipps 2013, p. 23).

## WHY IS THIS BOOK NEEDED? THE COLONIAL WORLD-SYSTEM AS CONTEXT

In this section we explore two connected ideas and what they mean for education: It is not a postcolonial world, and the world is an interconnected system. The idea that we are not in a postcolonial era has been argued by many postcolonial theorists who contend that even though political independence has been gained, a colonization of the mind continues (Sharp 2009; Dascal 2009; Thiong'o 1986). Dussel (2006) and Grosfoguel (2011) go beyond this to argue that the current world-system is a colonial world-system, because its very basis emerged from the "moments of the Portuguese expansion into the South Atlantic and toward the Indian Ocean, [and] Spain's 'discovery of America'" (Dussel 2006, p. 18). They also argue that modernity had its origins in these beginnings of colonialism in the late 1400s, rather than in the period of enlightenment in the 1600s in northern Europe (Burton and Flores Osorio 2011). These roots are important in providing a new understanding of the patterns of thought that characterize modernity – such as rationality, secularization (loss of religious influence at a societal level), objectivism, commodification (everything has a monetary value), separation of private and public spheres of life and universalism (Mitchell 2000). In locating modernity in the colonial expansion from Spain and Portugal in the mid-1400s, Dussel (2006) and Grosfoguel (2011) identify the nature of the relationship between the State and Religion at that time as a key factor in how the expansion took place. Catholicism and governance in Spain and Portugal was inseparable – there was not the notion of freewill separate from God's will that there is today – the ruling monarchs saw all their actions as being sanctioned by God. Thus, those who were sent to "discover" new worlds did not hesitate to appropriate lands because they embodied the God-given rights bestowed on them by their monarchs; they needed no other rationale than this. It is therefore argued that the new laws and institutions of modernity, and associated notions of citizenship and democracy, were "formed in a process of colonial interaction with, and domination/exploitation of, non-Western people" (Grosfoguel 2011, p. 12).

In essence, Dussel (2012) argues that modernity is itself a colonized and colonizing idea that assumes a way of thinking about development based on a categorization of periods and which entails moving from one period to the next, leaving the *old* and moving into the new, from which perspective premodern would be seen to be *backward* to modernity's *advanced* ways of being and thinking. It is therefore a necessary part of the decolonizing process to put forward a counter-narrative, a non-Eurocentric "trans[-]modern opposition to modernity's irrational violence based on the reason of the Other" (Burton and Flores Osorio 2011, p. 23). Trans-modern is a way of thinking that does not categorize by developmental stages, but sees the cultures that have been negated and ignored by the colonizers, as neither modern nor, therefore, postmodern.

> They are simultaneously *pre*-modern (older than modernity), *contemporary* to Modernity, and soon, *trans*-modern as well. *Post*-modernism is a final stage in modern European/North American culture, the "core" of Modernity. Chinese or Vedic cultures could never be European *post*-modern, but rather are something very different as a result of their distinct roots (Dussel 2012, p. 42).

Arguably, the most devastating aspect of colonialism (Said 1985) was the way in which the colonizers created a discourse about the "Other" that enabled them to justify the colonial project – taking ownership of indigenous lands, erasing language and culture and exploiting human and natural resources (Pennycook 1998). This was a discourse of exoticization, paternalism, dehumanization and infantilization – shown in a self-other dichotomy of us-them, like-unlike, natural-exotic, superior-inferior, human-savage, civilized-uncivilized – where the Other was marked by the visible difference of skin colour, resulting in the construction of race and racial hierarchies: "the black is not a man" (Fanon 1967, p. 8). In North America and Australia, British colonists were "of the view that Aboriginal peoples would eventually die out or become totally assimilated into European culture" (Cote-Meek 2014, p. 47). This deeply racist ideology had a profound effect on how the world was constructed from then on, economically and politically, along what De Sousa Santos (2007) has called *abyssal lines*,[1] and has been experienced as extreme ontological and epistemological violence (Fanon 1967; Grosfoguel 2011; Cote-Meek 2014) leading to generational trauma the effects of which have pervaded all social systems including education, as we argue below.

## THE INFLUENCE OF THE COLONIAL WORLD-SYSTEM ON EDUCATION

In this section we argue that the colonial world-system has had a profound influence on education – from the ways in which schools are organized and the nature of classroom relationships, to the curriculum that is taught and how students are assessed. In discussing the evidence for this statement we draw on the work of scholars from the field of indigenous studies and English as an Additional Language Program, arguing that their work has implications for education globally. In this work, settler colonialism refers to the colonial expansion into those areas of the world (Australia, Canada, USA) where White Europeans, particularly those from the UK, took possession of indigenous lands and imposed Eurocentric systems of governance, education and society, leading to those countries being seen to be Anglo-Saxon (Cote-Meek 2014).

Tuck and Gaztambide-Fernández (2013) argue that settler colonialism "operat[es] with a logic of *elimination*" where "the primary motive for elimination is not race (or religion, ethnicity, grade of civilization, etc.) but access to territory" (p. 73). This "logic of elimination is embedded into every aspect of the settler colonial structures and its disciplines" (Tuck and Gaztambide-Fernández 2013, p. 73) and represents invasion as a structure, rather than an event. In other words, school policies, the systems in which they operate, and the curriculum for instruction have all been colonized and thus constructed in the dominant, Eurocentric image. The purpose of such an education system is to create a model of imagined nationhood (Anderson 1983) to which everyone has to conform. Cote-Meek (2014) argues that this, in the Canadian context, was felt as a series of violences as indigenous people were robbed of their lands, their identities and their children. "No branch of learning was left untouched by the colonial experience" (Cote-Meek 2014, p. 48) and "one of the primary tolls of colonialism was the education system" (Cote-Meek 2014, p. 49).

As two of the chapters in the book attest, one of the most damaging and traumatic colonial structures that lasted into the latter decades of the twentieth century was the residential school system (Canada, Pete, Chapter 3), known as mission schools in Australia (Daly, Chapter 10). The systems used race as a marker of the imagined community/nation (Anderson 1983), with residential schools specifically designed to eradicate Aboriginal ways of being and to replace them with white settler ways of being, the effect of which has been to mark the memories/collective consciousness of indigenous communities forever (Cote-Meek 2014). In Canada, there have been various moves from the 1970s onwards to address this through legislation that gave "Indian Control of Indian Education" (Cote-Meek 2014, p. 46) with a focus on language, culture and cultural preservation, followed by a shift towards remedial programmes that aimed to "provide a 'remedy' for Aboriginal's lack of success in education. Often... [including] upgrading reading and writing or developing writing skills" (Cote-Meek 2014, p. 56). Despite these efforts, there continues to be a huge attainment gap between Aboriginal students and their non-Aboriginal counterparts. Cote-Meek (2014) argues that this is because, with a focus on remediation, "the gaze is turned towards the Aboriginal student as lacking" (p. 59) – a deficit orientation typical of colonial thinking; and "if white teachers can learn the appropriate cultural rules, we need not hire black teachers" (Razack 1998, pp. 9–10), so there is no need to diversify the teacher population. Underlying both of these is the argument that a focus on cultural revitalization is in the Settler Europeans' interest because,

> while a very important and worthwhile goal for Aboriginal peoples, [it] assisted with getting colonial institutions of the hook by decentering the racism and *violence* [emphasis added] that is so inherent in the colonial regime and in the education of Aboriginal peoples (Cote-Meek 2014, p. 57).

Following Fanon (1967), Cote-Meek (2014) emphasizes the importance of naming (colonial violence and abuse) and telling (bearing witness, narrative testimonies). This is part of a project of making visible the traumas that are held in indigenous bodies and their collective consciousness, and of speaking back to, or against, the dominant narratives that deny the continuing presence of colonialism. She also warns of the dangers of doing so. Naming violence can also invoke the dominant patronizing and deficit discourse of pity for the Other used by white settlers. There is a history of pathologizing indigenous peoples, but Cote-Meek poses the question, who is sick, the abused or the abuser? There is also a need to move the focus away from abnormality and individualism and to refocus on the perpetrators – on white peoples and whiteness and *their* need to change, to disrupt their colonial patterns of behaviour and to disrupt systems and structures that continue to harm.

We agree with a focus on violence and argue that the ways of thinking about education as a colonial tool can be applied to contemporary westernized education systems whether in settled nations or not. We and the other authors in this book see violence being done in every situation – violence towards English as Additional Language (EAL) students, violence to indigenous students, and violence to minoritized and marginalized students. For example, it is no accident that in each of the education contexts discussed by the authors in this book, English is the medium for instruction. Janks (2010) argues that the high symbolic value accorded to English "is an effect of powerful colonial discourses which continue into the present" (p. 128). Further, it is standard English that holds symbolic value, with other Englishes (e.g. Aboriginal English, Daly, Chapter 10) being positioned as inferior. Due to the inextricable connection between language and culture (Gunderson 2000) the use of English as the medium for instruction immediately puts EAL students at a disadvantage; in viewing those features of EAL speakers' English that are not standard as immature, teachers use this "as evidence of imperfect or poorly developed language . . . [which is] taken to signify lack of intelligence or ability to learn" (Gunderson 2000, p. 694). This is accompanied by concerns of EAL students and their loss of their heritage language and sense of identity, and how these students exist in the between spaces, no longer feeling centrally connected to their home culture, nor being able to see themselves in the imagined community (Anderson 1983) of their new country. The effects of this are often seen in higher drop-out rates of immigrant students from high schools (Gunderson 2008; Pirbhai-Illich 2006).

There is nothing in westernized education systems that does not create violence, from the assumptions about what counts as education and whose knowledge counts in the curriculum to the teacher–learner relationships and the methods of instruction that are used. The abyssal line is thriving in schools. This begins from the first moment students step inside school – at the age of 3 in some countries – and begs the question: What fundamental changes are necessary for the situation to improve? We are not the first to raise questions about the state of education in the twenty-first century, but the majority of critiques are linked to neo-liberalism (Apple 2004, 2006, 2014; Ball 2001, 2012; Bourdieu 1998; Campbell and Pederson 2001; Giroux 2014; Kohl 2006; Lipman 2004, 2011; Madrid 2003; Sleeter 2011) and we perceive this to be a further example of Eurocentric analysis that avoids acknowledgment of colonialism as integral to neo-liberal structures.

Often the birth of neoliberalism is traced to recent history – "Future historians may well look upon the years 1978–80 as a revolutionary turning point in the world's social and economic history" (Harvey 2005, p. 1), and "one of the difficulties of providing a history of neoliberalism is that it has emerged at different times and in different guises over the last 30 years" (Davies and Bansel 2007, p. 250), – focussing on the differing degrees to which nations applied the market-economy model to education through "heightened individualism", a reduction in central government responsibility, increased local accountability, performativity, competition for funding and evaluation by results (Davies and Bansel 2007, p. 251). While we do not dispute this analysis, we contend that the attribution of neoliberalism to the recent past sidesteps the longer history that traces back to colonialism, in the same way that western accounts of modernity find their roots in European enlightenment rather than colonization in the late 1400s. As Cote-Meek (2014) argues for an explicit naming of violence and trauma, we also argue (supported by Dussel 2006; Grosfoguel 2011) for an explicit naming of the current world-system as colonial. The structures that hold together schools and the academy are colonial and influence what is taught, how it is taught and who does the teaching (Cote-Meek 2014). It is our view that a response to this *has* to be de-colonial, to view the relationships within classrooms as intercultural, and to draw on indigenous and de-colonial scholarship to inform how this intercultural space might be understood in order to develop pedagogies that better serve those students who continue to be marginalized and pathologized by the current system. In this book we are therefore making pedagogy political (Giroux 2000) by identifying the ways in which the colonial exists in education systems worldwide, proposing that CRPs in their current form are insufficient for addressing this issue, and offering a variety of ways in which we (all authors) are extending CRP in our respective contexts.

## WHAT IS THIS BOOK ABOUT? CRP AS A DECOLONIZING PRACTICE

CRP, also called culturally relevant teaching and culturally relevant pedagogy, has been the subject of many publications (Ladson-Billings 1992, 1994, 1995; Gay 2000; Berryman et al. 2013). It grew out of the need to address the ways in which education in multicultural societies systematically disadvantaged students whose cultures are not reflected in mainstream pedagogies, curricula and organizational structures. Gloria Ladson-Billings

(1992, 1994, 1995), generally acknowledged to be the founder of CRP, developed the theory and associated pedagogical approaches in the USA during the 1990s. Concerned about the significant educational underachievement of African Americans, she drew on Critical Race Theory (CRT, Ladson-Billings and Tate 1995) to inform her work. CRT examines the appearance of race and racism across dominant cultural modes of expression. It has a dual focus of revealing how institutional inequalities based on race pervade the experiences of people of colour in every aspect of their lives, and on giving a voice to those whose experiences have been silenced by using story-telling and other narrative forms to "heal the wounds of pain caused by racial oppression" (Ladson-Billings and Tate 1995: 57). As Tuck and Gaztambide-Fernández (2013) describe, the settler colonial curricular project as one "of *replacement*, which aims to vanish Indigenous peoples and replace them with settlers, who see themselves as the rightful claimants to land, and indeed, as indigenous" (p. 73), so do Ladson-Billings and Tate (1995) examine the intersection of race and property and its connection to education. Property is understood in three ways: people of colour were the property of whites (slavery); Native American lands were appropriated by whites; and whiteness is portrayed "as the ultimate property" (Ladson-Billings and Tate 1995, p. 58) to have, due to the privileges it receives, and yet it is only possible for white peoples to possess (see McIntosh 1990 for a discussion of white privilege). Whiteness is therefore a key target for CRT, with narratives of the marginalized and dispossessed peoples being a crucial tool for speaking back to the constructions of race that are endemic in dominant discourses and felt on a daily basis as microaggressions and institutional racism.

Ladson-Billings' (1995) goal, through a CRT analysis, was to name the educational "failure" of African Americans as a racialized phenomenon and a product of colonialism.

In Black America, the main [colonial] instrument, though not the only one, of deculturalization is "mis-education", [which is] responsible for [the] "destructive effects on the Black mind by schools that use a pedagogy and curriculum that deliberately omits, distorts or trivializes the role of African people in and their seminal contributions to world history and culture" (Dascal 2009, p. 310).

Multicultural education was the initial response to these processes of deculturalization, but it was taken up by white educators in ways that made it palatable to them, and thus became assimilationist (Ladson-Billings 1995), superficial and focussed on essentialist views of culture (Sleeter and McClaren 1995). Ladson-Billings therefore saw a tension between multicultural education and the tenets of CRT.

In developing CRP, Ladson-Billings (1995) aimed to apply CRT's central ideas to pedagogical approaches that teachers could use in the classroom:

> Culturally relevant pedagogy rests on three criteria or propositions: (a) Students must experience academic success; (b) students must develop and/or maintain cultural competence; and (c) students must develop a critical consciousness through which they challenge the status quo of the current social order (p.160).

To this she added five key characteristics that were shown by teachers who were culturally responsive in their teaching: a belief that all students were capable of academic success; pedagogy is an art; that teachers saw themselves as members of the community; they saw teaching as a way to give back to the community; and they held the belief that teaching was mining – or pulling knowledge out, and that the curriculum was therefore created and shared by teacher *and* students (Ladson-Billings 1995). CRP works from the assumptions that much of mainstream education is framed on the cultural, historical and social norms of the dominant group. The approach not only unpacks these norms through the development of critical consciousness but also focusses on the diverse knowledges of minoritized students as derived from home and community (Moll et al. 1992). Culturally relevant teachers, rather than positioning minoritized students as deficient, encourage them to utilize their funds of knowledge in the process of developing "a community of learners" (Ladson-Billings 1995, p. 163) that includes the teacher "self" in the equation. The teacher, alongside the learners, collectively explores issues of social inequality that they all experience with the aim of deepening the understanding about the transient nature of knowledge (curriculum, resources, the purpose of schooling and social change) and of co-constructing critical consciousness. In this way, CRP serves to disrupt the dominant idea of the white teacher as racially neutral while at the same time challenging the assumption of the white teacher as knower imparting wisdom upon racially diverse learners.

CRP has been extended through the Te Kotahitanga project to a culturally responsive pedagogy of *relations* (Bishop et al. 2007),

accomplished when teachers create contexts where learners can be more self-determining; where pedagogy is interactive and dialogic; where the cultural experiences of all students have validity; where knowledge is actively co-constructed; and where participants are connected through the establishment of a common vision of what constitutes educational excellence (Berryman et al. 2013, p. 6).

However, in the application of CRP there have been barriers that have affected its successful implementation in schools, which Sleeter (2011) identifies as: "persistent simplistic conceptions about its meaning, a research base that while promising is thin, and political backlash prompted by fear of its potential to upset the existing social order", with "the growing impact of neo-liberal reforms" (p. 8) being seen as a key influencing factor. While these barriers exist, the argument we put forward in this book is that there are far more fundamental barriers than those attributed to neoliberalism – notably the systemic violences that continue to pervade westernized education systems, and that have their roots in colonialism. We have also noticed a trend in the ways in which CRP has been adopted by white teachers for CRP to be transformed into an easily implemented list of teacher behaviours, which focus on raising educational achievement of the students, and do not require the teachers to raise their own critical consciousness – thus distancing CRP from its original roots in CRT. In effect, CRP as often practiced by white teachers does not require them to consider their own complicity in the ongoing project of colonialism. In the countries where students of colour and indigenous students are minoritized this is a particular issue because, although student populations from diverse backgrounds are increasing, the proportion of the teaching population from diverse backgrounds is not keeping pace. For example, in the USA only 52% of the student population was white in 2011–12, yet "eighty-two percent of public school teachers are white" (Ahmad and Boser 2014, p. 4).

We recognize that systems often work against our attempts towards socially just education by requiring high levels of conformity for all educators, be they members of the dominant group or those who have been minoritized. In the face of the pressure to conform, the work of deconstructing dominance is left to already marginalized educators and to the allies who support this work;

while those educators who inhabit dominant ways of being are rarely encouraged to play any role at all. In our pedagogical practices we work towards higher levels of consciousness about this tendency and practice re-positioning power, authority, voice and praxis. As we've grown in our practices of Culturally Responsive Pedagogies, a political practice in itself, we have engaged with the ideas of culture, race, racial dominance, colonialism and systems of oppression as they are expressed in education.

## Overview of the Book

This book offers a unique view of the effects of colonialism as a global phenomenon. As educators of colour and as allies who work alongside them towards the goal of social justice, we are a diverse group of contributors. We come from various communities of origin and work in seven countries. Collectively our voices offer a variety of approaches to culturally relevant pedagogy that work towards *critical relationality*, by that we mean, our connectedness to place, our connectedness to our various experiences of colonization, oppression and dominance, our desire for a more socially just education system and our expressed commitments to navigate the troubling spaces of these relationships with one another. The importance of classroom relationships, and the need to go beyond these to relationships with families, communities, lands, spaces and places, are a common thread through the chapters that follow. So too is the concept of care, which is problematized through questions about who cares, how that care is expressed, who is invested in different modes of caring and why. Finally, all authors conduct critical analyses of the political and historical circumstances within which their research is located. This is accompanied by each author naming those discourses that are so often silenced in Eurocentric accounts of difference (whiteness, white privilege and racism) and being hyper-self-reflexive in consideration of their own relation to these discourses. Each of the authors is doing something to change the status quo. They are working in different ways with culturally responsive/relevant pedagogies and, according to their personal and professional orientations, are extending our understanding of CRP and how it might transform not only classroom practices, but also the structures that support them including the education of pre-service and in-service teachers. To honour each author's way of being expressed through their writing, and in keeping with the focus of this book, we have not imposed a common structure on the chapters. The reader will find diversity in the content, style and structure as well as in authors and their subjectivities.

The book is organized into four parts. The chapter under Part 1 sets the context. Part 2 has four chapters, which have a common focus on decolonizing higher education and the professional development of teachers. In Chapter 2, Abdul Jabbar and Mohammed Mirza illustrate the complexity of supporting culturally diverse students in the UK Higher Education Business Schools and how this complexity is compounded by the pedagogy commonly employed, which is shaped and dominated by aspirations of western culture. They investigate the cultural constructs of culturally responsive teaching within the structured framework of the five pillars of Jabbar and Hardaker (2013), proposing that within higher education there are fundamental gaps that should be developed to consistently engage with students in a fair, equitable manner. In Chapter 3, Shauneen Pete offers a self-study view of her efforts to indigenize her teaching in a required undergraduate course designed to provide mostly white, middle-class pre-service teachers with a better understanding of pedagogy. She uses the Idle No More (INM) movement, which emerged in the winter of 2013 in resistance to a government bill that called for changes to the Fisheries Act and the Navigable Waters Act, resulting in the diminishing of First Nations inherent rights. The dramatic events became the focus of the emergent curriculum in her course, while self-study allowed her the opportunity to interrogate dominant views of pedagogy and the "good teacher", resulting in a commitment to radical indigeneity in her own teaching. Chapter 4 continues the theme of decolonization of teacher education, this time in the context of English as a Second or Other Language endorsement programme at a south-eastern university in the United States. The chapter is co-authored by the programme leader, Gertrude Tinker Sachs, and the participants in the programme, Barbara Clark, Meral Durkaya, Annmarie Jackson, Charles Johnson, William Lake and Patty Limb. The course aimed to challenge the hegemony of English and a Eurocentric world view, and included a 10-week English literacy practicum in the homes of multilingual refugee mothers. The chapter provides a rich account of how the nontraditional teacher/student classroom site, in which the mother is positioned as knower and leader, and in which the teachers become collaborators and respecters of the mother's funds of knowledge. In the final chapter of this section, Andrea Blair reflects on her attempts to develop herself as a culturally responsive and ethically responsible practitioner in Brazil. Using an autoethnographic methodology, she draws on her experiences of teaching English to marginalized children in Brazil, coming to the conclusion that CRP cannot be applied as a prescriptive solution to practice. Deconstructing norms and assumptions so that difference is no longer understood as deficit, disrupting ethnocentrism to critically reflecting on practice and curriculum design as well as developing more ethical, caring and loving relationships are all important steps to take in practice if CRP is to become more than mere rhetoric.

Part 3 brings three chapters together each of which investigates culturally responsive pedagogies as they are practiced and developed when working with Aboriginal students. In Chapter 6 Anna-Leah King discusses how, as a new teacher placed in urban schools and assigned to co-choreograph Aboriginal student dance troupes, she found herself challenged by teacher's comments and questions about the troupes' merit and validity. This prompted her to undertake some research into the question: "What is the significance of song and drum in schools?" Drawing from Elders teachings, archives and literature she inquired into the traditional practice of song and drum and its significance in different communities. Her chapter provides a vivid illustration of the ways in which western education systems do not easily afford spaces for Aboriginal teachers' initiatives, despite the rhetoric of wishing to be culturally responsive. In Chapters 7 and 8, Iti Joyce and Therese Ford both discuss how they worked in different ways to develop culturally responsive pedagogies of relations with Māori students and communities. Their work grew out of the Te Kotahitanga project (Bishop et al. 2003) in New Zealand. Iti Joyce explores the use of Māori metaphors as a means of being culturally responsive. Her research highlights the fundamental importance of relationships between Māori students and their teachers that enable them to bring their cultural knowledge and experience into the educational setting as a basis for new learning. She also argues that teachers need to understand the political-historical reasons behind the educational disparities that exist between Māori and non-Māori students as part of being culturally responsive if this issue is to be addressed. In Chapter 8, Therese Ford focusses on partnerships between school teachers and Māori whānau in literacy interventions. She argues that while research indicates *why* connections with whānau are important, what is not so clear is *how* these learning partnerships might be achieved. Four case studies are described to illustrate the varying levels to which schools have engaged whānau through the implementation of two literacy interventions. She concludes that the challenges of such partnerships should be considered by schools who seek to partner Māori whānau at a structural level if they are to successfully support culturally responsive literacy interventions in the classroom.

Part 4 contains two chapters that focus on standardized assessments with students for whom English is an additional language. In both cases, there is a textual analysis of the language and multimodal cues used in standardized tests and the extent to which these disadvantage minoritized students. In Chapter 9, Theresa Austin conducts an analysis on math tests and invigilator instruction in the USA. She argues that, if tests are to be culturally responsive, there is a need to understand how multimodal items in standardized testing affect second language learners' ability to demonstrate what they know and can do. Drawing on critical multimodal analyses (Kress and van Leeuwen 2006) the multimodal assumptions in invigilator instructions are made visible. The findings highlight institutionalized practices that not only neglect culturally and linguistically diverse learners but jeopardize their access to higher education and their potential to be productive contributors in their communities. The context for Chapter 10 is the performance of Indigenous Australian students in the New South Wales Department of Education and Training's (2005a, 2005b) *Basic Skills Tests* (BST) of literacy. Ann Daly described her work as an educator who was concerned to create assessment practices for indigenous students who are culturally responsive. The three studies conducted grew from a concern about the consistently low scores attained by Aboriginal students in comparison with their non-Aboriginal counterparts, and an historical account of the effects of colonialism is provided as context. Daly's analysis of the data focusses on the relationship between spoken and written language, and the possible ways in which literacy tests might disadvantage indigenous students. She concludes that the tests are more closely aligned with non-indigenous language structures; and that teachers (who are predominantly non-indigenous) require additional training in culturally responsive ways of assisting indigenous students. In the final chapter we bring everything together to argue for a critical intercultural approach that goes beyond CRP and works as part of a process of decolonizing teacher education.

## NOTE

1. De Sousa Santos (2007) defines abyssal thinking as:

> a system of visible and invisible distinctions, the invisible ones being the foundation of the visible ones. The invisible distinctions are established through radical lines that divide social reality into two realms, the realm of 'this side of the line' and the realm of 'the other side of the line'. The

division is such that the other side of the line vanishes as reality becomes nonexistent, and is indeed produced as nonexistent. Nonexistent means not existing in any relevant or comprehensible way of being. Whatever is produced as nonexistent is radically excluded because it lies beyond the realm of what the accepted conception of inclusion considers to be its other. What most fundamentally characterizes abyssal thinking is thus the impossibility of the co-presence of the two sides of the line. (p. 1)

## References

Ahmad, F. Z., & Boser, U. (2014, May 4). America's leaky pipeline for teachers of color getting more teachers of color into the classroom. *Centre for American Progress*. Retrieved from https://www.americanprogress.org.

Anderson, B. (1983). *Imagined communities. Reflections on the origin and spread of nationalism* (1st ed.). London, UK: Verso.

Apple, M. W. (2004). Creating difference: Neo-liberalism, neo-conservatism and the politics of educational reform. *Educational Policy, 18*(1), 12–44.

Apple, M. W. (2006). *Educating the "right" way: Markets, standards, God, and inequality* (2nd ed.). New York, NY: Routledge.

Apple, M. W. (2014). *Official knowledge: Democratic education in a conservative age* (3rd ed.). New York, NY: Routledge.

Bakhtin, M. M. (1986). *Speech genres and other late essays* (V. W. McGee, Trans.). Austin, TX: University of Texas Press.

Ball, S. J. (2001). Performativities and fabrications in the education economy: Towards the performative society. In D. Gleeson & C. Husbands (Eds.), *The performing school: Managing teaching and learning in a performance culture* (pp. 210–226). London, UK: Routledge/Falmer.

Ball, S. J. (2012). Performativity, commodification and commitment: An I-spy guide to the neoliberal university. *British Journal of Educational Studies, 60*(1), 17–28.

Berryman, M., SooHoo, S., & Nevin, A. (Eds.). (2013). *Culturally responsive methodologies*. Bedfordshire, UK: Emerald.

Bhabha, H. K. (1994). *The location of culture* (2nd ed.). London, UK: Routledge.

Bishop, R., Berryman, M., Tiakiwai, S., & Richardson, C. (2003). *Te Kotahitanga: Experiences of Year 9 and 10 Māori students in mainstream classrooms*. Wellington, NZ: Ministry of Education.

Bishop, R., Berryman, M., Cavanagh, T., & Teddy, L. (2007). *Te Kotahitanga: Phase 3 Whānaungatanga: Establishing a culturally responsive pedagogy of relations in mainstream secondary school classrooms*. Wellington, NZ: Ministry of Education.

Bonilla-Silva, E. (2014). The style of color blindness: How to talk nasty about minorities without sounding racist. In E. Bonilla-Silva (Ed.), *Racism without racists: Color-blind racism and the persistence of racial inequality in the United States* (4th ed., (pp. 101–122)). Lanham, MD: Rowman & Littlefield.

Bourdieu, P. (1998, December). The essence of neoliberalism. *Le Monde diplo-matique: English Edition (LMD)*. Retrieved from http://mondediplo.com/1998/12/08bourdieu.

Bowell, T. (2016). Feminist standpoint theory. *Internet Encyclopedia of Philosophy (IEP): A Peer-Reviewed Academic Resource*. Retrieved from http://www.iep.utm.edu/fem-stan/.

Burton, M., & Flores Osorio, J. M. (2011). Introducing Dussel: The philosophy of liberation and a really social psychology. *Psychology in Society, 41*, 20–39.

Campbell, J. L., & Pederson, O. K. (Eds.). (2001). *The rise of neoliberalism and institutional analysis*. Princeton, NJ: Princeton University Press.

Cote-Meek, S. (2014). *Colonized Classrooms: Racism, trauma and resistance in post-secondary education*. Black Point, NS, CAN: Fernwood Publishing.

Dascal, M. (2009). Colonizing and decolonizing minds. In I. Kuçuradi (Ed.), *Papers of the 2007 World Philosophy Day* (pp. 308–332). Ankara, TU: Philosophical Society of Turkey.

Davies, B., & Bansel, B. (2007). Neoliberalism and education. *International Journal of Qualitative Studies in Education, 20*(3), 247–259.

De Sousa Santos, B. (2007, June 29). Beyond abyssal thinking: From global lines to ecologies of knowledges. *Eurozine*, 1–33. Retrieved from http://www.eurozine.com/articles/.

Dussel, E. D. (2006). Transmodernity and interculturality: An interpretation from the perspective of philosophy of liberation. *Poligrafi, 11*(41/42), 5–40.

Dussel, E. D. (2012). Transmodernity and interculturality: An interpretation from the perspective of philosophy of liberation. *Transmodernity: Journal of Peripheral Cultural Production of the Luso-Hispanic World, 1*(3), 28–59.

Fanon, F. (1967). *Black skin, white masks (original French ed., 1952)*. New York, NY: Grove Press.

Gay, G. (2000). *Culturally responsive teaching: Theory, research, & practice*. New York, NY: Teachers College Press.

Gillborn, D. (2010). Reform, racism and the centrality of whiteness: Assessment, ability and the 'new eugenics'. *Irish Educational Studies, 29*(3), 231–252.

Giroux, H. (2000). Cultural Studies, public pedagogy, and the responsibility of intellectuals. *Communication and Critical/Cultural Studies, 1*(1), 59–79.

Giroux, H. (2014, April 8). Neoliberalism and the machinery of disposability. *Truthout*, Retrieved from http://www.truth-out.org.

Grosfoguel, R. (2011). Decolonizing post-colonial studies and paradigms of politi-cal-economy: Transmodernity, decolonial thinking, and global coloniality. *Transmodernity: Journal of Peripheral Cultural Production of the Luso-Hispanic World, 1*(1), 1–37.

Gunderson, L. (2000). Voices of the teenage diasporas. *Journal of Adolescent & Adult Literacy, 43*(8), 692–706.

Gunderson, L. (2008). The state of the art of secondary ESL teaching and learning. *Journal of Adolescent & Adult Literacy, 52*(3), 184–188.

Harding, S. (2009). Standpoint theories: Productively controversial. *Hypatia: A Journal of Feminist Philosophy, 24*(4), 192–200.

Harvey, D. (2005). *A brief history of neoliberalism.* New York, NY: Oxford University Press.

Jabbar, A., & Hardaker, G. (2013). The role of culturally responsive teaching for supporting ethnic diversity in British University Business Schools. *Teaching in Higher Education, 18*(3), 272–284. 10.1080/13562517.2012.725221.

Janks, H. (2010). *Literacy and power.* New York, NY: Routledge.

Kohl, B. (2006). Challenges to neoliberal hegemony in Bolivia. *Antipode: A Radical Journal of Geography, 38*(2), 304–326.

Kress, G., & Leeuwen, T. V. (2006). *Reading images: The grammar of visual design* (2nd ed.). London: Routledge.

Ladson-Billings, G. (1992). Culturally relevant teaching: The key to making multicultural education work. In C. A. Grant (Ed.), *Research and multicultural education* (pp. 106–121). London, UK: The Falmer Press.

Ladson-Billings, G. (1994). *The dreamkeepers: Successful teachers of African-American students* (1st ed.). San Francisco, CA: Jossey-Bass.

Ladson-Billings, G. (1995). But that's just good teaching! The case for culturally relevant pedagogy. *Theory Into Practice, 34*(3), 159–165.

Ladson-Billings, G., & Tate, W. F. (1995). Toward a critical race theory of education. *Teachers College Record, 97*(1), 47–68.

Lipman, P. (2004). *High stakes education: Inequality, globalization, and urban school reform.* New York, NY: Routledge.

Lipman, P. (2011). *The new political economy of urban education: New liberalism, race, and the right to the city.* New York, NY: Routledge.

Madrid, R. (2003). Labouring against neo-liberalism: Unions and patterns of reform in Latin America. *Journal of Latin American Studies, 35*(1), 53–88.

Martin, F., & Pirbhai-Illich, F. (2015). Service learning as post-colonial discourse: Active global citizenship. In R. Reynolds, et al. (Eds.), *Contesting and constructing international perspectives in global education* (pp. 135–150). Rotterdam, The Netherlands: Sense Publications.

Martínez-Alemán, A. (2015). Critical discourse analysis in higher education policy research. In A. M. Martínez-Alemán, B. Pusser, & E. M. Bensimon (Eds.), *Critical approaches to the study of higher education: A practical introduction* (pp. 7–43). Baltimore, MD: Johns Hopkins University Press.

McIntosh, P. (1990, Winter). White privilege: Unpacking the invisible knapsack. *Independent School, 1*(49), 31–36.

Mitchell, T. (Ed.). (2000). *Questions of modernity.* Minneapolis, MN: University of Minnesota Press.

Mohanty, C. T. (2003). *Feminism without borders: Decolonizing theory, practicing solidarity*. Durham, NC: Duke University Press.

Moll, L. C., Amanti, C., Neff, D., & González, N. (1992). Funds of knowledge for teaching: Using a qualitative approach to connect homes and classrooms. *Theory Into Practice, 31*(2), 132–141.

New South Wales Department of Education and Training (NSWDET. (2005a). *Year 3 basic skills test 2005*. Sydney, AUS: NSW Department of Education and Training.

New South Wales Department of Education and Training (NSWDET). (2005b). *Year 5 basic skills test 2005*. Sydney, AUS: NSW Department of Education and Training.

Pennycook, A. (1998). *English and the discourses of colonialism*. London, UK: Routledge.

Phipps, A. (2013). Intercultural ethics: Questions of methods in language and intercultural communication. *Language and Intercultural Communication, 13*(1), 10–26.

Pirbhai-Illich, F. (2006). *The educational pathways and outcomes of adolescent ethnic and linguistic minority students in the Vancouver School District*. Unpublished thesis submitted in part fulfilment of a PhD, University of British Columbia.

Pirbhai-Illich, F. (2010). Aboriginal students engaging and struggling with critical multiliteracies. *Journal of Adolescent & Adult Literacy, 54*(4), 257–266.

Pirbhai-Illich, F. (2013). Crossing borders: At the nexus of critical service learning, literacy, and social justice. *Waikato Journal of Education. Te Hautaka Mātauranga O Waikato, 18*(2), 79–96.

Razack, S. (1998). *Looking white people in the eye: Gender, race, and culture in the courtrooms and classrooms*. Toronto, ON, CAN: University of Toronto Press.

Said, E. 1985. *Orientalism*. Harmondsworth: Penguin.

Sharp, J. (2009). *Geographies of postcolonialism*. London, UK: Sage.

Sleeter, C. E. (2011). An agenda to strengthen culturally responsive pedagogy. *English Teaching: Practice and Critique, 10*(2), 7–23.

Sleeter, C. E., & McLaren, P. L. (Eds.). (1995). *Multicultural education, critical pedagogy, and the politics of difference*. Albany, NY: State University of New York Press.

Soja, E. (2009). Thirdspace: Toward a new consciousness of space and spatiality. In K. Ikas & G. Wagner (Eds.), *Communicating in the third space* (pp. 49–61). New York, NY: Routledge.

Thiong'o, N. W. (1986). *Decolonizing the mind: The politics of language in African literature*. Nairobi, KE: East African Educational Publishers.

Tuck, E., & Gaztambide-Fernández, R. A. (2013). Curriculum, replacement, and settler futurity. *Journal of Curriculum Theorizing, 29*(1), 72–89.

**Dr. Fatima Pirbhai-Illich** is an associate professor and chair of the Language and Literacy Education Department in the Faculty of Education at the University of Regina, Saskatchewan. Fatima has taught initial and in-service teachers in various parts of the world. Her community-based interest and research focusses on critical multicultural literacy education for marginalized and disenfranchised youth.

**Dr. Shauneen Pete** is a Nehiyaw (Cree) woman from Little Pine First Nation, Saskatchewan. She is an associate professor, Faculty of Education (University of Regina). She served as Vice-President (Academic) and Interim President at First Nations University of Canada. She is a teacher educator and served as the Executive Lead: Indigenization, at her university.

**Fran Martin** University of Exeter, works in Initial Teacher Education. Her research interests are global education and intercultural learning. From 2009 to 2013 she worked with researchers in The Gambia and India on a project titled: "Global Partnerships as Sites for Mutual Learning". She is currently researching with colleagues in Canada and China.

# PART II

# CHAPTER 2

# Identification of Cultural Heuristics for the Creation of Consistent and Fair Pedagogy for Ethnically Diverse Students

*Abdul Jabbar and Mohammed Mirza*

## INTRODUCTION

This chapter seeks to illustrate the challenges that many educators and organizations face within the shifting cultural landscape of UK Higher Education. Hence this chapter seeks to develop discussion and raise awareness around the complex issues of pedagogy development, academic awareness and institutional support in creating a consistent UK Higher Education experience for ethnically diverse students in the UK Business Schools. The key output of this chapter is the proposal of cultural heuristics to support academic staff in the creation of pedagogy (Table 2.1). In developing this debate, the key discussions and gaps to emerge which impinge on the Higher Education experience for ethnically diverse students are the creation of inconsistent pedagogy design, poor pedagogy implementation and inadequate guidance, support and training for academic staff. This emerges from a literature review analysis within the fields of multicultural educational and culturally responsive teaching (Gay 2000, 2002; Jabbar and Hardaker 2013; Villegas and Lucas 2002; Villegas 2007).

A. Jabbar (✉) · M. Mirza
University of Huddersfield, Huddersfield, UK
e-mail: a.jabbar@hud.ac.uk

© The Author(s) 2017
F. Pirbhai-Illich et al. (eds.), *Culturally Responsive Pedagogy*,
DOI 10.1007/978-3-319-46328-5_2

**Table 2.1**   Heuristics of culturally responsive teaching

| Heuristics | Cultural consciousness | Resources | Moral responsibility | Cultural bridging | H.E. curriculum |
|---|---|---|---|---|---|
| Affirming cultural heritage (Villegas and Lucas 2002) | X | X | X | X | X |
| Pedagogy that is validating (Gay 2002) | X | X | X | X | X |
| Empowerment through academic success (Nieto 1999) | X | | | | |
| Transformative academic (Banks 1995) | X | X | | | |
| Confidence to develop relevant pedagogy (Gay 2000) | | X | | | |
| Multidimensional approach to resource design (Gay 2002) | | X | | | |
| Passion to act as an agent of change (Villegas and Lucas 2002) | | | X | | |
| Expectation to succeed (Nieto 1999) | | | X | | |
| Disruption of oppressive constructions (Gatimu 2009) | | | X | | |
| Knowledge construction process (Nieto 1999) | | | | X | |
| Self-reflection to construct tangible meaning (Kirkland and Gay 2003) | | | | X | |
| Modify instruction and curriculum for equity pedagogy (Banks 1995) | | | | X | X |
| Conducive Climate to the achievement of diversity (Hurtado 1999) | | | | | X |
| Deconstruction of a "white syllabus" (Allen 1998) | | | | | X |

*Note*: Copyright 2016 by Jabbar and Mirza

In order to develop this debate, this chapter defines ethnically diverse students as *students whose background, ethnicity and experiences differ from that of the dominant culture* (Gay 2000, 2002; Ladson-Billings 1995b; Nieto 1999). In discussing the challenges of Western pedagogy on ethnically diverse students this chapter puts forward innovative cultural heuristics (Table 2.1), which are designed to act as a benchmark in the construction and development of cross-cultural pedagogy that is consistent and fair. These cultural heuristics (Table 2.1) will be structured and discussed around the five-pillar framework (Jabbar and Hardaker 2013), which is specifically designed as a template for culturally responsive teaching in UK Higher Education. The five-pillar framework is underpinned by the work of Gay (2002), Ladson-Billings (1995b) and Villegas and Lucas (2002) whose work in this area has a focus on the development of consistency and to create an engaging environment of learning for ethnically diverse students.

While the development of consistency and the creation of an engaging environment is not a new or a novel concept it is only recently that it has taken on a more significant prominence. This is due to a number of factors, which include widening participation (Sanders and Rose-Adams 2014), the view of the student as a customer (Molesworth et al. 2009; Shaw 2009) and the marketization of Higher Education (Woodall et al. 2014). What's clear is the increase of tuition fees that has created a pressurized environment where many organizations are now competing for students (De Vita and Case 2003; Meek 2000; Molesworth et al. 2009; Woodall et al. 2014). This competition is especially fierce in the international market where ethnically diverse students traditionally pay a higher tuition fee (Woodall et al. 2014). One of the biggest beneficiaries of these higher fees have been UK Business Schools, who in 2009/10 earned approximately £2bn in export earnings (Chartered Association of Business Schools 2015). The UK British Council (2013) further expands on these figures and provides statistics which show that there were over 90,000 students from an ethnically diverse international background studying a business-oriented degree (e.g. Economics, Business Studies, Accounting, Marketing) in the academic year 2013/14. This has led to a culture of competition where market forces dictate institutional strategies, and growth in income from overseas is increasingly seen as a form of financial stability (Connor et al. 2004; Molesworth et al. 2009; Woodall et al. 2014).

This focus on the market and financial stability has led to increased student social and geographical mobility, with ethnically diverse students developing a confidence to study in other countries. This places increased pressure on Higher Education Business Schools to develop an educational experience which differentiates them from their competitors (Zamudio et al. 2009). One of the key ways of developing this differentiation is the creation of pedagogy which is consistent, an experience which is enriching and expectations which are fair (Tomalin 2007; Turner 2006). In order to move towards this, institutions must meet the challenge in establishing teaching policies, pedagogy and practices that reflect the changing needs of an ethnically diverse student body.

## ETHNICALLY DIVERSE STUDENT EXPERIENCE

The impact of competitive market forces and the influence these have on organizational strategy and growth should not be the defining argument in the creation of a consistent experience for ethnically diverse students, there is also a moral argument to be made. The moral argument in the past has not always been a priority, with literature (Connor et al. 2004; Modood 2006; Turner 2006; Tomalin 2007; Richardson 2008) suggesting that current UK Higher Education practice, theory and policies favour the Western learner, and any pedagogy that does not conform to the Western practice is seen as either incomplete (Joy and Poonamallee 2013) or is referred to as the 'other' (Ngambi 2008). Current pedagogy design is shaped by Western business practice, and dominated by aspirations of the Western culture, hence if a student is not from this dominant culture that student is then at a disadvantage. This continued focus on the Western learner leaves many ethnically diverse students struggling to try and unravel the UK's academic culture, almost piecemeal from those tangible practice-based aspects of university life (Turner 2006), leading to lower achievement and attainment (Connor et al. 2004; Modood 2006; Richardson 2008; Schapper and Mayson 2004; Turner 2006).

The issue of achievement and attainment is a recurring debate with multiple authors (Connor et al. 2004; Modood 2006; Richardson 2008) arguing that a poor Higher Education experience is a key trigger for low achievement and attainment. Ethnically diverse students are fundamentally disadvantaged in terms of attainment and achievement (Richardson 2008). This is underpinned by the notion that students from an ethnically diverse background have poorer representation and lower admission rates at the *prestigious* pre-1992 universities (Modood 2006), which has led to poor social mobility and the Russell Group universities becoming less socially representative (Social Mobility and Child Poverty Commission 2013).

These issues continue to contribute to a poor ethnically diverse student experience. Ngambi (2008) argues that Business Schools have a moral obligation to develop teaching practices that are meaningful to ethnically diverse students. The moral imperative is just as important as the financial argument and in the past this has been overlooked. In order to meet the challenges discussed so far and to develop academic and institutional understanding alongside a moral responsibility, this chapter proposes that UK Business Schools should have a view of learning which is not only comprehensive but spans across multiple factors such as curricular and pedagogical approaches (Gay 2002) underpinned by strategies, programmes and policies (Nieto 1999). Hence this chapter is grounded in culturally responsive teaching (Gay 2002; Jabbar and Hardaker 2013; Ladson-Billings 1995b; Villegas and Lucas 2002) within the larger body of research known as multicultural education (Banks and Banks 1995, 2009; Gaffney 2008; Nieto 1999; Sleeter and Grant 2006).

## CULTURALLY RESPONSIVE TEACHING

Culturally responsive teaching is an approach that takes into consideration a student's background and culture in the development of pedagogy (Gay and Kirkland 2003; Ladson-Billings 1995a). This is a conversation that has taken place over many decades but inconsistencies and poor student experience are still prevalent (Joy and Poonamallee 2013). Culturally responsive teaching by its very nature is designed to combat these issues of inconsistencies by acting as an enabler for teaching methods that allow for the use of cultural characteristics, experiences and perspectives of ethnically diverse students as conduits for teaching them more effectively (Durden and Truscott 2013; Schmeichel 2012). For this approach to be successful there needs to be organizational support where issues of multicultural education and diversity need to be developed through clear policies, procedures, curriculum and institutional strategy (Nieto 1999).

However, culturally responsive teaching is not without controversy. Critics of culturally responsive teaching argue that they have little time, minimal resources or their subjects are incompatible with a culturally responsive teaching perspective (D'Souza 1991, 1995; Schlesinger 1991; Tancredo 2006). These criticisms are rejected by Gay (2002) who argues that in many cases these are based on superficial pedagogy, anecdotal

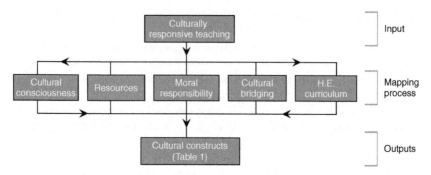

**Fig. 2.1**   Overview of the mapping process

Copyright 2016 by Jabbar and Mirza

incidents or distorted knowledge, which in many cases is conveyed through popular culture or mass media. In the view of Sleeter and Grant (2006) and Sleeter (2001), these distortions and misconceptions are based on educators being unfamiliar with the contributions made by ethnically diverse students to their subject.

In structuring this research, Fig. 2.1 outlines the key inputs, mechanisms and outputs for this chapter. The literature review is mapped onto the five-pillar framework (Jabbar and Hardaker 2013), this chapter then outlines in Table 2.1 the cultural constructs for consistent pedagogy development.

## THE FIVE PILLARS OF CULTURALLY RESPONSIVE TEACHING

In responding to these critics and creating a pedagogy that is fair and responsive, the five-pillars of culturally responsive teaching of Jabbar and Hardaker (2013) are proposed as a guiding mechanism to support the creation of consistent cultural heuristics to help academics in the creation of pedagogy. The five-pillar framework (Jabbar and Hardaker 2013) was one of the three different frameworks considered; the other approaches include the five essential elements of Gay (2000, 2002) and the six salient characteristics of Villegas and Lucas (2002). The five-pillar framework (Jabbar and Hardaker 2013) was deemed more of an appropriate framework due to its focus on UK Higher Education as compared to the five essential elements of Gay (2000, 2002) and the six salient characteristics of Villegas and Lucas (2002) which predominantly focus on pre-school and high school pedagogy in the United States.

The five-pillar framework (Jabbar and Hardaker 2013) proposes that UK Higher Education Business Schools, to undertake culturally responsive teaching successfully, must be organized around the five following concepts:

- Cultural Consciousness
- Resources
- Moral Responsibility
- Cultural Bridging
- Higher Education (HE) curriculum

The above five concepts are used as the basis to identify the key cultural heuristics for the development of culturally responsive teaching in UK Higher Education Business Schools. An overview of the cultural heuristics organized by the five concepts is available in Table 2.1.

### Cultural Heuristics Within Cultural Consciousness

This section of the chapter on cultural consciousness aims to explore the heuristics which illustrate the complex relationships that exist between Business School academics and their students. It is important to recognize that there is plurality in the way students think, talk, behave and learn, and also students are heavily influenced by variables such as their race, ethnicity, social class and language (Banks 1995; McGee Banks and Banks 1995; Villegas and Lucas 2002). In developing this plurality, Fig. 2.2 identifies the key cultural heuristics of cultural consciousness.

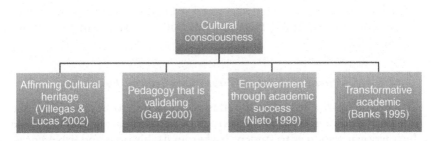

**Fig. 2.2** The cultural heuristics of cultural consciousness

Copyright 2016 by Jabbar and Mirza

These heuristics shown in Fig. 2.2 acknowledge difference and plurality as essential components within the remit of educators to comprehend and empathize with student experience and history. Empathy encourages academics to move away from their comfort zone, and create what is described by Villegas and Lucas (2002) as *social cultural environments*, or safe zones of learning.

However, developing cultural consciousness requires academics to be self-conscious, critical and analytical of their own teaching beliefs and behaviours (Choo 2007; Gay and Kirkland 2003; Nieto 1999). Hence the development of self-reflection and internal critical analysis is essential in not only helping to improve the educational opportunities of ethnically diverse students but also in creating a validating and affirming learning environment (Gay and Kirkland 2003; Howard 2003; Jabbar and Hardaker 2013; Nieto 1999). In order to create a consistent validating and affirming learning environment there are multiple approaches that can be adopted. One technique is for academics to be supported in getting to know their students better, and institutions allowing the utilization of home culture and language as part of the learning process (Nieto 1999; Vita 2001; Waistell 2011). Gatimu (2009) suggests a partnership between students and academic staff advocating students as creators of knowledge. This type of approach is powerful and brings meaning and context into the classroom, rooting knowledge in student background, history and culture, and can be transformative and empowering in the lives of students (Banks 1995, 2008; McGee Banks and Banks 1995).

Bringing culture and history into the classroom gives ethnically diverse students a platform to succeed. When students are taught in an environment which is designed to help them succeed, students from ethnically diverse backgrounds find it empowering and liberating, leading to higher levels of achievement and student satisfaction (Gay 2000, 2002; Ghere et al. 2007; Higbee et al. 2007; Ladson-Billings 1995b; Nieto 2009).

### Cultural Heuristics Within Curriculum Resources

In developing the heuristics for this concept and to contextualize the students' learning experience, there is a need for academics to relate instructional resources to student backgrounds, histories and experiences. When learning is situated within these contexts, the transformative academic recognizes that teaching in an increasingly diverse student environment poses learning challenges that need to be addressed through classroom pedagogy (Banks 1995; Ngambi 2008). Figure 2.3 outlines some of the key heuristics for this concept.

Culturally responsive pedagogy needs to be supported by resources that have context and relevance. The academic literature in this area (Ngambi 2008; Turner 2006) recommends that instructional resources should include diverse contexts and flavours which better represent the needs of the ethnically diverse student community. The importance of a balanced and consistent view towards resource development is evident as multiple authors (Allen 1998; Sleeter and Grant 1991) criticize current educational resources and curriculum as still very much targeted at the "white" European and American students.

The move towards implementing diverse curriculum resources requires academics to have confidence in themselves and in their subjects. Confidence gives academics the freedom and assurance to teach against prevailing stereotypes and also to become experienced in better judging the standard, quality and relevance of textbooks for Business School teaching. Confidence is a fragile thing, which can shatter in an instant, but is essential in developing a culturally responsive teaching base (Gay 2002; Maeroff 1988). To build confidence Gay (2002) talks about the need for a secure knowledge base, which should be supplemented within the cultural awareness of textbooks and supporting educational resources, which are not solely dominated with a Western resource framework. However, a knowledge base on its own is not enough, educators should take more responsibility for individual and group welfare, and should see their role as an advocate, educator and friend (Turner 2006).

This level of academic confidence requires academics to undertake a multidimensional approach to resource design, where they are comfortable with the multitude of educational resources used in the classroom in order to make learning more meaningful for students (Gorski 1997). Undertaking a multidimensional approach to resource design is a characteristic of a transformative academic who is defined as aiding "students acquire new perspectives" on history and society through the reformation of the curriculum (Banks 1995, p. 394). The concept of the transformative academic is interrelated to transformative academic knowledge, with the underlying notion being that "Transformative scholars assume that knowledge is influenced by personal values, the social context, and factors such as race, class, and gender" (Banks 2001, p. 10). Here, transformative

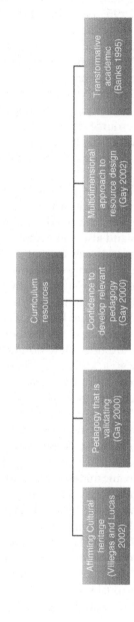

**Fig. 2.3**   Heuristics of curriculum resources

Copyright 2016 by Jabbar and Mirza

scholars argue for the need to focus the debate on creating knowledge that challenges mainstream academic understanding in its production and implementation (Banks 1995, 2001).

Hence mainstream academic knowledge needs to become more responsive in the creation and production of knowledge. This will mean that many academics may have to widen the net in the types of resources they develop (Avery and Thomas 2004) and start to include research chapters and evidence-based case studies that incorporate different ethnic minority groups (Villegas and Lucas 2002). This type of approach is not without consequence for Business School policies, procedures and pedagogy. In helping academic staff to move away from their comfort zones, Business School institutions may have to develop specific training courses that allow academics to build confidence in creating resources that offer a balanced view that reflects the increasing ethnic diversity of the student community.

### Cultural Heuristics Within Moral Responsibility

The cultural heuristics within this concept emphasizes the need for academics to develop a moral responsibility which transcends the classroom, and to acknowledge that teaching is not solely confined to the classroom (Nieto 1999). Figure 2.4 outlines the key heuristics of academic moral responsibility.

As part of this responsibility, academics should cultivate high expectations for all students not just for some (Goodlad 1994; Tom 1997). This concept views high expectations as a moral imperative that allows academics to increase learning and educational opportunities for students from an ethnically diverse background. As part of this responsibility there is a recognition that academics are in a privileged position to facilitate the growth and development of other human beings and are thereby in a position to challenge the status quo of the dominant group (Giroux 2004); it is these academics that are the real *agents of change* (Villegas and Lucas 2002).

An agent of change is defined as an individual who has empathy, passion and motivation for his/her students (Villegas and Lucas 2002). These qualities are not luxuries, they are essential elements of the teachers' toolkit which inspire students to achieve and develop themselves as human beings (Day 2004). Passion leads to high expectations which is essential in developing a positive student experience (Jussim 1989; McKown and Weinstein 2002; Rubie-Davies et al. 2006). This issue of academic expectations has also been discussed through the government funded Swann Report (Gillard 2007) which looked at the effectiveness of education for ethnic

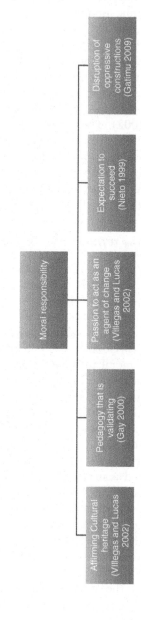

**Fig. 2.4**  Cultural heuristics of moral responsibility
Copyright 2016 by Jabbar and Mirza

minority groups in the United Kingdom. Pellegrini and Blatchford (2000) reported that one of its main findings was that low expectations for these students were a major factor in their poor academic achievement. This supports the view of Rubie-Davies et al. (2006) who argue that certain characteristics such as ethnicity may be a significant factor in educator expectations (Baron et al. 1985).

The danger in academics having low academic expectations especially in relation to ethnic minority students is that it can become a self-fulfilling prophecy. Ethnic minority students are highly influenced by low expectations, more so than their white counterparts, and this may serve to further widen the achievement gap when such students accept and confirm teachers' negative expectations (McKown and Weinstein 2002; Nichols and Good 2004; Sabry and Bruna 2007). In the development of high expectations, Durden and Truscott (2013) advocate the use of critical consciousness as a tool that explores and engages subjectivity and identifies issues of social struggle alongside helping educators develop understandings of culturally relevant pedagogy. Utilizing critical consciousness as part of pedagogy development gives academics the confidence to disrupt oppressive constructions. Disrupting oppressive constructions is not about breaking rules and regulations and overseeing general anarchy, it is about giving marginalized groups a voice, a stage to air their grievances and analyse the forms of oppressive policies and regulations that they encounter in their lives, underpinned by a critical approach (Freire 2000; Gatimu 2009; Giroux 2004). It also allows educators to take responsibility to identify and rectify areas of inequality in curricular and structural issues.

Developing a moral responsibility requires a multifaceted approach that explores academic intentions and passions and implements them within a culturally responsive framework. For many Business School academics this will require dedication, hard work and a genuine passion to see students succeed (Gay 2002). The concept of moral responsibility requires high levels of commitment and in order to do so, academics need to embody passion to fight social inequities and reconstruct education in order to provide all students with equal and equitable opportunities (Gatimu 2009; Nieto 1999).

### Cultural Heuristics Within Cultural Bridging

Cultural bridging is an approach that academics can use to equip students with the skills and confidence to build bridges between their pre-existing knowledge and what they are expected to learn (Sabry and Bruna 2007;

Villegas and Lucas 2002). This is primarily undertaken through the identification and implementation of a clear equitable pedagogy (Banks 1995, 2008), curriculum (Tomalin 2007; Turner 2006) and cultural consciousness where there is a need for academics to both understand the student and the subject matter they teach (Villegas and Lucas 2002). Figure 2.5 outlines the key cultural heuristics of cultural bridging.

The process of cultural bridging builds on the discussion around cultural consciousness with the additional focus on implementation. There is still a requirement for academics to acknowledge student background and behaviour (Banks 1995; Durden et al. 2014), but these elements need to be considered within the context and creation of learning opportunities which utilize culture as a vehicle for learning (Ladson-Billings 1995b; Moll and Gonzalez 1997). However, cultural bridging is not an arbitrary process and requires not only careful planning and scaffolding of students' personal knowledge alongside their academic knowledge, but also curriculum content and material that is relevant to the experiences and backgrounds of ethnically diverse students (Gay 2002; Ngambi 2008). In the view of Turner (2006), current attempts to create conducive knowledge construction processes are hampered by Western epistemological assumptions that frustrate the ethnically diverse learner due to a lack of opportunity to explicitly contextualize and discuss these issues within the framework of formal learning.

Thus, to overcome these frustrations and try to implement learning opportunities which help develop the knowledge construction process, Nieto (1999) makes the case for the development of a more equitable learning environment. To achieve this equity, Nieto (1999) identifies the need for educators to recognize that there is a plurality of learning styles within culturally responsive teaching and these styles have multiple viewpoints and characteristics. In developing this plurality, research (Gay and Kirkland 2003; Nieto 1999; Sabry and Bruna 2007) suggests that academic self-reflection allows the acknowledgement and understanding of student backgrounds and how students learn and think. This process of self-reflection builds up a reserve of knowledge which identifies that in many cases students from diverse backgrounds come with a variety of skillsets, which should be valued. Academics should focus on building on what students do have, rather than lament about what they do not have (Nieto 1999; Sabry and Bruna 2007; Villegas and Lucas 2002). Discussions of self-reflection by numerous authors (Houser 2008; Howard 2003; Ladson-Billings 1995b; Nieto 1999) very much focus on

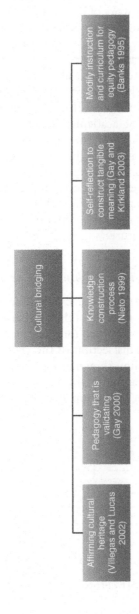

**Fig. 2.5**   Cultural heuristics of cultural bridging

Copyright 2016 by Jabbar and Mirza

turning the critical eye inward and interrogating personal attitudes, beliefs and actions. This supports the work of Freire (Freire 2000) who argues that educators cannot effectively support critical growth among students unless they too are willing to identify, acknowledge and resist personal complicity in existing systems of oppression.

Finally, it is important to recognize that cultural bridging has a crucial role to play in stitching together students' previous knowledge with what they are expected to learn. In the development of this concept, Villegas and Lucas (2002) argue that academics need to view all students as capable learners, who should view their role as *adding to* rather than *replacing* what students already have, hence the term cultural bridging. In order to accomplish this effectively, Gay and Kirkland (2003) talk about the importance of self-reflection and critical consciousness in understanding how academic behaviour and beliefs affect the process of implementing instruction that allows students to identify links between student home and school culture.

### *Cultural Heuristics Within HE Curriculum*

The final concept within the adapted five-pillar framework of Jabbar and Hardaker (2013) investigates the role of the Higher Education institution in the experience and support provided for the achievement and success of ethnically diverse students. This section of the chapter identifies the key heuristics of the HE Curriculum shown in Fig. 2.6.

The final concept of Jabbar and Hardaker (2013) outlines the role of the institution in creating an environment of learning. The institutional

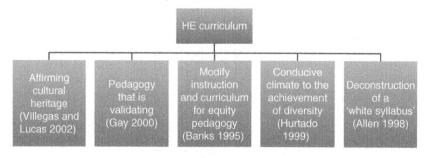

**Fig. 2.6**   Cultural heuristics of HE curriculum

Copyright 2016 by Jabbar and Mirza

curriculum is a key driver in the creation of an educational climate that facilitates the success and achievement of ethnically diverse students. Hurtado et al. (1999) argue that educational climates and perspectives are heavily influenced by the heritage and history of an institution. It is this heritage and history that shapes how institutions view culture, and how this then shapes policies, procedures and academic practice, and in their view the past influences the present.

The Higher Education institution has a key role in creating a climate that treats learning as an active process in which meaning is developed based on experience as opposed to the static pedagogical approach of direct transmission (McGee Banks and Banks 1995; Nieto 1999). In consigning this static approach to the past, Nieto (1999) calls for drastic changes to all school policies and practices, not simply pedagogy and curricula. In the view of Nieto (1999), a focus on specific strategies such as *Black History Month* is no longer enough; educational institutions need to go through a critical transformation process to create conditions of learning that are conducive for ethnically diverse students. This is a politically charged view not without its merits of how education needs a revolutionary change against oppression (Freire 2000), thus leading potentially to a radical shift in Higher Education Business School strategy, thinking, focus and course design (Ngambi 2008).

The creation of this conducive climate requires institutions to go through a process of change and reflection to fully realize their role in the deconstruction of the *white syllabus* also referred to as a Eurocentric perspective (Allen 1998; Gatimu 2009). This deconstruction is defined as a process where climate and curriculum are carefully sculpted to meet the learning requirements of ethnically diverse students. For Business Schools the key output of this deconstruction process should be a culturally responsive curriculum that allows for the creation of what Hurtado et al. (1999) refer to as a "climate of learning that is conducive to the achievement of diversity" (p. 6). In support of this, Ngambi (2008) advocates a conscious approach that explores student needs by developing a personalized understanding of student perceptions and history. For this process of deconstruction to be effectively implemented educational organizations need the support of all faculties and staff to create strategic awareness of culturally diverse challenges and how these can be overcome (Ladson-Billings 1995b; Villegas and Lucas 2002).

## CONCLUDING COMMENTS

Table 2.1 maps the heuristics identified within the five concepts of culturally responsive teaching (Jabbar and Hardaker, 2013). The cultural heuristics are spread evenly across the five pillars and show that there is still a lot of work to do for academics and institutions in expanding the debate and raising awareness in the implementation of a responsive and consistent approach in the adoption of equitable pedagogy within UK Business Schools. The cultural heuristics are intended to help refocus the debate on the student experience by proposing a framework of consistency that expands on the notion of cultural responsiveness (Gay 2000, 2002; Nieto 1999) within the parameters of a responsible approach. In order to achieve and develop this responsible approach the cultural heuristics depicted in Table 2.1 emphasize the need for educators to prepare and develop practice that acknowledges the requirements of culturally responsive teaching within teacher training (Gay and Kirkland 2003).

Hence the role of the academics and institutions within this environment is integral to a consistent and fair student experience. First, there needs to be recognition that individual academics need to take on responsibility for their ethnic minority students, with the expectation that culturally responsive educators develop intellectual, social and emotional learning by bringing back cultural associations to impart knowledge, skills and attitudes (Ladson-Billings 1995a, 1995b). This should be undertaken and underpinned by critical reflection, where the focus is on understanding the internal and external environments. This reflection is critical in developing an understanding of how students think and behave, and how this is deeply influenced by factors such as race, ethnicity, social class and language (Villegas and Lucas 2002). This also leads to the creation and support of structured development activities that progressively increase the students' abilities while reducing teacher-led direction, a process termed as *scaffolding* (Coulson and Harvey 2013).

However, these activities, training support and time for critical reflection is not possible without the support of Business School institutions, for they have a key role in facilitating the consistent learning approach. This must start with the acknowledgement that the mastery of content knowledge is not enough, it needs to be underpinned with teacher education to provide skills, knowledge and attitudes that are essential to develop teaching practices that are consistent (Gay 2000). Changing the mindset of institutions is the first step. There is also the process of rethinking and reconceptualizing pedagogy for different ethnic minorities and acknowledging that Western pedagogy is not necessarily the best approach for all (Howard 2003; Joy and Poonamallee 2013). It is not intended that institutions in the development of their curriculums need to undertake wholesale changes (Nieto 1999) or to create policies that lack detail (Villegas and Lucas 2002), but this chapter proposes a strategic vision which embeds teaching and learning in a multicultural society through the implementation of the proposed constructs depicted in Table 2.1.

## REFERENCES

Allen, P. M. (1998). Towards a Black construct of accessibility. In T. Moodood & T. Acland (Eds.), *Race and higher education* (pp. 86–95). London: Policy Studies Institute.

Avery, D. R., & Thomas, K. M. (2004). Blending content and contact: The roles of diversity curriculum and campus heterogeneity in fostering diversity management competency. *Academy of Management Learning & Education, 3*(4), 380–396.

Banks, J. A. (1995). Multicultural education and curriculum transformation. *The Journal of Negro Education, 64*(4), 390–400. doi:10.2307/2967262.

Banks, J. A. (2001). Citizenship education and diversity: Implications for teacher education. *Journal of Teacher Education, 52*(1), 5–16. doi:10.1177/0022487101052001002.

Banks, J. A. (2008). *Teaching strategies for ethnic studies* (8th ed.). Boston, MA: Pearson/Allyn & Bacon.

Banks, J. A., & Banks, C. A. M. (Eds.) (1995). *Handbook of research on multicultural education.* New York, NY: Macmillan.

Banks, J. A., & Banks, C. A. M. (2009). *Multicultural education: Issues and perspectives* (7th ed.). Hoboken, NJ: John Wiley & Sons.

Baron, R. M., Tom, D. Y. H., & Cooper, H. M. (1985). Social class, race and teacher expectations. In J. B. Dusek (Ed.), *Teacher expectancies* (pp. 251–269). Hillsdale, NJ: Lawrence Erlbaum Associates.

British Council. (2013). *British council data.* Retrieved May 6, 2015, from https://hesadata.britishcouncil.org.

Chartered Association of Business Schools. (2015). The Association of business schools participates at party conferences. Retrieved from http://charteredabs. org/association-business-schools-participates-party-conferences/.

Choo, K. L. (2007). Can critical management education be critical in a formal higher educational setting? *Teaching in Higher Education, 12*(4), 485–497. doi:10.1080/13562510701415524.

Connor, H., Tyers, C., Modood, T., & Hillage, J. (2004). *Why the difference? A closer look at higher education minority ethnic students and graduates* (Research Report No. 552). Retrieved from The National Archives Department for Education website: http://www.education.gov.uk/publica tions/standard/publicationDetail/Page1/RR552.

Coulson, D., & Harvey, M. (2013). Scaffolding student reflection for experience-based learning: A framework. *Teaching in Higher Education, 18*(4), 401–413.

D'Souza, D. (1991). *Illiberal education: The politics of race and sex on campus.* New York, NY: Free Press.

D'Souza, D. (1995). *The end of racism: Principles for a multiracial society.* New York, NY: Free Press.

Day, C. (2004). *A passion for teaching.* New York, NY: Routledge, Psychology Press.

De Vita, G. (2001). Learning styles, culture and inclusive instruction in the multicultural classroom: A business and management perspective. *Innovations in Education and Teaching International, 38*(2), 165–174.

De Vita, G., & Case, P. (2003). Rethinking the internationalisation agenda in UK higher education. *Journal of Further and Higher Education, 27*(4), 383–398. doi:10.1080/0309877032000128082.

Durden, T., & Truscott, D. (2013). Critical reflectivity and the development of new culturally relevant teachers. *Multicultural Perspectives, 15*(2), 73–80.

Durden, T., Dooley, C. M., & Truscott, D. (2014). Race still matters: Preparing culturally relevant teachers. *Race Ethnicity and Education,* 1–22 [ahead-of-print].

Freire, P. (2000 30th Anniversary ed.). *Pedagogy of the oppressed.* New York, NY: Bloomsbury Academic.

Gaffney, S. (2008). Teaching and learning in a multicultural environment: A mild polemic. In P. Martensson, M. Build, & K. Nilsson (Eds.), *Teaching and learning at business schools: Transforming business education* (pp. 111–127). Burlington, VT: Gower.

Gatimu, M. W. (2009). Undermining critical consciousness unconsciously: Restoring hope in the multicultural education idea. *Journal of Educational Change, 10*(1), 47–61.

Gay, G. (2000). *Culturally responsive teaching: Theory, research, & practice.* New York, NY: Teachers College Press.

Gay, G. (2002). Preparing for culturally responsive teaching. *Journal of Teacher Education, 53*(2), 106–116.

Gay, G., & Kirkland, K. (2003). Developing cultural critical consciousness and self-reflection in preservice teacher education. *Theory into Practice, 42*(3), 181–187.

Ghere, D. L., Kampsen, A., Duranczyk, I. M., & Christensen, L. L. (2007). Adopting and integrating multiculturalism: A closing assessment of general college. In J. L. Higbee, D. B. Lundell, & I. M. Durancyzk (Eds.), *Diversity and the postsecondary experience* (pp. 25–36). Mineapolis, MN: University of Minesota, Center for Research on Developmental Education and Urban Literacy.

Gillard, D. (2007). *The Swann Report 1985: Education for all* (Report of the Committee of Enquiry into Education of Children from Ethnic Minority Groups). Retrieved from http://www.educationengland.org.uk/documents/swann/.

Giroux, H. A. (2004). Cultural studies and the politics of public pedagogy: Making the political more pedagogical. *Parallax, 10*(2), 73–89. doi:10.1080/1353464042000208530.

Goodlad, J. I. (1994). *Educational renewal: Better teachers, better schools.* San Francisco, CA: Jossey-Bass.

Gorski, P. (1997). *Initial thoughts on multicultural education-multicultural pavilion.* New York, NY: Macmillan.

Higbee, J. L., Siaka, K., & Bruch, P. L. (2007). Student perceptions of their multicultural learning environment: A closer look. In J. L. Higbee, D. B. Lundell, & I. M. Durancyzk (Eds.), *Diversity and the postsecondary experience* (pp. 3–23). Mineapolis, MN: University of Minesota, Center for Research on Developmental Education and Urban Literacy.

Houser, N. O. (2008). Cultural plunge: A critical approach for multicultural development in teacher education. *Race Ethnicity and Education, 11*(4), 465–482. doi:10.1080/13613320802479034.

Howard, T. C. (2003). Culturally relevant pedagogy: Ingredients for critical teacher reflection. *Theory into Practice, 42*(3), 195–202.

Hurtado, S., Milem, J., Clayton-Pedersen, A., & Allen, W. (1999). Enacting diverse learning environments: Improving the climate for racial/ethnic diversity in higher education. *ASHE-ERIC Higher Education Report, 26*(8), 1–116. Retrieved from http://eric.ed.gov/?id=ED430514.

Jabbar, A., & Hardaker, G. (2013). The role of culturally responsive teaching for supporting ethnic diversity in British University Business Schools. *Teaching in Higher Education, 18*(3), 272–284. doi:10.1080/13562517.2012.725221.

Joy, S., & Poonamallee, L. (2013). Cross-cultural teaching in globalized management classrooms: Time to move from functionalist to post-colonial approaches? *Academy of Management Learning & Education, 12*(3), 396–413.

Jussim, L. (1989). Teacher expectations: Self-fulfilling prophecies, perceptual biases, and accuracy. *Journal of Personality and Social Psychology, 57*(3), 469–480.

Ladson-Billings, G. (1995a). But that's just good teaching! The case for culturally relevant pedagogy. *Theory Into Practice, 34*(3), 159–165.

Ladson-Billings, G. (1995b). Toward a theory of culturally relevant pedagogy. *American Educational Research Journal, 32*(3), 465–491.

Maeroff, G. I. (1988). *The empowerment of teachers. Overcoming the crisis of confidence.* New York, NY: Teachers College Press.

McGee Banks, C. A., & Banks, J. A. (1995). Equity pedagogy: An essential component of multicultural education. *Theory into Practice, 34*(3), 152–158.

McKown, C., & Weinstein, R. S. (2002). Modeling the role of child ethnicity and gender in children's differential response to teacher expectations. *Journal of Applied Social Psychology, 32*(1), 159–184.

Meek, V. L. (2000). Diversity and marketisation of higher education: Incompatible concepts? *Higher Education Policy, 13*(1), 23–39.

Modood, T. (2006). Ethnicity, muslims and higher education entry in Britain. *Teaching in Higher Education, 11*(2), 247–250. doi:10.1080/13562510500527826.

Molesworth, M., Nixon, E., & Scullion, R. (2009). Having, being and higher education: The marketisation of the university and the transformation of the student into consumer. *Teaching in Higher Education, 14*(3), 277–287. doi:10.1080/13562510902898841.

Moll, L. C., & Gonzalez, N. (1997). Teachers as social scientists: Learning about culture from household research. In P. Hall (Ed.), *Race, ethnicity, and multiculturalism: Policy and practice* (pp. 89–114). New York, NY: Garland.

Ngambi, H. (2008). Diversity dynamics in teaching. In P. Martensson, M. Build, & K. Nilsson (Eds.), *Teaching and learning at business schools: Transforming business education* (pp. 101–110). Burlington, VT: Gower.

Nichols, S. L., & Good, T. L. (2004). *America's teenagers—myths and realities: Media images, schooling, and the social costs of careless indifference.* New York, NY: Routledge.

Nieto, S. (1999). *The light in their eyes: Creating multicultural learning communities.* New York, NY: Teachers College Press.

Nieto, S. (2009). *Language, culture, and teaching: Critical perspectives* (2nd ed.). New York, NY: Routledge.

Pellegrini, A. D., & Blatchford, P. (2000). *The child at school: Interactions with peers and teachers.* London, UK: Arnold.

Richardson, J. T. E. (2008). The attainment of ethnic minority students in UK higher education. *Studies in Higher Education, 33*(1), 33–48.

Rubie-Davies, C., Hattie, J., & Hamilton, R. (2006). Expecting the best for students: Teacher expectations and academic outcomes. *British Journal of Educational Psychology, 76*(3), 429–444. doi:10.1348/000709905X53589.

Sabry, N. S., & Bruna, K. R. (2007). Learning from the experience of Muslim students in American schools: Towards a proactive model of school-community cooperation. *Multicultural Perspectives, 9*(3), 44–50. doi:10.1080/15210960 701443730.

Sanders, J., & Rose-Adams, J. (2014). Black and minority ethnic student attainment: A survey of research and exploration of the importance of teacher and student expectations. *Widening Participation and Lifelong Learning, 16*(2), 5–27.

Schapper, J. M., & Mayson, S. E. (2004). Internationalisation of curricula: An alternative to the Taylorisation of academic work. *Journal of Higher Education Policy and Management*, *26*(2), 189–205. doi:10.1080/1360080042000218258.

Schlesinger Jr., A. M. (1991). The disuniting of America: What we all stand to lose if multicultural education takes the wrong approach. *American Educator: The Professional Journal of the American Federation of Teachers*, *15*(3), 14, 21–33.

Schmeichel, M. (2012). Good teaching? An examination of culturally relevant pedagogy as an equity practice. *Journal of Curriculum Studies*, *44*(2), 211–231. doi:10.1080/00220272.2011.591434.

Shaw, J. (2009). The diversity paradox: Does student diversity enhance or challenge excellence? *Journal of Further and Higher Education*, *33*(4), 321–331. doi:10.1080/03098770903266018.

Sleeter, C. E. (2001). Preparing teachers for culturally diverse schools research and the overwhelming presence of whiteness. *Journal of Teacher Education*, *52*(2), 94–106.

Sleeter, C. E., & Grant, C. A. (1991). Mapping terrains of power: Student cultural knowledge versus classroom knowledge. In C. E. Sleeter (Ed.), *Empowerment through multicultural education* (pp. 49–67). Albany, NY: SUNY Press.

Sleeter, C. E., & Grant, C. A. (2006). *Making choices for multicultural education: Five approaches to race, class and gender* (5th ed.). Hoboken, NJ: Wiley.

Social Mobility & Child Poverty Commission. (2013). *Higher education: The fair access challenge* (Policy Paper). Retrieved from https://www.gov.uk/government/publications/higher-education-the-fair-access-challenge.

Tancredo, T. (2006). *In mortal danger: The battle for America's border security*. Nashville, TN: Cumberland House.

Tom, A. R. (1997). *Redesigning teacher education*. Albany, NY: SUNY Press.

Tomalin, E. (2007). Supporting cultural and religious diversity in higher education: Pedagogy and beyond. *Teaching in Higher Education*, *12*(5/6), 621–634. doi:10.1080/13562510701595283.

Turner, Y. (2006). Chinese students in a UK business school: Hearing the student voice in reflective teaching and learning practice. *Higher Education Quarterly*, *60*(1), 27–51. doi:10.1111/j.1468-2273.2006.00306.x.

Villegas, A. M. (2007). Dispositions in teacher education: A look at social justice. *Journal of Teacher Education*, *58*(5), 370–380.

Villegas, A. M., & Lucas, T. (2002). Preparing culturally responsive teachers: Rethinking the curriculum. *Journal of Teacher Education*, *53*(1), 20–32.

Waistell, J. (2011). Individualism and collectivism in business school pedagogy: A research agenda for internationalising the home management student. *Higher Education Research & Development*, *30*(5), 595–607. doi:10.1080/07294360.2011.598450.

Woodall, T., Hiller, A., & Resnick, S. (2014). Making sense of higher education: Students as consumers and the value of the university experience. *Studies in Higher Education*, *39*(1), 48–67. doi:10.1080/03075079.2011.648373.

Zamudio, M., Bridgeman, J., Russell, C., & Rios, F. (2009). Developing a critical consciousness: Positionality, pedagogy, and problems. *Race Ethnicity and Education, 12*(4), 455–472.

**Abdul Jabbar** joined the University of Huddersfield Business School in 2001 as a Learning Technology Advisor, with a remit to support academic staff in developing their teaching in the online environment. Within his current role, Abdul is a Senior Lecturer in Digital Business with a focus on learning technologies and their application within blended and flexible learning courses.

Abdul has a B.A. (Hons) in Interactive Media, an M.Sc. in Internet Application Development and he is a Fellow of the Higher Education Academy (FHEA). Abdul recently completed his Ph.D. in Business Management Education at the University of Huddersfield.Abdul is also a very active researcher, he has a wide variety of research interests including Information Science, Big Data, Business Digital Skills, Technology Entrepreneurship and Culturally responsive teaching.

**Mohammed Mirza** is a Principal Lecturer in Marketing and has extensive expertize in marketing, communications and customer care.

Mohammed has 20 years of teaching multicultural students in Higher Education and was responsible for initiating a series of international student support initiatives in the Business School at the University of Huddersfield, which were subsequently adopted university-wide. He is now the Director of International Student Learning and Development for the Business School.

Beginning his career in the private sector, Mohammed later entered the training sector from where he went on to teaching and learning, and subsequently Mohammed's approach to teaching and learning has always been to push boundaries and incorporate innovative practices to enhance the student experience.

# CHAPTER 3

# *Idle No More*: Radical Indigeneity in Teacher Education

## Shauneen Pete

### BACKGROUND: THE EMERGENCE OF IDLE NO MORE

"Idle No More calls on all people to join in a peaceful revolution, to honour Indigenous sovereignty, and to protect the land and water" (Idle No More [n.d.]). Idle No More (INM) emerged as an act of resistance to the proposed federal Omnibus Bills.[1] Many Indigenous peoples believed that these Bills were going to further reduce Indigenous sovereignty, by making changes to the Indian Act, and reducing environmental protections that were designed to ease the expansion of resource extraction. INM brought international attention to the Canadian government's plans for expansion of the tar sands and the expansions of the Keystone and Energy East pipelines for example. The movement foretold the ways in which resistance to the expansion of development would be met with force by Indigenous peoples.

At the same time, Chief Theresa Spence (Attawapiskat) was engaged in her 6-week-long hunger strike. She asserted that after years of being ignored by the federal government her community could no longer wait for the houses, new school, or employment opportunities that had been promised and not delivered upon. Both of these events, the global INM movement and the very public hunger strike by Chief Spence became the

S. Pete (✉)
University of Regina, Regina, Saskatchewan, Canada
e-mail: Shauneen.Pete@uregina.ca

© The Author(s) 2017
F. Pirbhai-Illich et al. (eds.), *Culturally Responsive Pedagogy*,
DOI 10.1007/978-3-319-46328-5_3

focus of discussion in our class. The politics of the land, development, and Indigenous sovereignty were all coming to a head. This chapter explores how INM influenced my decision-making around the scope and the focus of my undergraduate class.

Note: INM began with a call for a conversation about the proposed Bills on Facebook. The INM founders include Sylvia McAdam, Nina Wilson, Jess Gordon, and Sheila McLean. I am very grateful for these women. Through their leadership and their vision they inspired me to greater levels of academic activism and a more radical indigeneity.

## A Self-Study in Radical Indigeneity

Like many other First Nations people in Canada, the emergence of the INM movement in the winter of 2013 was deeply personal for me. In my community, some people first denied the federal legislative changes and then dismissed the impact these changes would have on our nation. Conflicts arose between the chief and council and the community members; tensions were obvious between the young and the old, as well as the urban and on-reserve members. Some of the elders and many of the youth gathered to discuss treaty rights, legislative reforms, and the UN Declaration on the Rights of Aboriginal People. Daily, my father would call me to update me on the growing conflicts in the community. He was particularly concerned about the growing pressure by some adults to "not agitate the youth." These same individuals cautioned band members that their actions could be detrimental to the federal finances that the band relied on.

In my home (in an urban setting where I work and reside), my daughter and I updated one another on our growing understanding of the Omnibus Bills and the UN Declaration. We shared the writings of Chelsea Vowel, Russ Diabo, and many other Indigenous public intellectuals and academic scholars. My daughter and I participated in local teach-ins, round dances and marches, to raise awareness about the impacts of the legislative changes. On campus, my colleagues and I hosted a panel discussion on INM and later hosted RED/Talk, an event which asked four Indigenous intellectuals to imagine a post-Indian Act future in Canada. My identities as an urban Cree woman/mother and activist/educator coalesced that winter. While I already embraced that my personal life was highly political I came to understand in a deeper way how my teaching work too was shaped by my growing "radical indigeneity." By this I mean, I embrace my responsibilities as an Indigenous educator to teach from and to re-center indigenous knowledges, scholarship, epistemologies, and ontologies; and, I do so within mainstream teacher education so that my white middle-class learners will gain some understanding of indigenous knowledges, communities, and peoples.

As the INM movement grew in its visibility, and the tensions grew within my own community, I found that my understanding of the complexity of the continued oppression of Indigenous peoples also grew, and so did my anger, fear, and frustration. You see, I am also a university educator committed to decolonizing, anti-oppressive, and social justice education. My service to our academic community has included being a member of the Aboriginal Advisory Circle (AAC) to the President. More recently, I have served for two terms as the Executive Lead: Indigenization. In these roles, I have worked with my colleagues to create a pathway toward indigenizing our university. For members of the AAC, we agree that indigenizing the university means a radical transformation of the academic programs and operations of the university. For us this work includes: policy reform, academic decolonization, the development of professional development sessions on Indigenization, and many other activities. As well as serving as the Executive Lead, I have also taught one course per term these past 2 years.

My teaching, like my activism, was shaped by the events unfolding that winter and I was increasingly aware of how little my learners understood or cared about the magnitude of social injustices directed toward Indigenous peoples that we were witnessing. My education students, like other Canadian citizens wondered what INM was all about; some even asked why the movement mattered – but few went out of their way to seek out any information about the issues. Fewer still saw any relevance to these issues with their own experiences as Canadians, or as future educators. As I worked to draw their attention to the issues, my attempts were met with loud resistance: "just teach us how to teach" they implored.

The great tensions (Berry 2004) that I struggled with during that time was how to model social justice education with learners who were white and were learning to identify their own white privilege; many whom voiced their fear that they would have to teach First Nations peoples their "culture" in a teacher-directed way; and some who expressed that there was already too much Aboriginal content in our teacher education program. I wrestled briefly with the idea that perhaps I was letting my personal priorities for indigenous social justice get in the way of my professional responsibilities: were my political urgencies being imposed on these learners? I reminded myself that as an Associate Professor in a Faculty of Education designed with social justice, indigenizing, anti-oppression, and decolonizing priorities: I was doing my job.

This chapter offers a self-study into my efforts to indigenize my curricular practice (as inspired by the INM movement). Self-study guides the researcher to engage reflexively with the artifacts of their work (course outlines, required readings, notes, lesson plans, and student assignments and feedback) as well as with their own reflections and (in)formal conversations with colleagues, and with our students.

Self-study allowed me to "interrogate the uncertainty of practice" in the work of "teaching about teaching" (Loughran 2006) or as I define it here "teaching about teaching for social justice." To go further, self-study provided space to consider the tensions which exist when I, a professor of Indigenous ancestry, teach white pre-service teachers, whom I hope will begin to decolonize their teaching practices for the sake of Indigenous learners. Teaching work is framed on the tensions between "telling and growth," whereby the educator (researcher) strives to move away from transmission approaches which students want – "just teach us how to teach" toward a deeper and more meaningful engagement with the ambiguity that social justice education creates. This is where our learner's desire from their professor "the right answer" or the "right way" to facilitate social justice education, and I insist that they join with me in the messiness and ambiguity, which is how the social justice teaching is.

This chapter is limited to three tensions which arose in my teaching and will conclude with my self-study reflections on my growth toward decolonizing my pedagogical practices. By presenting the self-study in this way my hope is to better understand the orientations to teacher preparation informative of the goals of social justice and how this will transform my work as an Indigenous educator of white, pre-service teachers.

## THEORETICAL FRAMEWORKS

This chapter like others in this book is (loosely) framed by Culturally Relevant Pedagogy (Howard 2012), Critical Multiculturalism (May and Sleeter 2010), and more specifically by both Tribal Critical Theory (Brayboy 2005) and Red Pedagogy (Grande 2004). In my view, these theoretical frameworks are useful for disrupting white pre-service teachers' ideas about professional practice. These frameworks also underpin how I view my own responsibilities as a critical educator to white learners.

Culturally responsive pedagogy (CRP) works from the assumptions that much of mainstream education is framed on the cultural, historical, and social norms of the dominant group. CRP not only unpacks these norms through the development of critical consciousness but shifts the focus to the diverse knowledges of racial minority students. Tyrone Howard (2012) states, "Culturally responsive pedagogy is a multidimensional approach" (p. 3). He continues by stating,

> Culturally responsive pedagogy embodies a professional, political, cultural, ethical, and ideological disposition that supersedes mundane teaching acts, but is centered in fundamental beliefs about teaching, learning, students, their families, their communities, and an unyielding commitment to see student success become less rhetoric, and more of a reality (p. 1).

In my teaching work, I attempt to redirect my white student's attention from their desire to "learn how to teach" (as a teacher-centered focus) to learning to respond to the experiences and voices of diverse learners (a student-focused exercise). Gay (2002) states, "Culturally responsive teaching is defined as using the cultural characteristics, experiences, and perspectives of ethnically diverse students as conduits for teaching them more effectively" (p. 106). CRP along with critical multiculturalism serves to disrupt the dominant idea of the white teacher as racially neutral while at the same time challenging the assumption of the white teacher as knower imparting wisdom upon racially diverse learners.

Critical multiculturalism helps us to understand the persistence of race in schooling. It helps us to understand structural inequality in access and achievement. May and Sleeter (2010) state that critical multiculturalism "gives priority to structural analysis of unequal power relationships, analyzing the role of institutionalized inequalities, including but not necessarily limited to racism" (p. 10). Critical multiculturalism challenges the idea that "culture" is the issue that so many of my education students assume. It offers educators an opportunity to move beyond celebrating difference by focusing on the ways in which identities are shaped by the social construction of raced bodies, including white bodies. While Critical Multiculturalism emphasizes race, Tribal Critical Theory (TribalCrit; Brayboy 2005) posits that colonialism plays a more prominent role in domination for Indigenous peoples. For me, both critical multiculturalism and TribalCrit together help me to guide my learners to a deeper understanding of race in relation to colonization, racial superiority, and racial domination; as well as systemic and institutionalized oppression.

As I explain within this chapter my courses were designed to explore the unequal access to power in relation to the land, resource development, resource extraction, and resource revenue sharing that are reinforced through the federal Omnibus Bill changes. Brayboy (2005) states, "policies toward Indigenous peoples are rooted in imperialism, white supremacy, and a desire for material gain" (p. 429). He continues by adding, "Indigenous people desire to obtain and forge tribal sovereignty, tribal autonomy, self-determination and self-identification" and "government policies and educational policies toward Indigenous peoples are intimately linked around the problematic goal of assimilation" (p. 429). In this case, increased resource exploration on Treaty lands has very real assimilative outcomes for Indigenous peoples. To go further, TribalCrit allows us to identify how resource extraction serves white supremacy while undermining the self-determination of Indigenous peoples. Critical Multiculturalism, TribalCrit, and Red Pedagogy combined provide a theoretically layered way of engaging in anti-oppressive education.

Red Pedagogy (Grande 2004) creates space for the intercultural investigations into how we are shaped by our history as white and Indigenous peoples; and how this shared history shapes us as educators. Grande challenges us to consider the "Deep Structures of Colonialist Consciousness" or those underpinning dominant group ideals which hold white superiority firmly in place. I will focus on three of these ideals: (1) the belief in progress as change and change as progress, (2) subscription to ontological individualism, and (3) belief in human beings as separate from and superior to the rest of nature (Grande 2004, p. 69). Grande suggests that these deep structures shape schooling by assuming that our learners must be independent, achievement oriented, detached from sources of local and personal knowledge, and also detached from nature and educators. She suggests that the deep structures actualized in school maintain the colonialist project. Her work suggests that schooling operates as another location for the maintenance of Western hegemony and needs to be unpacked as a part of social justice practice.

Together these theoretical foundations offered me a layered, yet precarious perch from which to take up critical, culturally relevant curriculum practice with my white pre-service teacher candidates. I knew that I was actively disrupting the norms of the class and these learners, and I remained committed to engaging in this process nonetheless. The whole season seemed steeped in the politics of discontent; the convergence of normative politics came to a head that term. As an Indigenous educator committed to the practice of a radical indigeneity, my considerations for course design were shaped by the emerging INM movement. I explore the tensions that emerged in my classroom in the following sections.

## Tension: Expectations for the Course

I teach a course called Pedagogy: Theory and Practice. This class is required of all third-year pre-internship students. These students are a mix of direct entry and after-degree candidates. Almost all of my students are white; there are more women than men, and many self-declare as middle-class.

Over the course of the past 5 years this class has evolved from a technical rational to a reflective practitioner model. While some of the faculty make this distinction clear through wording in outlines and repetition verbally in classes; students still perceive the course as being about the skills of lesson planning, classroom management, and assessment. Some students struggle with their impatience to gain skills to teach and our (faculty) desire to ensure that they enter the profession as socially aware educators. The tensions between these differing perceptions of what should happen in the course are complicated by my insistence that along the way they will also learn about Indigenous peoples, issues and communities reflective of the treaty territory in which we work, reside, and study.

I recognize that many of these learners have been structurally denied the opportunity to learn about First Nations and Métis (FNM) peoples in their own formal schooling. They express confusion about their roles in FNM education; they struggle with how they will teach FNM culture to their learners; and they are aware that they don't know very much about Aboriginal peoples. Many of our learners come to the faculty with deeply rooted ideas about First Nations. For them the dominant stereotypes of First Nations peoples are deeply entrenched. I regularly expect that students will comment that this "is not an Indigenous studies program" or that "there is too much First Nations content." I don't include Métis peoples here because my learners rarely mention them. I have learned that these white students require:

- An introduction to correct terminology (First Nations, Métis, Native, Aboriginal etc.);
- An introduction to who FNM peoples are politically and culturally;

- An introduction to what FNM curriculum could look like across the grades;
- An introduction/reminder about culturally responsive teaching;
- An understanding of why a focus on FNM learners does not detract from immigrant learners or mainstream learners;
- A reminder that social justice, anti-oppression, and indigenization are central to the design of our faculty;
- The practice of identifying and confronting dominance as it is reflected in assumptions of the role of teacher, curriculum, and pedagogy.

Few of my students are ready to seriously or critically engage with indigenous content. Yet, even though they admit that there is much to be learned about Indigenous peoples, schooling, and pedagogies, many also express that they have already grown restless with "theory." They communicate a pervasive need for "the facts of how to do that work" meaning "just teach me how to teach."

As their pre-internship (three-week school placement) date loomed they repeatedly called for a focus on classroom management, and instructional and evaluation strategies. In their view, the real curriculum work in this class should be the practice of teaching not social justice. They express that they are biding their time until they can get to what they perceive is the real work of teachers – instructing in front of a classroom of attentive young people. They communicate a very traditional view of the work of teachers; a view that was shaped by their assumption that they as white teachers occupy a racially neutral position. At that point in the course, my learners resisted any discussion about how their social positioning as white educators allowed them to assume that the work of "classroom management" or "instructional strategy choices" were somehow race neutral. They asserted that both classroom management and instructional strategies were neutral; often dismissing my attempts to draw their attention to a critical multicultural view of these professional choices. Their urgency to teach superseded my attempts to support their growth of a culturally responsive pedagogy. As my learners escaped to their field placements, I retreated to my office for the purposes of deeper reflection and the practice of self-study.

As I reviewed my course outline and my class notes, I reminded myself that self-study allowed me the space to (re)consider my intentions for this course. I wanted to prepare white educators who were aware of their privilege in relation to our shared profession. I wanted them to be able to demonstrate a variety of approaches to teaching which were reflective of a diversity of learners, including First Nations children and youth. I wanted them to recognize the role that they play in maintaining colonial ideas of nationhood, citizenship, and meritocracy, through their unexamined assumptions about teaching work. I wanted them to shift their focus on planning for learning through teacher-directed curriculum design to student-led inquiry. I wanted them to practice facilitating learning based on the priorities that their learners felt were relevant. I wanted them to be aware of the practice of disrupting whiteness in their own teaching practices. I wanted them to engage more effectively in the practice of critical multiculturalism in much the same way that my self-study was allowing me to gain a new awareness of my own practice.

In the next iteration of the course, several lessons were followed by the explicit declaration of the practice of critical reflection. I named my intentions, and the decisions that I was making about instructional resources, instructional strategies, and assessment strategies as a "process narrative of teaching talk." For example, I said to my learners,

> Many of you have been structurally denied the opportunity to learn about Aboriginal people; you say you have been ill-prepared to teach these learners; therefore you will focus your intentions in this class on a group of First Nations students in a fictional case study. You will plan with these learners' interests and needs in mind.

These undergraduate students were then expected to align their own intentions for unit planning with the information they had been provided about the case study students. They were required to submit not only a unit plan and lesson, but also a process paper which explicitly identifies their pedagogical decision-making process.

While it would have been easier to bend to their demands for a non-political, technical-rational course about instructional strategies and evaluation approaches; social justice teaching is so much more: it's the practice of self-correction from normative and dominant ways of knowing. Through this self-study I reaffirmed my commitments to practicing culturally responsive pedagogy in my own classroom. I set up these learners to be the teachers of a racially diverse class (the case study). This decision allowed my learners to reposition authority with their learners who offered up their own prior knowledge to guide the design of learning activities.

Through this practice, my own learners began to shift their gaze from their own assumed demands for learning to those of their own (fictional) students.

The self-study allowed me time and focus to review and renew my commitments to practicing Red Pedagogy and TribalCrit by recommitting to the indigenous content that framed the course because these learners have little other access to it. As faculty members, we wrestle with our learners' expectations for course design and our own. Instead of giving in these learners' expectations, I opted instead to continue to aim for a decolonizing curriculum design for this class.

## TENSION: TEACHING CULTURE/CULTURALLY RESPONSIVE PEDAGOGY

Even though these learners are in the third year of a program designed with social justice, anti-oppressive and indigenous frameworks, they still maintain the misunderstanding that they are expected to "teach culture to First Nations peoples." When pressed for what they think "cultural teaching" looks like, they often respond simply "bring in elders" or "community-based knowledge keepers," often missing the point that their learners come to the classroom with rich identities which could drive curriculum choice. When I challenge them about where they got this idea that it was their job to teach culture (in a teacher directed way) to brown children they are often unable to respond. When I ask them what they think that would look like, again, they cannot identify what they mean. Occasionally, I will have a student stay after class, who is honest/brave enough to admit that what s/he thought was culture might actually be is in fact of dominant stereotype of identity. I have come to understand that few if any of the learners know exactly what culture means for First Nations peoples. I wonder, whatever gave them the idea that they, as unknowing, white people, were in the best position to teach our culture to our people when they knew so little about us. My task was to help them to unpack these ideas about teaching culture and shift their attention to issues of social justice.

As I planned for the class, I wondered about how to create a situation whereby students would have to apply what they were learning about social justice education, and Indigenous peoples in relation to practicing planning for learning. I understood from my own teaching practice that the content needed to be relevant to have meaning for the learners, and therefore in order to make learning about Aboriginal peoples meaningful, I had to create a sense of urgency for these learners. Teaching about the events emerging from INM created the urgency that I sought as I attempted to model teacher responsiveness to current events.

In my teaching practice I work from the understanding that Canadian policies toward First Nations peoples are rooted in white supremacy and the goals of assimilation. The INM movement emerged because of the federal Omnibus Bills (No. 45). These bills included legislative changes to the environmental assessment requirements of industry, the protection for waterways, and changes to the Indian Act. Grassroots First Nations' leaders challenged these bills. In their view, the Omnibus Bills rejected the Duty for Free, Prior and Informed Consent (UN Declaration of the Rights of Indigenous Peoples) and proposed numerous legislative changes that would directly limit the rights of Indigenous peoples in Canada.

In my view these events were the emergent curriculum. There was no better time to introduce and model critical pedagogies. I tailored a required assignment to a case study we were working on; the learners in the case study were white and First Nations youth surrounded by oil and gas development. The fictional learners were impacted by the legislative changes, and their growing understanding of the health impacts of the oil and gas industry on the Lubicon First Nations peoples of northern Alberta. My students were tasked with planning for a unit of study with issues emerging from these various current events. As they planned for the unit, they were of course engaged in various forms of research about the Omnibus Bills, fracking, and pipelines. I directed them to undertake some research on Treaty Rights, Indigenous sovereignty, and self-determination to extend their units. I named these approaches as ways to decolonize curriculum practice. They wondered aloud about what any of this had to do with teaching.

Inspired by critical pedagogies (critical multiculturalism and TribalCrit), I challenged my learners to discover the manner in which these events could also be shaping their evolving teacher identities. Through question posing I attempted to help them realize that their white identities were also shaped by colonialism. I asked them to consider the ways in which the issues of water protection, intensive development in the west, and the continued oppression of First Nations peoples were their issues too. I offered these white learners new ways to examine the lived experiences of Indigenous and white relationships in our province, and our country. The truth-telling about INM informed by TribalCrit was intended to offer a deeper, richer, and more honest story of our colonial past and current experiences with one another. I hoped that this more honest version would allow for vigorous inquiry into our collective responses to these issues. By engaging in a critical social justice and decolonizing pedagogy we were all offered one way to rewrite the curriculum and change their orientation to teaching work for the purposes of social justice. My hope was that these learners would actively and critically engage in decolonizing practices from their positions of privilege as white educators. But few seemed to grasp that these events had any bearing on their teacher identity – it's just a nonissue for many of them. My decisions to continue to push the issue was and remains very much framed on my commitment to exposing oppression, social inequality, and domination in our professional practices.

In the next iteration of the course, self-study strengthened my resolve to continue on this path. I reexamined the milieu in which we were all working. I grounded the sense of urgency I was trying to create in our 30-year provincial policy frameworks in support of Aboriginal learners; as well as in the research that shows systemic inequality in graduation rates and the achievement gap for First Nations and Métis learners. I explored with my learners the professional responsibilities as identified in our Ministry policy document: the Continuous Improvement and Accountability Framework. By creating urgency around professional responsibility more of my third-year students began to embrace these expectations for their professional practice. Social justice work, they came to understand, is the work of teachers in our province. It became easier for many of these students in this second class to engage with the practice of critical pedagogy in their own planning for learning. Some reflected on how their social positioning as white peoples allowed them to carry forth ideas about teaching and learning which were shaped by colonization including the assumption that resource development was going to be good for all Canadians – these learners could begin to identify how a critical pedagogy allowed space for an examination into the ways in which more intensive resource extraction without resource sharing would perpetuate social inequalities for Indigenous peoples. As an experienced teacher in the academy I also recognized that these efforts to engage in culturally responsive and critical pedagogies were still met with resistance by many of my learners.

## TENSION: THE GOOD (WHITE) TEACHER

I understand from listening to my learners, reviewing assignments and course evaluations, that in their view "real" teachers are "nice, funny, and well-liked by their students" at the same time they imagine teaching work as instructional practices which are "fun, memorable, and engaging." Alternatively, these students express that teachers should not be "political" and curriculum experiences should not be "negative." I wonder aloud with them, "good teachers are good for whom?" In my view, these notions of the good teacher are tied up with an unacknowledged colonial consciousness (Grande 2004). These pre-service teachers see the good teacher as "neutral" and "normal," whereas I see the "good teacher" as deriving from white supremacy (Grande 2004).

We didn't have to go far to see how discourses of white supremacy played out in response to more intensive media coverage of the INM rallies, Chief Theresa Spence, and flash mob round dances. When these events were picked up by mainstream media, they were shrouded in racial stereotypes. They generally focused on the disorganized way in which the events were unfolding and at their worst referring to Chief Spence as "fat" or a "pig" and claimed that she was not really on a hunger strike but was merely "dieting" on fish broth. First Nations protestors were cast as unruly and disorganized in headlines, yet the real picture (photos posted on Twitter and Facebook) showed intergenerational groups of Indigenous peoples and allies joining together in great numbers, in an organized manner; and speeches were articulate and specific to Bill C-45 and to the Indian Act and Treaties. This was not at all the story that was making the headlines of the major Canadian media outlets. In the face of these representations, white journalists and politicians joined in the action by downplaying the growing resistance movement by failing to show it either in pictures or videos, or in the case of Christie Blanchford, who claimed that Chief Spence's actions were akin to terrorism. I asked my learners to consider how these representations of racial identity aligned with their developing understanding of racial identity construction.

The identities of the white learners in a class with an Indigenous professor are ripe for conflict. I have learned over the years, that for many of my learners I may be their first and only Indigenous professor they will have. Their views of my professional work are often shaped by the lifetime of stereotypes and negative characterization of First Nations peoples that they have been steeped in. Some of these students are fearful of saying something that I will perceive as racist, yet few have done enough critical work to see the ways in which much of what they say is shaped by raced ideology. I expect that one or two students each term will claim that I am racist against them for teaching in an anti-oppressive way. They claim, that by speaking about race I am making the possibility of racism greater, not realizing that I am making what for them is invisible – visible. For many of my learners the good professor like the good teacher is cordial, approachable and fun; not challenging, troubling, and brown.

For me, I have made a career of observing how my white learners process courses with anti-oppressive designs. Talking about the tensions in our perceptions of 'self' and 'other' is essential in my work. I build off an earlier required course which includes a hefty dose of inquiry into the construction of white racial identities in my third-year courses. I recognize that a "critical multicultural understanding of identity provides the opportunity to analyze the normative nature of whiteness and the process of racialization" (May and Sleeter 2010, p. 11). Gary Howard (2006) states,

> hegemonic groups do not consider their beliefs, attitudes and actions to be determined by cultural conditioning or the influences of group membership. As Whites, we usually don't even think of ourselves as having culture; we're simply right. Dominant groups don't hold "perspectives" they hold "truth." (p. 54)

I drew my students' attention to the ways in which their white identity allows for the assumption of rightness to operate; and in the case of INM, the way in which dominant identities allow for the assumptions of rightness to operate as evidenced in the comments sections following INM stories on CBC (Canadian Broadcasting Corporation), Global News, and other media outlets. The commonly identified stereotypes of First Nations peoples were steeped with racial hatred informed by a lack of understanding recast as common sense. This view shifted attention away from the ways in which white supremacy was being enacted from the legislative choices of politicians, to the invisibility then stereotypical way that dominant groups characterize 'other' as the events of INM unfolded.

Through question posing I was able to challenge my learners to examine the way in which the good teacher is shaped by whiteness. As much as I wanted them to understand deeply the ways in which their identities are framed by dominance and that their work as white educators is as political as the work that I engage in, many were unable or unwilling to take responsibility for their emerging professional and dominant identities in this way. Critical multiculturalism allows one entree point into the discussion that their identities like mine matter.

Instead, some students insist that they are "colorblind," that they will treat all children the same. Color blindness operates like the assumption of rightness to deny the institutional and systemic nature of dominance: if I don't see it, the social inequality can't be real. These comments open up the floor for another conversation. Often, one or two of my learners will state, "I am not white" to which I must respond, "What are you then?" In response, they proclaim their citizenship as Canadians, as if this were some sort of normative apolitical term. I challenge these learners to consider how their identity as white people allows them to proclaim some sort of artificial neutrality while First Nations have to insist on self-identification which is always labeled radical and a threat to Canadian nationhood. The question, "Who gets to be Canadian?" emerged from these discussions. At that point, the discomfort was palpable, and many of my students withdrew from participating in the discussion.

G. Howard (2006) says that the "luxury of ignorance" does not allow those of the dominant group to really know their power or have a responsibility for really knowing those people who are not of the dominant group (p. 61). Our teaching then, must expose ignorance, and the ways in which ignorance is rooted in supremacy. Brayboy (2005) states that "white supremacy is viewed as natural and legitimate and it is precisely through this naturalization that white supremacy derives its hegemonic power" (p. 432). The idea of the good teacher when unexamined does nothing to challenge white racial dominance in teaching work. Good teachers, don't know, don't see, and don't trouble the common sense approaches to curricular practice that has been shaped by dominance, and why would they? They are already privileged by the system, its works for them.

Our learners are introduced to the ideas of white privilege early on in the program and then they move through the program with the idea that it was only a topic for discussion and not a critical lens through which to examine teaching assumptions and practices. As an Indigenous educator in the faculty I am conscientious about disrupting these dominant views of teachers and teaching work. I draw my learner's attention back to the original discussions about white privilege. My intention is to demonstrate that there is a growing body of literature on white teacher identities; and that these are not simply the politicized opinions of their brown teacher. I recognize that these deeply engrained ideas can be difficult to shake in the 4 years these learners remain in our program. I recognize that the tensions of remaining committed to this way of teaching allowed for unprecedented professional growth on my part.

## GROWTH OF A RADICAL INDIGENEITY TEACHING PRACTICE

It's been over a year since I taught that course that was inspired by the INM movement. Since that time I redesigned the course based on my own self-study, and based on a series of collaborative conversations that I had with a colleague (McNeil and Pete 2014). I've learned that while it may have been easier to bend to the learner's desire to see a course that only focused on the theory and practice of pedagogy (as if it were some sort of race-neutral practice), this work would not have allowed me to model the ambiguity that social justice work creates for the educator. I recognize now that through my commitment to a practice of radical indigeneity I could also demonstrate for my learners one way of juggling the complex theoretical intentions that I had for the course, and in turn allow me to come to appreciate this complexity as well.

I recognize now the very special period of time that we were in. It was a time laden with the politics of identity, continued efforts toward assimilation, federal intensification for resource development, and continued domination of Indigenous peoples in Canada. The emergent curriculum was perfect for an investigation into the theory and practice of pedagogies which support social justice. The decisions to explore topics emerging from INM allowed us the opportunity to challenge our common sense ideas about the curriculum, good teaching, the good teacher, and so much more. Yet, at the end of teaching that term I was wracked with frustration, anger, and uncertainty. Some of these feelings were certainly directed toward my students who continued to insist that "this had nothing to do with teaching." Some of the feelings had to do with my own uncertainty about whether I had done anything right with this group of learners.

As I reviewed my course notes I discovered that I had written in the margins of one of my day plans, "I would love to shift my teaching focus to courses that support Indigenous sovereignty and self-determination, but I teach white students" (Pete 2013). Now that some time has passed, I understand how this statement was written in the heat of the frustration that I was experiencing with these learners in this particular class.

This self-study provided me the opportunity to take stock of how I am currently working to indigenize my curricular practices while teaching white learners. Some strategies include:

- I purposefully select readings by First Nations and Métis scholars;
- I have developed a case study for use in my ECS 350 class which guides students to consider the learning needs of diverse youth under a school merger (First Nations and rural school);
- I choose required assignments with a focus on Aboriginal/ Indigenous issues and concerns;
- I anticipate racism and stereotypes and I am prepared to respond;
- I ask questions that challenge my learners to reexamine their own identities in relation to teaching;
- I name and expose institutional racisms, oppressions, and systems of domination (curriculum, schooling, mascots, hiring practices, governance practices, etc.).

I would rephrase this statement today to read, because my learners are white, and have been structurally denied the opportunity to learn about indigenous histories and contemporary issues – I must teach in way that reflects culturally responsive pedagogy, critical multiculturalism, including Tribal Critical Theory and the practice of Red Pedagogy in order that they may learn to be socially just educators.

In this case, I rejected the notion that the pre-service students' dominant worldviews would remain central to the assumed course outcomes (teach me how to teach) and embraced both culturally responsive pedagogy and critical multiculturalism to purposefully and assertively direct my learners attention to a case study. CRP becomes the starting point for my course design. I assume that my white learners expect a certain kind of teacher preparation program: one that reflects the deeply held ideas, histories, and values characteristic of their dominant group membership. Yet, I design my undergraduate courses with an intention of reshaping their white identities away from the replication of domination to that of critical, socially just educators. I teach about, and model culturally responsive pedagogy with an aim of changing how these white educators serve our increasingly racially diverse schools, characterized by an ever-growing Indigenous student population. I want them to not only understand the ways in which education has normed their own experience in formal learning, but also the ways in which this normed education has limited their ability to understand racialized others including Indigenous peoples. I want them to come to appreciate that I am offering them the gift of understanding at a deeper level what it means to teach in Indigenous communities, and in schools with increasing Indigenous student populations. I want them to come to appreciate that this work is messy and requires a thoughtful assertion of their theoretical frameworks.

This self-study allowed me the opportunity to focus on three tensions: (1) the tension of expectations of learning to teach, (2) the tension of the assumption to teach culture, and (3) the tensions behind the identity of a good white teacher. Through my practice of CRP with a view for critical multiculturalism my learners were challenged to unpack their assumption that they, from a seat of authority, have to teach "culture" to racialized learners. I challenged them to be learner-centered, and let the priorities of their fictional class guide curriculum planning. I engaged them in a critical examination of their own white privilege in relation to authority, goodness, and knowing. I strived to disrupt their firmly entrenched idea that their role was to be the authority to an identification of the multiple ways that they can facilitate their own learners in sharing their own rich histories, perspectives, languages, and worldviews. In this case, the case study allows my students to assume the role of facilitator for learning as their fictional students identify the emergent curriculum through inquiry activities.

The use of a critical multiculturalism practice allowed my learners to question in this case, the impact that the Omnibus Bills would have on the First Nations community. They came to understand how these legislative changes undermined Indigenous sovereignty. The case allowed them to begin to consider the indigenous teaching that posits "We Are All Related," a teaching that troubles the colonialist consciousness suggested by Grande (2004), by re-centering indigenous worldviews. They also began to consider their own advocacy and activism from their own privileged positions as white educators, and through this disruption unpack their notion of the good teacher. Additionally, in a few cases, the recognition of the impact on their teacher identity also led to a better understanding of the impact these bills would have on their identities as white citizens/settlers in lands that are shared with Indigenous peoples. Through this critical examination we can begin to take those first tentative steps toward confronting the luxury of ignorance (Howard 2006) and histories of white supremacy (Brayboy 2005) that dominate white pre-service educators. As a social justice educator myself I have to hold onto the hope that through this critical examination these educators will teach and live differently.

Guided by critical pedagogy, TribalCrit, and Red Pedagogy we learned to choose a different view of curriculum and pedagogy. A view that inspired my learners to take up topics of fracking, and pipeline expansion, Indigenous sovereignty and Treaty rights in their own unit planning practice; albeit with much resistance.

## FINAL THOUGHTS

As a responsive educator I make particular decisions about the content that I teach and I aim to consciously demonstrate social justice educational practices in my own teaching about pedagogy: theory and practice. I assert the social justice, anti-oppressive, and critical frameworks of our pre-service program as essential to our collective emancipation from the colonial structures of public education. I assert that teaching work *is* political work. I hope that my students will reconsider their current understanding of the good teacher. I hope that they will embrace teaching in socially just ways. Their ideas of the good teacher challenge my work as an effective (good) social justice educator. I am learning to assert a radical indigeneity in my teaching work with these white learners in the hopes that they will move past their narrow, colonial views of teaching work.

## NOTE

1. The Omnibus Bill C-45 included sections that would impact on the Fisheries Act, and change the Navigable Waters Act; and would clearly diminish First Nations' rights to determine how their lands are used.

## REFERENCES

Berry, A. (2004). Self-study in teaching about teaching. In J. J. Loughran, M. L. Hamilton, V. K. LaBoskey, & T. Russell (Eds.), *International handbook of self-study of teaching and teacher education practices* (pp. 1295–1332). Dordrecht, ZH: Kluwer.

Brayboy, B. (2005). Toward a tribal critical race theory in education. *The Urban Review, 37*(3), 425–446.

Gay, G. (2002). Preparing for culturally responsive teaching. *Journal of Teacher Education, 53*(2), 106–116.

Grande, S. (2004). *Red pedagogy: Native American social and political thought*. Lanham, MD: Rowman & Littlefield Publishing.

Howard, G. (2006). *We can't teach what we don't know: White teachers, multicultural schools*. New York: Teachers College Press.

Howard, T. (2012). Culturally responsive pedagogy. In J. A. Banks (Ed.), *Encyclopedia of diversity in education* (pp. 549–552). Thousand Oaks, CA: Sage.

Idle No More. (n.d.). Retrieved from www.idlenomore.ca.

Loughran, J. (2006). Researching teaching about teaching: self-study of teacher education practices. *Studying Teacher Education: A Journal of Self-Study of Teacher Education Practices, 1*(1), 5–16.

May, S., & Sleeter, C. (Eds.;). (2010). *Critical multiculturalism: Theory and practice*. New York, NY: Routledge.

McNeil, B., & Pete, S. (2014). Self-study of a journey of indigenization. In D. Garbett & A. Ovens (Eds.), *Proceedings of the Tenth International Conference on Self-Study of Teacher Education Practices. Herstmonceux Castle, East Sussex, England* (pp. 154–156). Auckland, NZ: University of Auckland.

Pete, S. (2013). Unpublished course notes, Faculty of Education, University of Regina, Regina, Canada.

**Shauneen Pete** is a *Nehiyaw* (Cree) woman from Little Pine First Nation, Saskatchewan. She is an associate professor in the Faculty of Education, University of Regina and is serving in her final year as the Executive Lead: Indigenization of the university. She has previously served as vice-president (Academic) and Interim President at First Nations University of Canada, as Inaugural Tribal Scholar in Residence at New Mexico State University, as Inaugural Indigenous Scholar in Residence at Nipissing University, and was honored to be a Distinguished Professor at Brock University. Her publications include: *100 Ways to Decolonize and Indigenize Academic Programs; Indigenizing the Academy: One Story,* and *Toward Indigenizing University Policy.* Dr Pete has twice been nominated for Canada's Most Powerful Top 100 Women. She is the recipient of the YWCA Woman of Distinction Award (Cultural Heritage) and is the recent recipient for the "Raising a Generation of Peace Builders" Award presented by the Intercultural Dialogue Institute.

# CHAPTER 4

# Decolonizing Pedagogies: Disrupting Perceptions of "The Other" in Teacher Education

*Gertrude Tinker Sachs, Barbara Clark, Meral Durkaya, Annmarie Jackson, Charles Johnson, William Lake, and Patty Limb*

G.T. Sachs (✉)
Department of Middle and Secondary Education (MSE),
Georgia State University, Atlanta, GA, USA
e-mail: gtinkersachs@gsu.edu

B. Clark
Gwinnett County Public Schools, Georgia, USA
e-mail: Bclark8@att.net

M. Durkaya
Turkish Education Ministry, Ankara, Turkey
e-mail: Mdurkaya82@gmail.com

A. Jackson
University of North Georgia, Gainesville Campus, Dahlonega, GA, USA
e-mail: Annmarie.Jackson@ung.edu

C. Johnson · W. Lake
Georgia State University, Atlanta, GA, USA
e-mail: chuckjohnsonatl@gmail.com; Wlake1@gsu.edu

P. Limb
Cherokee High School, Marlton, NJ, USA
e-mail: pattylimb@gmail.com

© The Author(s) 2017                                                      73
F. Pirbhai-Illich et al. (eds.), *Culturally Responsive Pedagogy*,
DOI 10.1007/978-3-319-46328-5_4

## INTRODUCTION

In educational settings where the culture, language, or social experiences of minoritized students differ from the backgrounds of their teachers and the dominant culture, should teachers adjust their teaching techniques and methods to accommodate students from diverse backgrounds? After all, many teachers assume that since immigrant students are in American schools, if any adjustments are to be made, students should be the ones to do so by learning to acculturate. Many also believe that teaching these students are no different from teaching mainstream American children (Harper and De Jong 2005). However, given the enduring impact of racism, colorism, discrimination, classism, and immigration on education in the United States and elsewhere (Anzaldúa 1987; Darling-Hammond 2005; Gonçalves E Silva 2005; King 2005), it is imperative that educators find ways to provide experiences that challenge the status quo and its debilitating historical legacies (DeVillar et al. 2013).

In this chapter, through a specific focus on the education of refugees, we strive to show how a practicum course prepared certified educators to teach speakers of English as an additional language (commonly referred to as English to Speakers of Other Languages or as ESOL). The practicum, which is part of a teacher endorsement program, provides deeply scaffolded ethnographic experiences that are transformative for the teachers who participate. The experience is one of engaging with mothers and family members of refugee learners starting from those in pre-kindergarten (PK) up to Grade 12, in their home settings, an experience that acts as a catalyst for positively impacting teachers' knowledge, attitudes, and dispositions toward "the Other," which in turn leads to the development of more effective pedagogical practices. The ethnographic practicum is based on an ecological approach to learning that challenges Western scientific, rational notions of learning and development as a set of cognitive "processes that go on inside the head.... An ecological approach asserts that the perceptual and social activity of the learner, and particularly the verbal and nonverbal interaction in which the learner engages, are central to an understanding of learning" (Van Lier 2000, p. 246). From this perspective, understanding the learner *in context* is essential.

Adopting an ecological approach to our work therefore allows us to obtain glimpses of the "whole PK-12 child" by getting to know the personal contexts from which some of them come. Marsiglia and Menjivar (2004) hold that an ecological approach involves learning about the "struggles of these immigrant groups in their historical and political context" (p. 253). For example,

> [a] refugee family leaving a war-torn country has several environments to negotiate before it settles in the United States: the native country of origin, perhaps a series of refugee and transit camps, the journey to the United States, and often several temporary residences on arrival. (Fong 2004b, p. 6)

Our support for the development of deep understandings of, and respect for, "the Other" in teacher education programs is premised on the view that teachers' teaching and children's learning are more positively enacted when teachers are knowledgeable about children's culture, and when they respect and feel a kinship for them (Nieto 2008; Noddings 2005). Critical ethnography can play a strong role in deeply affecting teachers' values, knowledge, and overall effectiveness in their working relationships with "the Other." Shirley Brice Heath and Brian Street (2008) describe ethnography as "a theory-building enterprise constructed through detailed systematic observing, recording, and analyzing of human behavior in specifiable spaces and interactions" (p. 29) and that it "forces us to think consciously about ways to enter into the life of an individual, group, or institutional life of the 'other'" (p. 31). The deep immersion and critical reflections of critical ethnography are well suited to an ecological approach, and we contend in this chapter that when used in teacher education such orientations can serve to enhance teachers' work with those who may be socially, racially, culturally, and linguistically different from themselves. While our thrust is on the education of teachers to work more capably and empathetically with diverse PK-12 children, we recognize the significance of our task in working with mothers in general and refugee mothers in particular. The United Nations clearly states the importance of educating women; if we are to begin to come near to gender equity then giving mothers access to instruction in dominant world languages is an important objective to attain (UN Women 2015).

## CRITICAL PERSPECTIVES UNDERPINNING THE COURSE WORK AND THE LANDSCAPE OF TEACHING "THE OTHER"

Camarota (2012) of the United States Center for Immigration Studies (CIS) reports that "50 million immigrants and their minor children now comprise one-sixth of the United States residents" (p. 8). Camarota's report is based on CIS's analysis of the 2010 American Community Survey public-use file which shows that 86.7% of immigrant households speak languages other than English at home and of these immigrants between the ages of 5 and above, 30.3% self-reported that they speak English "not well or at all" (p.38). The results of the survey also show that there are 11.1 million school-aged children from immigrant households who comprise 21.5% of all children in public schools and 6.6% of children in private schools. Seventy-eight and a half percent of these children reported they speak a language other than English at home, which may be viewed as a deficit or a resource depending on the educators' knowledge, skills, and dispositions in those schools (Camarota 2012). In the state of Georgia which has seen a 300% increase in the number of immigrant children in the last decade, 24.6% of immigrants and their children "live in poverty" (Camarota 2012, p. 78) and 49.8% "live in or near poverty" (Camarota 2012, p. 76).

The majority of the immigrants who live "close to poverty" come from Central and South America and countries in Africa and Asia many of which have been given the appellation, "third world." Though many of the immigrants may have been in the United States for a long time (some up to 20 years) many still make slow progress in acquiring English. It is no understatement that immigrants' skills and proficiency in the English language play a major role in their having access to a "high or low quality" of life in the United States. Once arriving in the United States, these people and their children become "minoritized" and cast as "the Other" along with other minorities, given their color of skin and country of origin despite their linguistic and cultural resources.

Refugees are a special group of immigrants who are the focus of this chapter. The 1951 Refugee Convention spells out that a refugee is someone who,

> owing to a well-founded fear of being persecuted for reasons of race, religion, nationality, membership of a particular social group or political opinion, is outside the country of his nationality, and is unable to, or owing to such fear, is unwilling to avail himself of the protection of that country (UNHCR 2015a).

The United Nations Refugee Agency estimates that there were over ten million refugees of concern to their organization in 2013 who are spread out around the world and who face repatriation, local integration, or resettlement (UNHCR 2015b). Between 1983 and 2004, over 40,000 refugees were settled in the Atlanta region (Singer and Wilson 2007) and they continue to come as the United States accepted 70,000 refugees in 2015, a figure that is due to rise to 85,000 in 2016 and 1000,000 in 2017 in response to the Syrian crisis (Zong and Batalova 2015).

Bearing in mind the preceding data on the number of immigrants, we need to juxtapose this with the data on teachers. In 2011–12, 82% of all public school teachers were non-Hispanic White, a figure that rises to 88% for private schools (U.S. Department of Education Institute of Education Sciences, National Center for Educational Statistics 2015). When we consider that they are teaching minoritized students of color and historically disenfranchised youth one might form the conclusion that there is much work to do to increase teachers' familiarity and knowledge of the homes and cultures from which their students come. Because of the increasing numbers of children in the US for whom English is an additional language, "multicultural education is an imperative in the 21 century" (Banks 2006, p. xi). However, increasing teachers' knowledge of "the Other" is not sufficient; teachers also need to be skilled in intercultural competence. Deardorff's (2012) framework for intercultural competence that is based on attitudes, knowledge, skills, and internal and external outcomes is one approach that teacher educators can adopt to support teachers' work with diverse others. We also contend that to effectively incorporate multicultural education and the development of teachers' intercultural competencies, there is a great need for *deep scaffolded experiences* that support teachers thinking when working with diverse others. This imperative is especially acute due to the *diversity gap*, and the statistics shown by The National Center for Education Statistics that by 2021, 53% of the student population will be children of color (Aud et al. 2013).

In a talk given at Georgia State University, noted public interest lawyer, Bryan Stevenson (2013) detailed four ways educators could strengthen social justice activity: (1) get close to issues by proximity, (2) work to change the narrative, (3) orient the spirit and, the most difficult of all, (4) commit ourselves to being uncomfortable. Mr. Stevenson was addressing issues specifically related to the work of his nonprofit organization, the Equal Justice Initiative (2014), which challenges racial discrimination in the criminal justice system. The work of this chapter is devoted to social justice at two levels: (1) at the macro-level, social justice through the education of refugees in the United States and ultimately dismantling hegemonic ways of knowing; and (2) at the micro-level, through our (the authors of this chapter) collective work to orient our spirit to commit ourselves to being uncomfortable yet accountable to our adult, and ultimately our PK-12, learners. We will describe how through *scaffolded proximity* in the community and critical *reflections to disrupt the grand narrative* we worked toward these goals.

The data reported in this chapter consist of both teachers' and the instructor's reflections on their experiences in working with diverse Others. Reflections, scaffolded by the course activities, are seen to be crucial to learning from experiences. Our reflections are therefore based both on the experiences in the homes and scaffoldings from the course readings, assignments, and group discussions. Zeichner and Liston (1996) draw on John Dewey's early work (e.g., 1904) to help us appreciate the *deep roots* of reflection for educators. The researchers highlight three orientations which include: (1) open-mindedness, (2) responsibility, and (3) wholeheartedness. Open-minded educators "are continually examining what is taken as natural and right and take pains to seek out conflicting evidence"; responsible educators consider "the consequences of their actions" and who is impacted by those actions; and educators who are whole-hearted, "approach all situations with the attitude that they can learn something new" (Zeichner and Liston 1996, pp. 10–11). Particularly for teachers who teach speakers of English as an additional language, the reflective approach is about "critical self-examination and reflections as a basis for decision-making, planning, and action" (Richards and Lockhart 1994, p. ix). Our reflections are premised on the view that self-growth is always necessary when considering what action can be taken to improve teaching and learning.

As a group of educators we came to this class, open to critical ways of being and the development of respect for diverse others. The first author, Gertrude is a Teachers of English to speakers of Other Languages (TESOL) professor of African Bahamian descent. All other authors with the exception of William and Meral were part-time Masters of Education students and PK-12 teachers: Barbara is European American, Annmarie is African American of Caribbean descent; Charles is European American, and Patty is Asian American. William is a European American full-time student and Meral was a full-time Masters of Education international student from Turkey at the time of the course work. Our diverse ways of seeing the world greatly added to the richness of our class interactions, which were in themselves spaces of intercultural interaction from which we could learn in addition to those spaces afforded by the practicum.

## Contextual Course Information

This chapter will document the work and reflections of teachers of ESOL in an endorsement practicum in the homes of refugee mothers. The practicum is one of four courses along with a portfolio required for the ESOL endorsement (Tinker Sachs et al. 2008; Tinker Sachs et al. 2014). The practicum is taught in conjunction with a nonprofit organization, formerly Refugee Family Services (RFS) and recently renamed New American Pathways (NAP 2014). The practicum takes place in a community a few miles outside of the city of Atlanta. This course has been developed at Georgia State University by the first author and usually takes place every fall. Teachers meet biweekly, a lecture class in the university classroom and practicum session in the field. The lecture class provided the deep scaffolding as teachers debriefed about their practicum, developed curricula, and talked about the related assigned readings, reflections, and assignments.

In the second meeting of the course, a representative from NAP comes to the university classroom to fill out the necessary paperwork and requirements to work with the mothers. The liaison also informs teachers about the work in the homes – who the women are, countries represented and languages spoken, and some background on their English competencies. Any discomfits that teachers may have are addressed. Teachers learn that during their first meeting with the mother they will be accompanied by a caseworker and a translator if needed and that some initial assessments of the mother would be done. The initial assessments include basic literacy in the mother's home language and in English and a discussion on the English-learning goals of the mother. Teachers meet with the mothers at a time that is mutually convenient and classes are held once a week for an hour and a half in the mothers' homes. The course instructor conducts one home visit per family and also records her reflections which are shared with the teachers as feedback. During class time in the teacher education classroom, teachers discuss the development of curricula based on the learning goals of each mother/student. Much of the subsequent class discussion is a reporting on the development and enactment of the student's curriculum, observations on the observed funds of knowledge in the home, and reporting on the course readings with applications to the mother's learning and PK-12 classrooms. One of the major foci of the work in the homes of the mothers is to unlock the close-up and personal funds of knowledge that are inherent in every home regardless of class, religion, race, gender orientation, country of origin, or languages spoken. These are the "historically accumulated and culturally developed bodies of knowledge and skills essential for households or individual functioning and well-being" (González et al. 2005, p. 72). These may be visible/ invisible, tangible or intangible but very much present and important, and serve to disrupt hegemonic ways of knowing and dismantle any stereotypes and bias held by educators. The major texts for the course are:

- Bixler M. (2006). *The lost boys of Sudan. An American story of the refugee experience.* Athens, GA: University of Georgia Press. ISBN: 13-978-0-8203-2883-6
- Fong, R. (Ed.). (2004a). *Culturally competent practice with immigrant and refugee children and families.* New York, NY: Guildford Press. ISBN: 1-57230-931-8
- González, N. Moll, L., & Amanti, C. (Eds.). (2005). *Funds of knowledge: Theorizing practices in households, communities and classrooms.* Mahwah, NJ: Lawrence Erlbaum Associates. ISBN-10: 0805849181
- Stoops Verplaetse, L., & Migliacci, N. (2008). *Inclusive pedagogy for English language learners: A handbook of research-informed practices.* New York, NY: Taylor & Francis. ISBN: 13-978-0-8058-5720-7

## METHODOLOGY

Critical ethnography, as used in this chapter, recasts the traditional teacher/student classroom sites to a place where the student "belongs" and reigns as knower and leader, in her home, the site of home management, child rearing, organizing, and multiple varied linguistic negotiations with family, friends, coworkers, and community members. The teacher becomes a collaborator and a recipient of the resources of the mother through the teacher documenting of her/his learner's funds of knowledge through literacy engagements. This intimacy-building process aims to transform the perspectives of the teachers about how they engage with their own PK-12 learners, as they develop a healthy regard for the mother. Our data were built on this perspective and are derived from the reflections which were written after the literacy sessions in the homes of the refugee mothers. The reflections are connected to the literature read in class and capture the development, work and impact of the practicum on our minds, hearts, and practice. Due to chapter length restrictions, not all our reflections in our data pool are represented, but all authors played a role in the preparation of this chapter.

Our approach to data analysis is as follows. At the end of the course, our reflections were gathered and read multiple times by the first two authors and a list of recurring themes were created. All authors were then asked to assign their reflections to a theme and/or create another theme where appropriate and make any changes as they deemed necessary. The first two authors had agreed on the assignment of the various themes. The final themes and journal assignments were then collated and organized for the writing of this chapter. The following is a discussion of the prominent themes derived from the instructor's and teachers' reflections over different years from 2009 to 2013. In reflecting on our work, we use pseudonyms to talk about our insights into our participants' funds of knowledge, as well as to the insights gained about their countries of origin and/or the refugee camps where they lived. The names of the refugee participants were also changed to culturally appropriate pseudonyms. Six themes were identified: (1) teacher/teacher educator as learner and intercultural developer, (2) critically responsive curriculum as transformative ground, (3) deconstructing teacher/learner and researcher/participant roles, (4) school and family relationships, (5) navigating institutional structures, and (6) learner empowerment. We have selected the first three themes to report and discuss in this chapter. In accordance with the nature of ethnographic research, detailed "thick descriptions" (Gilbert Ryle 1971; in Geertz 1973, p. 6) are generated; in accordance with an ecological approach, the contexts within which reflections were made are central to making meaning from the data. For these reasons reflections are reported at length, following a paragraph or two that sets the scene. The findings are then discussed in the penultimate section of the chapter, and implications considered in the conclusion.

## TEACHER/TEACHER EDUCATOR AS LEARNER AND INTERCULTURAL DEVELOPER

One of the most prominent themes emerging from our collected reflections was *teacher/teacher educator as learner and intercultural developer*. Inherent in all teaching methods and classroom organizational patterns are social and cultural values that are both significant and deeply imbedded. According to Prabhu (1992), the function and status of both teacher and student are historically rooted within different cultures. These cultural learning styles are learned in early childhood and can be resistant to change (Nelson 1995). Teachers can create classroom environments that do not alienate students from cultures that are different from ours; however, the onus of learning and adjustment is on the teacher as well as the student. Intercultural communication begins with examining one's own cultural beliefs and then realizing that cultural differences do exist (Bennett 1993). Martin and Nakayama (2010) identify three approaches or orientations about intercultural communication:

> (1) the traditional social-psychological approach that emphasizes cultural differences and how these differences influence communication, (2) the interpretive approach that emphasizes understanding communication in context, and (3) the more recent critical approach that underscores the importance of power and historical context to understanding intercultural communication, including postcolonial approaches. (Preface, xx)

When we understand our students' cultural differences, we can begin to build bridges of commonalities between our own culture and that of our students. It all starts with our own openness to learning about others' cultures and ways of being as depicted in the reflections of William, Gertrude, and Meral below.

### William

> Regarding my deepened understandings from this experience, I have grasped Stolzenberg's (2001) notion of culture as "a placeholder for a set of inquiries" (p. 444). In other words, I can gain cultural knowledge about the history of a particular people considered as a group. Yet to preclude prejudicial actions or thoughts, I must regard that knowledge only as a placeholder which I may need to revise as soon as possible upon meeting someone whose experiences differ from a set that I have encountered in print or in person. I learned that I still have some growing left to do as a global citizen. One morning, I attempted to call Anandi to confirm our lesson. A voice on the other end of the line said, "this is not my phone." Having deduced that her sister was speaking on the other line, I ended up writing the following in her weekly progress report to her community liaison: "I called Anandi. Her sister answered the phone and said she was not available, but that Anandi would call me back. I have not received a call back." The liaison then informed me that

that particular day was part of the Nepali festival of lights and that all Nepali recipients and staff were celebrating at that time. This was a key experience in realizing that, before casting any doubt on the dedication of my students, I must remain fully aware that their lives contain many more structured facets of which I am not initially aware.

## *Gertrude*

Samakab and his wife, Fawzia, have been in the United States for more than 10 years. While Linda taught Fawzia, I worked with Samakab to develop his literacy skills in reading. Samakab referred to his home country as Somaliland and described the political situation there. He said that no one knew about Somaliland because it was in Somalia. Somaliland wanted to become independent from Somalia but he said that there were many struggles. Samakab was a competent speaker of English and spoke volumes and was eager to tell me about his home country as I asked about the various pictures posted around the room. There were two pictures from Somaliland which Samakab described. There was one that had a dwelling place which he called a hut. He said it was made of cloth and sticks and stones and whatever one could find in the environment. It was sheltered behind some shrubbery for added protection from the fierce desert winds I thought. In the foreground of that picture were some beautiful goats and cows which he told me were unique and indigenous to that area as they did not look familiar to me. A man and a woman were in the second picture and they were minding the animals. The animals were healthy-looking with strong colors. Samakab told me that if I got married, I would receive those goats and cows as part of my dowry. Next Samakab told me about the prayer rug that he had hanging on the wall. He used the one on the sofa to demonstrate how to use it. The rug had the Grand Mosque in Addis Abba, Ethiopia depicted on it. The mosque was always pointed east toward Mecca, and one had to pray five times every day on one's knees. Samakab demonstrated how to prostrate oneself. I asked him how he prayed five times a day when he was working. He said during breaks but that he did not always pray five times, now he can do it he said. I asked him what he prayed for five times a day. He said health, happiness, forgiveness, things like that. Later, Samakab told me about the Arabic ways of writing and I asked him to write my name. He was very happy to do so for me. He showed me how the letters ran together and how "h" was not pronounced in Arabic. He then showed me how to write his own name in Arabic. I could see how animated and proud Samakab was as he told me about things dear and familiar to him.

*Meral*

There are three members in the Turkish immigrant family. The mother of the family is Esin, who at 22 years of age, came to the United States after marriage; Esin has been living here for approximately 2 years. Her husband, Semih, came to the United States 7 years ago. Whenever I went to Esin's house, I could smell delicious foods from the kitchen, which were prepared for me. She always offered me something to drink or eat. If I refused, she forced me to eat or prepared them for me to take when I was leaving. She is very generous and hospitable person. Because she is Muslim, she wears a turban and it is necessary to take your shoes off when entering her house. While making some observations around the house, I noticed that there was a prayer rug on one of the chairs. These were all symbols of Islamic world and I reflected that she grew up with Islamic culture. This definitely shows that they are hospitable people since they are sharing the foods and drinks with me that they buy with their food stamps. Also, whenever I went there, their door is not locked and the neighbors and the relatives come in without knocking on the door.

These reflections provide insight into how each author positioned themselves at the time of writing, with regard to the family they were visiting. William positions himself as a knower of "the Other," but this is tempered by a realization that this knowledge can only ever be tentative and subject to revision with each encounter. He also shows how important it is to suspend judgement during intercultural interactions – that prior to the course he may have been swift to judge and that these judgements would have been made through a process of privileging of his own cultural norms and practices. Gertrude positions herself as the learner, and the father of the home as the expert. Her position is one of humility, as she centres Samakab and his funds of knowledge in the conversation. Meral also positions herself as learner, and focuses on the ontological aspect of her experiences in Esin's home – which centred around food, drink, and the physical environment. In being attentive to these "objects," she is moving beyond their surface features to reflecting on the deeper meanings that they convey – in short, she is learning from the differences rather than making judgements about them.

## CRITICAL CULTURALLY RESPONSIVE CURRICULUM AS TRANSFORMATIVE GROUND

The second prominent theme was *critical culturally responsive curriculum developer*. Teachers work to cocreate a curriculum that is responsive to the mothers' instructional and cultural needs. The mothers' skills in English, funds of knowledge, and their goals for living in the United States are incorporated into the teachers' instructional repertoire. One of the teachers' charges was to learn about the mothers' home countries and the camps where they have lived and to use this knowledge to develop stories as part of their curriculum. According to Diaz-Rico (2004), a narrative approach to teaching language reduces one of the affective factors in language learning, such as nervousness about producing new language. These affective variables are the learner's emotions, motivation, language, and culture shock, and ego-permeability (Schumann 1978). Krashen (1977) describes these affective concerns as motivation, self-confidence, and anxiety – a low affective filter (low personal anxiety) is conducive to acquisition. Stories also help refugees to preserve their cultural identity during the integration process. The use of narrative stories not only promotes literacy among adult and older teen refugees and immigrants, but also accommodates affective concerns and transmits culture. In the following, Barbara, Chuck, Meral, and Annmarie describe their experiences with developing curricula for the mothers.

### Barbara

Nella and her family, refugees from Burundi, live in an apartment complex that is also home to many other refugee families. In her clean, but sparsely furnished apartment, a large blue area rug covered the stained dining room carpet and a green fringed lace curtain was tacked up and draped across the sliding door in the dining area. At the end of the second lesson, I recorded Nella's story using the language experience approach (LEA) and she was able to read it. Each week, Nella and the children practised literacy skills, but for Nella, the highlight of each lesson was rereading her LEA stories. We collected her stories in a binder and they became her narrative and a source of pride when she read them to her children and visiting friends. Nella told stories about her daily life: the struggles and challenges of adjusting as a refugee in a new country. After a few weeks, Nella's husband Didier was waiting for me at the dining room table to join the lesson. Didier dictated a short history of his life. Then he read it easily aloud. He was so pleased and surprised. The next week, Didier dictated another story. After I copied Didier's new LEA, he smiled with pride as he read the pages. He read it a second time more fluently, and will continue to gain fluency as he practises on his own time. Nella is eager to help her husband. While Didier read his story, his daughter, Estella, listened respectfully. For the rest of our sessions, Didier joined the Saturday lessons around the dining room table.

### Chuck

Although my meetings with Nanu were just another representative slice of the overall experience of helping her improve her English literacy, a profound understanding of the meaning of that exercise emerged in me. At the end of each of our tutorial sessions, I left feeling grateful to be a part of the efforts she was making to improve her life and the lives of her family. In the scheme of things, I was a small part of her amazing life journey. It is a privilege to be able to provide critical pedagogy to Nanu – and for her willingness to accept my instruction as helpful and valid to her life's goals. We have developed a reciprocal relationship. Her efforts to improve her English literacy sprang from her belief in the promise of a better life for her children. It was the desire to speak to her children's teachers that motivated her. It was the need to communicate effectively with her children's health-care professionals that drove her to learn. Nanu's goals were a given to most of us – but to Nanu, it was an avenue for her to be active in her children's lives. I endeavored to provide her with the basic literacy skills she needed to take on the tasks she had set for herself. I created a vocabulary list of essential terms related to school and doctor. We worked diligently on reading, speaking, writing, and listening to the vocabulary. Eventually, Nanu was able to ask basic questions, read simple sentences, write fundamental vocabulary, and understand vital language related to school and doctor.

### Meral

There are six members in the Bhutanese family, the mother and father and children from 12–20 years of age. The family had been living in the United States for 4 months when I first met with them. However,

I couldn't learn the reasons to leave their country and live in the United States as a refugee family exactly from them because of the language barriers. Sabarna, the mother of the family, is not literate in her first language and doesn't have enough proficiency in English to live in a society where English is used as a first language. Besides this family literacy project, she attends the classes given in the church. However, she cannot find a job because of her language proficiency. Even though Aadarsh, the father, has better proficiency in English than Sabarna because he learned English before coming to the United States, he cannot work anywhere because of his health problems. Since all the children have to go to school, they cannot work, either. They get aid from refugee family service and can buy foods with stamps but this aid will end at the end of 6 months. By taking her needs into consideration, I prepared the unit overview on filling out the job application form. In each lesson, I introduced the possible questions in the job application form and how to write the response to those questions. By teaching one point in each lesson and asking her to complete the sections that she knows in the application form, I aimed to teach how to fill out the application form to help her find a job.

*Annmarie*

Sanaa shared that her number one goal was to be able to help her children and to be able to communicate effectively with their teachers at their schools. It bothered her that she could not speak English sufficiently and would not be able to support her children. She wanted to be "taken seriously." That is, it was important to her that her children's teachers knew that although she was a refugee and had limited English, she was interested in helping them. Fong (2004a) posits that the goal in working with immigrant and refugee families is empowerment. In an effort to empower Sanaa to navigate the U.S. school system, I provided personalized instruction for her including sentence starters, phrases, questions and practice in conversation, replete with pronunciation. Through repeated practise with Sanaa, by the end of the 10 weeks, she felt more confident about advocating for her children.

It is evident from these reflections that what was important to the mothers was the acquisition of English that would enable them to take control over everyday activities such as speaking to their children's teachers, liaising with health-care professionals, and applying for jobs. These are all things that they would hold cultural capital for them in their countries of origin; in providing a language curriculum that responded to these needs, the teachers were supporting the mothers' agency and ability to represent themselves rather than to be reliant on others. What motivated the parents was the desire to articulate their own narratives and centering these in the literacy curriculum is consistent with a central tenet of Critical Race Theory, that of "'naming one's own reality' or 'voice'" (Ladson-Billings and Tate 1995, p. 56). Less explicit is the transformative potential of working with the families in their own homes; whether creating a curriculum that directly responded to the families' cultural contexts represented a transformation in orientation in the teacher is difficult to state without additional data. What is evident, however, is a growing understanding of the educational relationship as reciprocal – both teachers and mothers were learning from each other.

## DECONSTRUCTING TEACHER/LEARNER AND RESEARCHER/PARTICIPANT ROLES

Murray Thomas (2005) proposes that the relationship between the researcher observer and participant can fall anywhere along a continuum between closeness and distant objectivity. González et al. (2005) write that ethnographic research creates a relationship between researcher and participant that is "formed interpersonally, evocatively, and reciprocally" (p. 93). Moreover, Murray Thomas (2005) writes that researchers should understand the "language, ambitions, and values" of their subjects (p. 63). To achieve this kind of understanding, a researcher must develop a cordial and respectful relationship with the participants. Also in this relationship of teacher/student, traditional teacher roles became blurred in the homes of the mothers. Teachers felt like "kin" (William), receiving a gift (Barbara), and a learning experience (Chuck), and because they saw themselves in their students (Annmarie).

### William

In the session before last, Anju was home during the day for Thanksgiving vacation. As Anandi changed Kanti's diaper, I gave Anju a copy of *Brown bear brown bear, what do you see?* and told her that she can become a doctor. While I would encourage Anju to choose the career for which she felt most passionate, knowing that she can succeed is an important first step in raising self-esteem. Even at her pre-K program, she has already faced bullying at the hands of a neighbor boy. Despite this turbulence, her English proficiency had seemingly doubled after just 2 months of her program. I want her, and other refugee children, to grow in an environment favorable to their circumstances. Accordingly, I am thankful for the existence of this ESOL endorsement program which will permit us to become part of the solution for these immigrants. I discovered that the setting of my instruction, in the family's home with all members present, resulted in a closer relationship than if I had met the mother in more neutral territory – like a school or library. I was welcomed as if I were one of their extended kin, as part of their in-group.

*Annmarie*

Sanaa and her husband Yusuf have been in the United States for close to 4 years. She is a mother of three school-age children who works at home while her husband works as an apartment manager. She recalled the wonderful life they had in Iraq, where her husband was a pilot and she worked as a preschool teacher. To build a relationship with Sanaa, I decided to find ways to point out similarities between us. Since, I knew she wanted to return to teaching, I encouraged her to continue learning English and to pursue Early Childhood Education at a community college, as I did when I just arrived in the United States. It was important to show Sanaa that her previous teaching experience was a strength that she had within her which would ultimately empower her and the family (Furuto 2004).

*Barbara*

My teacher/learner relationship with Nella reconfirms for me that teaching is as much about finding out about myself, as it is about learning about the learner. Teaching is a gift – a passport to the learner's mind – a virtual document of agreement of trust issued by the learner – a boarding pass that guarantees the teacher a seat on the learner's life adventure train.

*Chuck*

As I arrived for our last meeting, I found Nanu and her daughter Pavitra waiting for me. Dressed in a pink jacket and a baby-blue knit cap, Pavitra was pleased to see me. We all knew the routine by then. I had special permission from Nanu to take my shoes off inside her home – her gracious way of welcoming me. We sat on the floor, shoulder to shoulder, with Pavitra between us – on top of us – and all over us. As always, we started with a little chitchat about her week as we prepared to proceed with the day's lesson. And then the work began.

With each meeting my awareness of the surrounding funds of knowledge was sharpened by what I observed during the course of the visit. I noticed the residents of the apartment community sitting outside on their doorsteps when I arrive. I noticed a group of children playing nearby as the adults talk with one another. I once again observe the trail of people walking from the main highway down the residential street to their apartment community. They carry their purchases in their arms and shepherd their children from the center of the street.

The hope of the future and the determination of Nanu and her family to learn are mirrored here – on the living room floor of Nanu Gurung, a 25-year-old refugee with two children and a husband – a woman who for the first time since she was an infant is living outside of a refugee camp. I admire her and I feel fortunate to know her. She has taught me about me while I taught her.

In this practicum, teacher learning was taking place at two levels: (1) the teachers were identifying the funds of knowledge of the families they visited in order to become culturally responsive in their literacy teaching and (2) the teachers and the first author were also noticing the impact of an ESOL endorsement practicum course on the teachers' own familiarity and knowledge of the learners' home cultures, and the ways in which this transformed their pedagogical practice in the specific context of the practicum. The above reflections show mixed success. All four provide evidence of having built an interpersonal relationship that was reciprocal and valued by them. Within this, Annmarie seems to position *herself* as being an agent of change ("I want her...."; "It was important to show Sanaa...") and the language used by William is Othering and self-serving ("I am thankful for this ESOL...program which will permit 'us' to become part of the solution for these 'immigrants'"). On the other hand, Barbara and Chuck focus on the family as key agents in their (the teachers') professional development. In addition, Chuck's learning is sharpened by what he notices on each visit to the home. This careful attention seems to be what Noddings (2005) argues for and that Gay (2002) suggests is "very different conception of caring than the often-cited notion of 'gentle nurturing and altruistic concern'" (p. 107).

## DISCUSSION

Peggy McIntosh (2000) writes that self-reflection is especially important for members of dominant groups, who tend to "disparage, fear, neglect, or be oblivious to anything outside of the dominant cultural forms" (p. 118). When teachers from dominant cultural groups are provided with critical and reflective scaffolded ethnographic ecological approaches to work with diverse others, stereotypes are challenged through "close-up and personal" extended encounters – stereotypes about "poor people," people of different skin color, people of different cultural and linguistic backgrounds, and most of all people from different countries with varying schooling experiences. There is no denying that we were "fearful" of the "unknown" at first as Barbara says here:

> Initially, many of us were uncomfortable working inside the homes of our refugee families, and struggled to identify areas of strengths in face of poverty, however, we learned to view our learners through a different lens.

The experiences were not, on their own, sufficient to bring about transformations. Through our class discussions, the readings, and the focus on identifying the strengths of each family through their "funds of knowledge," we began to develop a kinship and comfort as we saw and experienced our common humanity. Chuck says it best in one of his reflections:

> Nanu and I have a common belief – we believe justice exists for all of us regardless of who we love; where we came from; the color of our skin; and what God we believe in – and we will have it because we are entitled to it. The idea of advocacy is fundamental to the obtainment of justice when you consider the message about teaching as a reciprocal relationship.

A strengths approach highlights "healing and wholeness" (Furuto 2004, p. 25) of every individual, group, family and community, and how the individual immigrant or refugee can find his or her own strengths within themselves and around them. We saw the strong resilience of the women we worked with as we learned about their family histories and the contexts from which they had come. This learning about them served to build empathy, critical understanding of who they were, and helped us to advocate for them. We discussed numerous times in our class meetings how many of us went over, above, and beyond our course requirements to accompany a mother to the doctor, to call the telephone company about a bill or set up a service, to help a family member fill out forms, and to write notes to teachers to explain why a form had not been signed by a mother or why a child had been absent from school. Our class discussions, as well as our reflections encouraged critical self-examination (Richards and Lockhart 1994) and pushed us to be more open-minded, responsible, and wholehearted (Zeichner and Liston 1996) as we challenged our assumptions and stereotypes.

## Concluding Remarks

We began this chapter discussing the need for *scaffolded proximity* and *reflections* to change the narrative of working with diverse Others in the context of the United States and elsewhere. We contend that a critical ethnographic approach that allows scaffolded proximity and reflective practice be incorporated in teacher education programs so that teachers experience firsthand what it means to work in multicultural contexts with diverse others. In this chapter we shared some of our reflections on this process. We identified and discussed our key themes: (1) teacher/teacher educator as learner and intercultural developer, (2) critical curriculum development, and (3) the blurring of teacher/learner roles and researcher/participants in ethnographic settings. The practicum, undertaken in partnership with New American Pathways (2014), was central to the four ways that Bryan Stevenson (2013) has identified as strengthening educators' social justice activity. It provided us with proximity to the everyday lives and concerns of our students, it demanded that we "oriented" the spirit and invested in the mothers' educational goals, and the discomfort experienced forced us to examine our attitudes and values and, as a result, to change our narrative.

There is no denying the need for breaking down barriers and facing ourselves by looking at these themes in the work we do in teacher education and ultimately how we enact them and apply them in our practice. This is the work of the critical educator – one who aims to change behavior, who sees culture as a site of struggle, and who "[r]ecognizes the economic and political forces in culture and communication; [who] asserts that all intercultural interactions are characterized by power" (Martin and Nakayama 2010, p. 51). We end with reflections from Patty about the work we have done and its applications to PK-12 settings.

As educators, we have the power to determine whether students feel included or excluded in our schools and classrooms. By bringing students' languages from their homes into the classroom, we can validate their culture and their history as topics worthy of study. Therefore, the role of culture in education is paramount. The student should be the cornerstone of all instructions, and culture plays a key part since one cannot be separated from his/her cultures. Instructors must teach students to be culturally competent by helping students to appreciate and honor their own beliefs and practices while acquiring access to the majority culture, where they are likely to have a chance of improving their socioeconomic status and making informed decisions about the directions of their lives (Ayers 2008). The goal of a compassionate sensitive teacher is to take the learners' individual differences into account and to create a learning environment in which more learners can be successful in learning a second language.

## REFERENCES

Anzaldúa, G. (1987). *Borderlands/La frontera: The new mestiza*. San Francisco, CA: Aunt Lute Books.

Aud, S., Wilkinson-Flicker, S., Kristapovich, P., Rathbun, A., Wang, X., & Zhang, J. (2013). *The Condition of Education 2013 (NCES 2013-037)*. Retrieved from the U.S. Department of Education: National Center for Education Statistics, Institute of Education Sciences. Website http://nces.ed.gov/pubs2013/2013037.pdf.

Ayers, R. (2008). Classrooms, pedagogy and practicing justice. In W. C. Ayers, T. Quinn, & D. Stovall Eds., *Handbook of social justice in education* (pp. 657–660). New York, NY: Routledge.

Banks, J. A. (2006). Series foreword. In A. F. Bail, *Multicultural strategies for education and social change: Carriers of the torch in the United States and South Africa* (pp. xi–xv). New York: NY: Teachers College Press.

Bennett, M. J. (1993). Towards ethnorelativism: A developmental model of intercultural sensitivity. In R. M. Paige (Ed.), *Education for the intercultural experience* (2nd ed., pp. 1–51). Yarmouth, ME: Intercultural Press.

Bixler, M. (2006). *The lost boys of Sudan: An American story of the refugee experience*. Athens, GA: University of Georgia Press.

Brice Heath, S., & Street, B. V. (2008). *On ethnography: Approaches to language and literacy research*. New York, NY: Teachers College Press.

Camarota, S. (2012). *Immigrants in the United States: A profile of America's foreign-born population*. Retrieved from the Center for Immigration Studies website http://www.cis.org/sites/cis.org/files/articles/2012/immigrants-in-the-united-states-2012.pdf.

Darling-Hammond, L. (2005). New standards and old inequalities: School reform and the education of African American students. In J. E. King (Ed.), *Black education: A transformative research and action agenda for the new century* (pp. 197–224). New York, NY: Routledge.

Deardorff, D. K. (2012). Framework: Intercultural competence model. In K. Berardo & D. K. Deardorff (Eds.), *Building cultural competence: Innovative activities and models* (pp. 45–52). Sterling, VA: Stylus.

DeVillar, R. A., Jiang, B., & Cummins, J. (2013). Introduction. In R. A. DeVillar, B. Jiang, & J. Cummins (Eds.), *Transforming education: Global perspectives, experiences and implications* (pp. 1–16). New York, NY: Peter Lang.

Dewey, J. (1904). *The educational situation*. Chicago, IL: University of Chicago Press.

Diaz-Rico, L. T. (2004). *Teaching English learners: Strategies and methods*. Boston, MA: Pearson/Allyn and Bacon.

Equal Justice Initiative. (2014). Retrieved from http://eji.org/.

Fong, R. (Ed.). (2004a). *Culturally competent practice with immigrant and refugee children and families*. New York, NY: Guildford Press.

Fong, R. (2004b). Overview of immigrant and refugee children and families. In R. Fong (Ed.), *Culturally competent practice with immigrant and refugee children and families* (pp. 1–18). New York, NY: Guilford Press.

Furuto, S. B. C. L. (2004). Theoretical perspectives for culturally competent practice with immigrant children and families. In R. Fong (Ed.), *Culturally competent practice with immigrant and refugee children and families* (pp. 19–38). New York, NY: Guilford Press.

Gay, G. (2002). Preparing for culturally responsive teaching. *Journal of Teacher Education, 53*(2), 106–116.

Geertz, C. (1973). Thick description: Toward an interpretive theory of culture. In C. Geertz (Ed.), *The interpretation of cultures: Selected essays* (pp. 3–30). New York, NY: Basic Books.

Gonçalves E Silva, P. B. (2005). A new millennium research agenda in black education: Some points to be considered for discussion and decisions. In J. E. King (Ed.), *Black education: A transformative research and action agenda for the new century* (pp. 301–308). New York, NY: Routledge.

González, N., Moll, L. C., & Amanti, C. (Eds.). (2005). *Funds of knowledge: Theorizing practices in households, communities, and classrooms*. Mahwah, NJ: Lawrence Erlbaum Associates.

Harper, C. A., & De Jong, E. J. (2005). Working with ELLs: What's the difference? In A. Huerta Macias (Ed.), *Working with English language learners: Perspectives and practice* (pp. 107–135). Dubuque, IA: Kendall Hunt.

King, J. E. (Ed.). (2005). *Black education: A transformative research and action agenda for the new century*. New York, NY: Routledge.

Krashen, S. (1977). Some issues relating to the monitor model. In H. Brown, C. Yorio, & R. Crymes Eds., *Teaching and learning English as a Second Language: Trends in research and practice* (pp. 144–158). Washington, DC: Teachers of English to Speakers of Other Languages.

Ladson-Billings, G., & Tate, W. F. (1995). Toward a critical race theory of education. *Teachers College Record, 97*(1), 47–68.

Marsiglia, F., & Menjivar, C. (2004). Nicaraguan and Salvadoran children and families. In R. Fong (Ed.), *Culturally competent practice with immigrant and refugee children and families* (pp. 253–273). New York, NY: Guilford Press.

Martin, J., & Nakayama, T. (2010). *Intercultural communication in contexts* (5th ed.). New York, NY: McGraw-Hill.

McIntosh, P. (2000). White privilege: Unpacking the invisible knapsack. In J. Noel (Ed.), *Sources: Notable selections in multicultural education* (pp. 115–120). Guilford, CT: McGraw-Hill/Dushkin.

Murray Thomas, R. (2005). *Teachers doing research: An introductory guidebook*. Boston, MA: Pearson Education.

Nelson, G. (1995). Cultural differences in learning styles. In J. M. Reid (Ed.), *Learning styles in the ESL/EFL classroom* (pp. 3–18). Boston, MA: Heinle & Heinle.

New American Pathways (NAP). (2014). Retrieved from http://newamerican pathways.org/.

Nieto, S. (2008). Nice is not enough: Defining caring for students of color. In M. Pollock (Ed.), *Everyday antiracism: Getting real about race in school* (pp. 28–32). New York, NY: The New Press.

Noddings, N. (2005). *The challenge to care in schools: An alternative approach to education* (2nd ed.). New York, NY: Teachers College Press.

Prabhu, N. S. (1992). The dynamics of the language lesson. *TESOL Quarterly, 26*(2), 225–241.

Richards, J., & Lockhart, C. (1994). *Reflective teaching in second language classroom*. Cambridge, UK: Cambridge University Press.

Ryle, G. (1971). *Collected papers*. London, UK: Hutchinson.

Schumann, J. (1978). The acculturation model for second-language acquisition. In R. C. Gingras (Ed.), *Second language acquisition and foreign language teaching* (pp. 27–50). Arlington, VA: Center for Applied Linguistics.

Singer, A., & Wilson, J. (2007, March 1). Refugee resettlement in metropolitan America. *Migration Policy Institute.* Retrieved from http://www.migrationpo licy.org/article/refugee-resettlement-metropolitan-america/.

Stevenson, B. (2013, November 12). *25th Annual Benjamin E. Mays Lecture.* Atlanta, GA: Lecture presented at Georgia State University.

Stolzenberg, N. M. (2001). What we talk about when we talk about culture. *American Anthropologist, 103*(2), 442–444.

Stoops Verplaetse, L., & Migliacci, N. (2008). *Inclusive pedagogy for English language learners: A handbook of research-informed practices.* New York, NY: Taylor & Francis.

Tinker Sachs, G., Hendley, M. L., Klosterman, S., Muga, E., Roberson, A., Soons, B., Wingo, C., Yeo, M. (2008). Integrating funds of knowledge in the ESOL practicum: The missing element. *GATESOL in Action, 21*(2), 23–30.

Tinker Sachs, G., Carr, K., Limb, P., Choi, J., & Odo, D. M. (2014). An award-winning ESOL endorsement program: A case for ethnographic approaches in teacher education. *GATEways to Teacher Education: A Journal of the Georgia Association of Teacher Educators, 15*(1), 2–12.

UNHCR: The UN Refugee Agency. (2015a). *Refugees: Flowing across borders.* Retrieved from http://www.unhcr.org/pages/49c3646c125.html.

UNHCR: The UN Refugee Agency. (2015b). *Refugee figures.* Retrieved from http://www.unhcr.org/pages/49c3646c1d.html.

UN Women. (2015). About UN women: Meeting the needs of the world's women. Retrieved from http://www.unwomen.org/en/about-us/about-un-women.

U.S. Department of Education Institute of Education Sciences, National Center for Educational Statistics. (2015). *Fast facts: Public and private school comparison.* Retrieved from https://nces.ed.gov/fastfacts/display.asp?id=55.

Van Lier, L. (2000). From input to affordance: Social-interactive learning from an ecological perspective. In J. P. Lantolf (Ed.), *Sociocultural theory and second language learning* (pp. 245–260). Oxford, UK: Oxford University Press.

Zeichner, K., & Liston, D. (1996). *Reflective teaching: An introduction.* Mahwah, NJ: Lawrence Erlbaum Associates.

Zong, J., & Batalova, J. (2015, October 28). Refugees and Asylees in the United States. *Migration Policy Institute.* Retrieved from http://www.migrationpo licy.org/article/refugees-and-asylees-united-states.

**Gertrude Tinker Sachs** Ph.D., is chair of the Department of Middle and Secondary Education (MSE) at Georgia State University and associate professor of ESOL, Language and Literacy. As a critical teacher educator professor, Dr. Tinker Sachs' research focuses on inquiry-oriented local and international teacher professional development through transformative culturally responsive literacy pedagogies in English as a first or additional language in low-income communities. She can be contacted at gtinkersachs@gsu.edu.

**Barbara Clark** teaches middle school Language Arts in Gwinnett County in Georgia and has previously taught ESOL and Special Education Language Arts at the high school level. She is a graduate of the University of Florida and earned M.Ed. in Reading, Language, and Literacy at Georgia State University. Barbara lives in Norcross, Georgia. She can be contacted at Bclark8@att.net.

**Meral Durkaya** obtained her B.A. degree from the English Language Teaching Department, College of Education, Hacettepe University (Ankara, Turkey) in 2005. In 2010, she obtained M.Ed. Degree in Reading/Language & Literacy Education. with an ESOL endorsement from College of Education, Georgia State University (Atlanta, GA). She currently teaches in the Turkish Education Ministry in Turkey. She can be contacted at Mdurkaya82@gmail.com.

**Annmarie P. Jackson** Ph.D., is an assistant professor of Literacy and Elementary Education at the University of North Georgia, Gainesville Campus. Her research interests include preservice teacher development, teacher literacy understanding, and culturally relevant pedagogy. She prepares teachers to have a deep grasp of literacy instruction and approaches for integrating literacy in the content area. She can be contacted at Annmarie.Jackson@ung.edu.

**Charles Johnson** is a graduate of Georgia State University with a Master of Arts in Teaching (M.A.T.) for Middle Level Math/Science and an endorsement in ESOL. He holds a MPS with a concentration in Finance from Cornell's School of Hotel Administration, and a B.F.A. from the University of Florida. He can be contacted at chuckjohnsonatl@gmail.com.

**William Lake** is a second-year doctoral student in Applied Linguistics at Georgia State University and has an ESOL endorsement from the same university. His research interests include Spanish corpus linguistics, blended learning, teacher education, and academic writing pedagogy. His current work examines the role of the flipped classroom methodology in Spanish as an instructional aid for high need college students. He can be contacted at Wlake1@gsu.edu

**Patty Limb** currently teaches ESOL at Cherokee High School. She serves as an advocate for English Language Learners in the content areas through co-teaching. Her educational background includes a Bachelor of Science in Education in Social Studies Education with an emphasis in history from the University of Georgia, a Master's in Education in Social Studies Education from Georgia State University, and an ESOL endorsement from Georgia State University. She can be reached at pattylimb@gmail.com.

# CHAPTER 5

# Becoming Culturally Responsive: Reflections from an Autoethnographic Exploration of Teaching and Learning English in Brazil

*Andrea Blair*

## INTRODUCTION

My skin is white and my face is covered in freckles. I was born and raised in Northern Ireland during the 1980s. Television time was limited and the house was filled with books. After I graduated from a bachelor's degree in accounting, I felt that the corporate life was not for me and I decided to become a teacher. I qualified as a secondary mathematics teacher in England where I lived and worked for six years before moving to Brazil to live with my husband in 2011. Given my background, upbringing and formal education, it is rather unsurprising that I should quite unwittingly find myself on a civilizing mission when confronted with difference in relation to my normative whiteness (Ladson-Billings 1999) in Brazil. For someone with my background it is pretty hard not to be violently ethnocentric. It is fairly easy to assume that one's own experience is "normal" and any deviation from that norm would be seen as "different". The way I

A. Blair (✉)
Pedagogical Coordinator, Instituto Povo do Mar (IPOM), Fortaleza, Brazil
e-mail: blair_a6782@hotmail.com

© The Author(s) 2017　　　　　　　　　　　　　　　　　　　　　99
F. Pirbhai-Illich et al. (eds.), *Culturally Responsive Pedagogy*,
DOI 10.1007/978-3-319-46328-5_5

respond to or explain those differences reflect certain assumptions about me and my culture. As an educator, I have a responsibility to critically examine those assumptions, so I do not mindlessly (re)produce the kinds of social injustices and racial inequalities which exist beyond the reach of my professional practice. Culturally responsive pedagogy proposes exactly that. In this chapter I will explore some of the key principles of culturally responsive pedagogy in relation to my own lived experience teaching English as a foreign language to children and adolescents in a marginalized *favela* community in North-East Brazil.

When I moved to Brazil, the uncomfortable process of (un)learning my norms and assumptions about education, culture and difference was magnified and distorted in ways which would not have been possible had I remained teaching in the United Kingdom. This process led me to culturally responsive pedagogy via a postcolonial critical framework which allowed me to develop my practice towards what Andreotti (2011) calls a pedagogy of "unconditional love" (p. 180). Howard and Terry (2011) propose that culturally responsive pedagogy (CRP) is located in a paradigm built on five key principles:

- The eradication of deficit-based ideologies of culturally diverse students.
- Disrupting the idea that Eurocentric or middle-class forms of discourse, knowledge, language, culture and historical interpretations are normative.
- A critical consciousness and sociopolitical awareness that reflects an ongoing commitment to challenging injustice, and disrupting inequities and oppression of any groups of people.
- An authentic and culturally informed notion of care for students, wherein their academic, social, emotional, psychological and cultural well-being are promoted.
- Recognition of the complexity of culture, in which educators allow students to use their personal culture to be used as an enhancement in their quest for educational excellence (p. 5).

My focus in this chapter contribution is less on the postcolonial theoretical framework which I use to critically reflect on my practice and more on the lived experience and practical example of culturally responsive pedagogy which arose from critically reflective practice during my doctoral studies. The critical stance and embracing of complexity resonate with the core principals in critically responsive pedagogy and cannot be reduced to a simple list of what to do in culturally diverse and hybrid contexts but relate to a posture or way of being in the world which faces humanity (Todd 2008) for all that it is. When I moved to Brazil I was halfway through my doctoral studies and it happened that I wrote an autoethnography over a period of 2 years during my teaching practice in Brazil. I aim to share some reflections from this autoethnography and in doing so illustrate that culturally responsive pedagogy or any other pedagogy, like research, is a messy iteration which cannot be applied as a prescription solution for problems in practice. Like any critical issue in education, it is necessary for the practitioner to develop a constant habit of critical reflection (Brookfield 1995) rather than searching for external or global prescriptive solutions to apply in specific local contexts. Any solution is only ever partial, always evolving and, simply put, "culturally responsive pedagogy embodies a professional, political, cultural, ethical, and ideological disposition that supersedes mundane teaching acts" (Howard and Terry 2011, p. 2).

## Autoethnography: A New Epistemology for Educators

Autoethnography has given me a way to participate in a new epistemology which makes no difference between practicing education, doing research and living a life (Muncey 2005). Autoethnography, as a research methodology, is an approach to knowledge construction which, whilst emphasizing the auto-, can also emphasize the interconnectedness of my selves and other selves, as well as the interaction of selves and cultures. It offers an ethically responsible position for me as a practitioner-researcher because it permits me to move beyond the confines of researcher/researched or teacher/learner dichotomies and write through the messy iterations of human interaction.

Autoethnography therefore allows me to create knowledge by critically reflecting on my practice and using writing as a form of inquiry (Richardson and St. Pierre 2004). When I left teaching in England I was able to capture a version of my experiences as I began to set up a (potentially neocolonial) project for teaching English, and put them into interaction with educational theory and the reactions of colleagues, mentors and students. The resulting autoethnography allowed a form of culturally responsive pedagogy for teaching and learning English to emerge in my specific context in Brazil. The beauty of autoethnography lies in exploring these kinds of hybrid spaces that I and others inhabit in the twenty-first century research and classrooms so that theory is generated from practice. Educators can share stories as cautionary tales or offer them as inspiration to other educators, a storytelling which Ladson-Billings (1999) attributes to critical race theory and which acts as a catalyst "to jar dysconscious racism" (p. 16). What I offer in this chapter are reflections from my autoethnographic journey and the knowledge constructed with and through others.[1]

## LOCAL CONTEXTS: BRAZIL IS NOT FOR BEGINNERS

> There are children and adults on the street throughout the city, painfully thin figures begging at traffic lights or pushing rubbish carts. Sometimes the squirt of suds hits my windscreen and I jump, then a toothless smile reaches across with a squeegee and I watch lines of bubbly water and dirt dribble onto the wiper blades. The signal turns green and I lower my window just enough to squeeze a fifty cent coin into an outstretched hand. "Never drive with your windows down!" I am reminded by friends and family, "it's too dangerous!" The *catadores*, the rubbish collectors, who walk barefoot picking up scrap metal or plastic, are a shocking sight for me. I regularly drive past other nameless adults two blocks away from my apartment condominium, smoking crack beside overflowing rubbish carts at the side of the road. An Al Jazeera documentary, "Brazil: Forced to the Streets" (Corba 2013) speaks to children and teenagers on the streets of Rio de Janeiro, one of whom explains that surviving repeated rape attacks becomes part of daily life for the girls, but the worst part of street life is the lack of attention and love, the fact that no one cares. (Blair 2013, pp. 71–72)

Culturally responsive pedagogy emerged in my practice teaching English as a foreign language at IPOM, which stands for *Instituto Povo do Mar* or "The People of the Sea Institute" in Portuguese. At the time, IPOM was attending to approximately one hundred children and adolescents in a community known as *Serviluz* in Fortaleza. Fortaleza is the state capital of Ceará, home to over 3 million inhabitants and said to be the fifth most unequal city in the world (United Nations Human Settlements Programme 2012). Located on the periphery of the city, *Serviluz* has grown from a small fishing colony in the 1950s to one of the largest favelas in Fortaleza, with a population of approximately 23,000 residents. The original fishing colony was relocated from a neighbouring beach favoured for the installation of the industrial and navy port during the 1960s and has suffered with the expansion of the port and neighbouring petroleum works ever since. The community suffers from the indifference of the local government in providing adequate public services and infrastructure which in turn perpetuates many violent tensions within the Serviluz community. There is a high prevalence of crack cocaine use and associated trafficking. The community is a common scene of violent Brazilian social and economic inequalities, but also a unique juxtaposition of violence and poverty alongside a thriving local surf and fishing culture. The saving grace of *Serviluz* is the sea. Geographically privileged, the community stretches along the beachfront, waves breaking at three main points where many seek refuge from the misery and violence in the streets (see *IPOM Documentário Buca Dantas* [IPOM 2011] & *Titan Kids* [Curren 2011]).

As I began my ambiguous interventions in Brazil, I was undoubtedly motivated by an unexamined charitable benevolence (Andreotti 2011, p. 117), wishing to improve the lives of less fortunate others. For an educator moving against the flow of global wealth and resources, entering subaltern spaces (Spivak 1988, 2004), I know now to guard against taking up a new "civilising mission" as part of a generation encouraged and motivated to "make a difference" (Andreotti 2006, p. 1). At the time unaware of culturally responsive pedagogy and related discourse I used a postcolonial critical framework with which to reflect upon my practice. It was a critical conversation with Dr Fran Martin, shortly after moving to Brazil, which prompted me to engage in a process of deconstructing my beliefs about practising education with IPOM. Andreotti (2006) warns against the projection of my (Eurocentric) beliefs and myths as universal which might reproduce "power relations and violence similar to those in colonial times" (p. 41). During this time postcolonial perspectives began to give me a new language with which to articulate the complexity of my presence and practice in Brazil. My doctoral thesis (Blair 2013) became a response to Andreotti's (2011) invitation to "a type of scholarship that engages with both the gifts and limitations of any theory in an attempt to imagine dialogue, relationships, and education otherwise" (p. 7). A process of decolonizing my professional practice and relationships is the story I share in this chapter using excerpts from my doctoral thesis and can be understood as a living theory (Whitehead 2012) of culturally responsive pedagogy.

## WIDE OPEN MINDS: TEACHING AND LEARNING ENGLISH IN BRAZIL

"Wide Open Minds" is the name of the project for teaching and learning English in Brazil which I created within IPOM. The idea for the name represents the struggle to maintain an open mind, to develop a habit of critical scrutiny and reflection on the (Eurocentric) norms and assumptions of Teaching English as a Foreign Language (TEFL). When the IPOM founders invited me to work with them, their desire was to offer English classes to the children and young people in *Serviluz* as a skill which would help them to negotiate their way through potential sponsorship on the competitive surf scene, on a global stage. In September 2011, accompanied by a bilingual colleague and friend, we attempted to evaluate the children's level of English and how we might begin to organize English classes. I can see with hindsight how oblivious I was to the local realities and cringe to remember the naïveté with which I began a weekly "Storytime" session, unable to speak fluent Portuguese or build meaningful relationships with local people. I have since watched how this naive positivity, as a form of unexamined charitable benevolence, manifests in students – studying abroad for undergraduation degrees in Europe or America – who have visited the project. The language limitation represents an extreme inhibitor in terms of mutual understanding but the media representations and single stories (Adichie 2009) also shape the imagined geographies (Sharp 2008) of others from different cultures.

My first Storytime session was in early February 2012, and although it was the one for which I prepared the most resources, I think it was the worst Storytime session I did. Far away from the intimacy I enjoy with the children now, I had chosen to read *The Very Hungry Caterpillar* by Eric Carle (1989), having loved the book as a child. I had printed lots of flashcards to use with the children and to teach them some vocabulary, just like the English teacher in the film *Trash* (Bevan et al. 2014). Even after all the theorizing I had done, it seemed so difficult to put this theory into practice. I look back now and see that I had no caring, loving relationship with the children, and I was not really responding to them. It was me alone who had decided to bring the storybook to the children, totally submerged in my own ethnocentric perspective, I didn't even consider how it might relate to the children or how they might relate to the book – or me.

After this awkward beginning, the primary focus of the Storytime sessions became building relationships with the children, and it gave me time to improve my Portuguese. These relationships were defined by the love, care and attention which I gave and received and did not require the spoken word. This pre-empted any attempt to define objectives or outcomes for the learning of English. Even after the Wide Open Minds classroom was ready and more formal classes began in October 2012, I continued to do Storytime sessions on Fridays. Apart from anything else, it was an opportunity to continue to open space for friendship and new beginnings, to have fun with a storybook. I felt that the Storytime sessions were a time for the students to respond to myself, the storybook, each other or whatever else they chose to bring to the space.

As I began deconstructing my intentions, I also became concerned that I did not wish to offer a predefined, one size fits all, English course on students, whereby I would be constructed as superior and there would be little opportunity to respond in any meaningful way to local language and culture. I began to listen, (un)learn and observe the local culture so that I could respond to it in a more ethical manner. A continual state of critical reflection, and hyper self-reflexivity (Andreotti 2011) in particular, led me to a state of paralysis, where I felt unable to act without reproducing epistemological violences in my practice. It didn't take long for me to become overwhelmed with guilt and anxiety about my presence in the community. Where I thought I could make a difference to those who I once perceived as less fortunate, I became aware of the risk of perpetuating the kinds of injustices which contribute to the uneven distribution of global wealth and resources.

The arrival of a German student volunteer who had seen the project advertised in a magazine as "Surfing as a Way Out of Poverty" brought the Wide Open Minds project into presence in a way which was previously unimaginable to me. Suddenly life threw us into interaction – an anxious theorist from Northern Ireland with a bilingual German girl, both of whom were willing to devote their time and energy to the children at IPOM and neither of whom could speak fluent Portuguese. I was anxious that Hannah was also from Europe and together we represented two Eurocentric lenses driving the project. Before Hannah arrived, IPOM had designated a (class) room for the Wide Open Minds project. They installed air-conditioning and asked me what colour I wanted to paint the walls. I chose white, so that the students could fill the room with colour. The implications of it being my choice, and not something negotiated with the children bothered me immensely, but I found myself trapped into a position of authority whose opinion was sought and acted upon. It seemed to be impossible to turn things around and ask even my own husband (one of the four original founders of IPOM), what do you think? I was working within IPOM, and as the person responsible for setting up an English course, my opinion was sought by those with the means of creating a structure for the project, but I did not want that authority: me, the white European acting in Brazil to help the less fortunate. Something which as unexamined charitable benevolence (Andreotti 2011, p. 117) felt so good and so rewarding, suddenly felt so complicated. The (class)room was ready for use at the end of September 2012 and the white walls represented a physical space for the emergence of that which was previously unimaginable (Biesta 2010). In 2011 when I first started to visit Titanzinho, the room was a storage room full of old books and school materials from another era. The books were cleared out into another room, a new floor put down, the walls painted white, air-conditioning installed and there it was: a colonized space in the middle of a *favela* community in North-East Brazil.

Another arrival from the Global North compounded the issue. My best friend since we were 4 years old, Tori, had taken a sabbatical year from her work in London as an events coordinator to travel around South America. "It's like you're reluctantly teaching them English," she said to me one day, and she was right. I was preoccupied with a fear of (re)producing (neo)colonial power relations based on my own cultural heritage, but it had taken me 2 years of doctoral study and critical reflection to develop this hypersensitivity. As such, my comparatively uncritical colleagues were major catalysts in helping me to overcome this state of paralysis. I realized and accepted that I had to act from somewhere, that I could not erase my own culture and difference. I could continue to think education "otherwise" in a process of critical reflection while being open to (un)learning and carefully examining my assumptions, but I also had to have praxis: practice upon which to critically reflect. Time had to pass. My concerns were balanced by Hannah and Tori's relatively unexamined charitable benevolence, and the classroom came to life, the walls painted by the coming together of difference. Tori, who spent a month volunteering in the project, later gifted a few words to me about the experience:

Personally I had not given much thought to the consequences of teaching English as a foreign language – to me, it was a great opportunity for the children to learn one of the most popular/useful languages so that they could use this to create a better life for themselves. However, Andrea challenged my "western" perception of this and of education in general – why should our ideas be the best? Why should we put emphasis on learning English? I admire that Andrea was able to pull herself out of this way of thinking, challenge these traditional concepts of education and create a new means of educating, one that doesn't impose our mindset on the children, and come up with a mutually rewarding educational structure for children and volunteers/teachers, taking into consideration the cultural impact as well.

Wide Open Minds means...maintaining an open mind/not falling into the traditional way of thinking/being open to new and different methods of doing things/being an inspiration – having a wide open mind and thus inspiring this in the students that one teaches. Showing that there is not necessarily one "right" way/taking into consideration the viewpoints and opinions of others and learning from these different viewpoints. (Adapted from Blair 2013, pp. 104–105)

Around this time I began working closely with a local photographer and community leader, Raimundo Cavalcante, known as Raimundinho, who opened the window to the favela so that I could see the beauty inside. His photography work focusses on the positive aspects of life in the *Serviluz* community, he is proud of where he is from and works to promote an image which is not solely focussed on the misery and suffering of his neighbours, relatives and friends.

My work here contributes to the people, like IPOM and others who come here, who we [community leaders] think will do something good for the neighbourhood, and my contribution is showing Titanzinho in another way, not marginalised, but a neighbourhood developing every day, so that the politicians look more towards here, with more heart, to develop the beautiful work that IPOM does here. I think it's very important to work with developing the children, because this is what we want, that they grow up with good relationships and friendships so their future is much better than what was in the past here. We didn't have hope for a child, and nowadays these children of the street, children who are the street, there are some who we see playing...all of them enter too easily into marginalisation. Surf is one option that takes these children off the streets and to the water, then IPOM arrived with a surfing mentality, and you now are asking me to do this work taking photographs, to develop the work telling a story of the neighbourhood. I think that you will further enrich our work here, on the "inside".

Development for us in the neighbourhood would be to clean everything up, this is very flawed here. I think the local government could come here "inside" you know? Fix up our housing, we are paying taxes for this. The health service here is precarious, the health centres do not work in the way they should. The public schools are just a façade, there is no good education here. It is even worse for those who do not have financial conditions, they are not well attended in the schools, even by the directors. So I think development for us here is school, health, a well-made infrastructure and a good standard of living. We live in an area of risk, at the same time it is an area of privilege – with the fishing, the surf, football and leisure space on the beach and in the sea. We have lived here for many years, I think for about 70 years there are people living here in Serviluz so we can't just leave, it has to improve.

Every day I become more impressed when I arrive and see these children speaking English, I never saw a thing like this in my life. I don't know, it's emotional, I get emotional with this here, I arrived here and the children are presenting themselves in another language that I don't even know how to speak – I only speak Portuguese, and even that is bad! It is a beautiful work of yours, a work of the heart, you do it with love and it's very well done. It's very pleasurable for the children, I always say that to the surfers, because a lot of them don't bother to come here and they're missing out and they will come here because they know that this is very important. We see these children speaking English and we live right beside the harbour. A lot of gringoes come on these ships and they always pass through here on their trips, so it's important. Some day one of these gringoes will arrive here and one of these children will be speaking English with them. I think that the day this happens, the people will see, the community will see, they won't believe what they are going to see. I think that they are going to think that they are dreaming, because a lot of people haven't seen the reality of IPOM, this English work with you . . .

The children here are very intelligent, they have a very strong local culture. They are fighters, spending the whole day in the middle of the streets, on the beach, created free on the shoreline, this isn't something we see everywhere. They are very strong, they learn things easily, they are bad at studying because they want to be free, they don't want to be like those children locked inside a classroom. I think they see this difficulty, they feel this difficulty in their skin, what is it to teach them? They are very free children, free from the family, because the family liberates them a lot. The father has to work or the mother has to work or the parents are separated, so the children live in the middle of the streets. It's really difficult to teach them, but for those who want to learn it's really easy because they are really smart and they pick things up very quickly. (Adapted from Blair 2013, pp. 66–70)

Today the Wide Open Minds project is a window to a diverse range of cultural backgrounds. I have hosted around twenty students and volunteers from Brazil, South and North America and Europe to watch or volunteer their time during the English lessons and I try to share a sense of critical reflection and an openness to different ways of teaching and learning English in Brazil. Engaging with the Wide Open Minds project is about engaging with difference and imagining beyond our selves and cultures; being willing to occupy hybrid spaces and (un)learn both language and culture. In this context, I often find these questions useful for provoking critical reflection in colleagues, students and volunteers:

- Why teach English?
- What systems have led to the role I occupy as an educator in this context?
- How do I present myself to learners?
- Do I act superior because I see myself as more educated than my students?
- What assumptions underpin my practice?
- What are my motivations for being involved in this project?
- What is shaping mine and others' understandings/knowledges?
- Who decides (what is taught, can be known or needs to be done) and for whose benefit?
- What are the implications of claims (past/present/future: social, environmental, economic, etc...) to know or to act for my students?
- What are the sanctioned ignorances (blind spots) and contradictions in my knowledge and practice?
- How can I create the conditions for a non-judgemental space where unique differences can be valued?
- What style of teaching is appropriate here?
- What assumptions about English can I explore with learners? (Adapted from Learning to Read The World Through Other Eyes, Andreotti and De Souza 2008)

## BECOMING CULTURALLY RESPONSIVE: CURRICULUM DESIGN

In the context of Wide Open Minds, the curriculum I design or use is always subject to critical reflection and scrutiny in terms of what should or ought to be taught and learnt. The objectives of formal qualification are concerned with language acquisition and the technical concerns of teaching and learning English as a foreign language. I have found that there is a wealth of free resources on the Internet for use in teaching English as a foreign language. While these resources are diverse and useful, they are quite often ethnocentric in that they reflect the kinds of epistemological violence which I am anxious not to (re)produce. White skin, Euro/North-American housing, leisure and transport thematics are the norms. I am reminded of the awkward beginnings of Storytime, a time when I was unaware of the local contexts and how English might be taught in such a way as to develop vocabularies and expressions appropriate to the lived realities of the children and adolescents in *Serviluz*. I am also reminded of a scene in the Brazilian–British film *Trash* (Bevan et al. 2014) which shows a pretty, (white) foreign female, teaching English to the children living in a *lixão* or dump. In powerful juxtaposition, the boys pick through mountains of waste and rubbish and scramble through sewage pipes, the young teacher is showing them flashcards of animals and performing a classic "listen and repeat" exercise as they memorize the pronunciation of "cat", "dog", "snake" and so on.

In response to the students I teach at IPOM, I have therefore dedicated many hours to drawing and writing customized worksheets and language tasks which might be termed as culturally responsive. The materials I have used for qualification purposes therefore draw on themes relating to the local culture, particularly a connection with the sea and surfing. I cannot replace by imposition all resources so that they relate only to my perceptions of local culture, but I can make it a priority to constantly critically reflect and create resources which are culturally relevant and responsive. The thematics which I have used to write the curriculum for Wide Open Minds include (a) Greetings and Introductions (b) Numbers and Colours, (c) Under the Sea, (d) Animals, (e) My Family, (f) My Body, (g) My Daily Routine, (h) Nature and Weather, (i) School Supplies, (j) Food and Drink, (k) Hobbies and Interests, (l) Surf Season and (m) *Serviluz*. Within each of these themes culturally responsive pedagogy foregrounds endless issues for critical reflection: (a) hair and skin colour (e.g. this raises issues about Afro, Indigenous, black or mixed race identities, particularly for young females exposed to media representations which devalue blackness and glorify whiteness); (b) bodies (e.g. the historical subjugation, objectification and sexualization of Afro descendant bodies); (c) family structures (e.g. many children in *Serviluz* are raised by their grandmothers, or have absent parents for a variety of reasons, or have aunts, uncles and siblings who are not blood relatives); (d) telling the time (e.g. I found that many of the children could not tell the time and had little need for doing so until we found common ground in the ebb and flow of the tides and the cycles of the sun and moon); and (e) local and regional foods (e.g. rice and beans is staple food; often children have never tasted an expensive item like an apple or a pear, fruits commonly included in TEFL resources as basic vocabulary; with time I have included foods like cashew fruit and guava, coconut water and symbolic meals such as *feijoada* – Do you like *feijoada*? – showing that not everything has or ought to have a direct translation from Portuguese to English and vice versa, that foods can be cultural products as much as music or art). These issues are represented orally and symbolically as I struggle with my whiteness, my (Eurocentric) norms and assumptions.

Over time, these themes have also evolved from beginner to pre-intermediate-level English. These levels have evolved in the local context and do not reflect the application of formal assessment strategies. Our beginner (Groms) level is aimed at children from 7 to 11 years old, and the pre-intermediate (Pro-Surfer) level is for children and adolescents aged 12–17 years old. As I write these words I am also working in collaboration with a friend who, in the spirit of the gift economy (Vaughan 2002), is transforming my hand-drawn worksheets into graphic illustrations in order to put together two course books which have grown organically with the experiences of educators and students in the first two years of Wide Open Minds at IPOM and represent a product of culturally responsive pedagogy. This resource lays a foundation for opening minds and conversations through the teaching and learning of English in Brazil, particularly for communities such as *Serviluz* whose skin colours, bodies and local realities are not (re)presented in mainstream English teaching resources.

Although Wide Open Minds, as a project for teaching and learning English in Brazil, has formal objectives for the teaching and learning of English, these technical concerns for qualification do not exhaust the task of the educational project (Biesta 2006, 2010). In the context of IPOM, relational ethics, or "an authentic and culturally informed notion of care for students, wherein their academic, social, emotional, psychological and cultural well being are promoted" (Howard and Terry 2011, p. 5) also play an important role in culturally responsive pedagogy. In the next section I share something of what I have learnt about not teaching the subject I've been contracted to teach at the expense of caring to know my students and knowing how to love them for being who, not what, they are (Andreotti 2011, pp. 175–190).

## Ethical Responsibility: Caring to Know, Knowing to Love

I slowed my car and creaked over the awkward speed bump on the road leaving IPOM. I saw Raimundinho standing under the shade of the surf shack. The sea glittered behind him as he waved and returned my thumbs-up hand signal. He hoisted himself up from his perch on the wall, his camera in his hand. The water full of surfers, young and old, carving out manoeuvres on the waves below, Raimundinho would spend hours photographing them. The shack was a corrugated tin roof held up by six posts, perched on the edge of the large boulders installed during the building of the industrial port, as one of two enormous breakers to stop the sand drift. It provided the perfect vantage point from which to watch the waves breaking onto the beach below, offering protection from the sun's rays directly overhead. I stopped and Raimundinho bent towards my car, leaning his free hand against the doorframe. "Tudo bem?" he inquired, smiling. "Tudo joia!" I replied, returning his smile.

He agreed to take me on a walk around the community the next day. This walk would give me a unique glimpse of an imagined unknown, "the inside". I was too scared, and had been told that it was too dangerous for me to walk around alone. I had always driven "in" and "out" of the community by car, always by day. I do not feel safe, the way I do "at home", inside my condominium apartment or in the UK. Raimundinho's company, as a man and a community leader, would ensure that no *ladrões*[2] would approach me as we walked through narrow streets lined with open sewers. Some streets were sandy paths, strewn with uncollected bags of rubbish, as we walked to the abandoned *Mucuripe* lighthouse at the edge of *Serviluz*. The lighthouse was constructed by slaves between the years 1840 and 1846. Nowadays it is quite symbolic of the social exclusion of the community, on the periphery of Fortaleza's postcard cityscape. The lighthouse was deactivated some time during the 1960s and is at the centre of a proposed development project which threatens to remove current residents from their beachfront homes.

As we walked up the steps of the lighthouse Raimundinho explained that the state and city governors were locked in a bitter argument about who was responsible for refurbishing and maintaining the lighthouse. Meanwhile it stood on uneven concrete steps amongst the tumbleweed, its walls wearing peeling paint covered in graffiti and *pixação*. The inside of the lighthouse gave me a strong feeling of unease. The obvious signs of transient occupants ranged from the human excrement on the floor to the pixação covering every inch of the walls. The floor was covered in dust and broken cement. We made our way up the rusted iron staircase that seemed to float up the central shaft of the lighthouse. It moved with every step but I felt ridiculous to be scared, Raimundinho stepped ahead of me and offered me a hand to steady myself. The view from the top of the lighthouse was breathtaking. I stood and took in the bizarre blend of beachfront, industrial port, shipping yard, the prohibited green space meeting the perfect waves on *Praia Mansa*,[3] cityscape, the *favela* on the hill beyond and the *Serviluz* community stretching from across the railway track. Raimundinho told me that there are around 15,000 people living in *Serviluz*. My head spun at the number and I looked across the vast sprawl of jumbled red brick houses squeezed beside and on top of each other, a swollen and entangled meshwork of lives.

We descended, my legs shaking on the swaying spiral staircase. I eyed the broken joints that had torn themselves away from the concrete walls and tried not to panic as I imagined the whole thing falling away from underneath me. At the bottom I followed Raimundinho around the back of the lighthouse, the sun now behind us, it was a relief to stand in the cool shade. There were some children sitting around. They were dancing to funk music from Rio de Janeiro, battering a crumbled old wooden shack and staring at me and Raimundinho, who continued chatting away to me unperturbed. My own mind was racing, looking at the children, I was a little bit speechless. Dressed in too-small and worn-out clothes with sun-bleached hair and skinny limbs, they seemed so abandoned to my Western gaze. Their dance was, to me, overtly sexual and although Raimundinho laughed, I admitted to being rather shocked by what I saw. They looked and smiled so shyly. I shuddered to think of who else might approach these children, one of whom was jiggling her bottom in front of Raimundinho's camera. The children peered into his viewfinder to see the recording. I wanted to "reach out" to all of them, invite them to IPOM to play and learn and have fun in a "safe" environment, but the longing to care was balanced by the voice in my head asking "what right do you have, to judge?... to offer something better?" I didn't say anything to the children, I simply returned their stares and shy smiles. I knew that this kind of "reaching out" was based partly on pity, an emotional reaction to what I saw. Even though by now I had carefully examined my own cultural norms, I realised that it was hard not to judge these children by my Western standards of living. (Adapted from Blair 2013, pp. 70–71)

These children, children of the street, are somebody's children. Many have been abandoned by parents and by society. I include this story because Raimundinho continues to show me the real meaning of facing humanity (Todd 2008). I do not have to give something to these children to make their lives better. At the lighthouse, I watched how Raimundinho shared the video footage with them, leaning down to chat with two or three children, speaking in his gentle, smiling voice. I see him almost every day and the way that he engages with people who some might consider to be subaltern (Spivak 1988, 2004). There is something in this idea of facing humanity, as Todd (2008) suggests, which isn't something that ought to be avoided in education but somehow "rooted in the difficult relations between actual persons" (p. 3). What I have come to understand is that every person is living a human experience as I recognize the other as both equal and different. In a recent meeting with the educators at IPOM he spoke with emotion about the children living in precarious conditions, surrounded by drugs and guns, whose immediate family and circle of friends are most likely the gang leaders, drug traffickers and assassins of the community.

Leonardo Boff (2010, 2007) argues that essential care is an ethics of human nature that the world needs healers and those who are willing to stand in solidarity with those who are suffering. To stand in solidarity means to not let the other to suffer alone, but to be there *with* the other, to recognize the human experiences different from my own, to care to know. Carol Gilligan (2011) too refers to the ethic of care as "a human ethic" (p. 175) and for me this signifies a learning to love. Boff (2007) aligns essential care with interconnectedness, a consciousness that sees itself as part and parcel of the universe (p. 7). In this view, care is a fundamental mode-of-being which represents "an attitude of activity, of concern, of responsibility and of an affective involvement with the other" (Boff 2007, p. 14). Gilligan (2011) suggests that in reference to the women whose acts saved hundreds of lives during the Second World War,

> rather than asking how do we gain the capacity to care, how do we develop a capacity for mutual understanding, how do we learn to take the point of view of the other or overcome the pursuit of self-interest, they prompt us to ask instead: how do we lose the capacity to care, what inhibits our ability to empathise with others, and most painfully, how do we lose capacity to love? It is the absence of care or the failure to care that calls for explanation (pp. 164–165).

Gilligan (2011) argues that an ethic of care is integral to the functioning of a global society, a "resistance both to injustice and to self-silencing" (p. 175). I therefore feel less inclined to justify an attitude of essential care and more inclined to continue questioning an absence of care or of the capacity to love "difference".

One of the biggest challenges of my current role as the Coordinator for IPOM is establishing norms and limits for excluding or including children or young people who participate in the projects. How far, my team asks, do we tolerate displays of aggression or challenging behaviours? I do not want to exclude the children and young people already abandoned by parents and society. Our work is to love and care for these children, to respond to the ways that they have been raised in a different culture, on the street or in the midst of a gang or brothel, however shocking that difference might be to me and my ethnocentric experiences. Raimundinho's words in that meeting resonate with me: "*precisamos conviver com isso*", meaning that instead of searching for ways to exclude children who present challenging behaviours, we need to live with and face this reality. We do not look upon these children or their families as inferior, we replace judgements with curiosity; we need to face this humanity (Todd 2008).

## Conclusion(s)

It is hard to do justice in one chapter to the stories I have lived, with and through others in Brazil. There are many people who have helped me to (re) negotiate meanings in practice and develop culturally responsive pedagogy which embraces a new paradigm for education (Howard and Terry 2011). Deconstructing norms and assumptions so that difference is no longer understood as deficit, disrupting ethnocentrism to critically reflecting on practice and curriculum design as well as developing more ethical, caring and loving relationships are all important steps to take in practice if culturally responsive pedagogy is to become more than mere rhetoric.

I close this chapter with lyrics from the song *Janela da favela* by the Brazilian band Ponto do Equilíbrio (Do Salgueiro 2007),

Não quero dizer que lá não existe tristeza
Não quero dizer que lá não existe pobreza
Porque favela sem miséria não é favela
Porque favela sem miséria não é favela
Abre! Abre a janela da favela
Você vai ver a beleza que tem por dentro dela
Abre a janela moço!
Abre a janela da favela
Você vai ver a beleza que tem por dentro dela (n.p.).

Below is my translation of the lyrics a reflection on its title, which means "Point of Balance".

I don't want to say that sadness does not exist there
I don't want to say that poverty does not exist there
Because a *favela* without misery is not a *favela*
Because a *favela* without misery is not a *favela*
Open! Open the window of the *favela*
You will see the beauty inside

Open the window my friend!
Open the window of the *favela*
You will see the beauty inside.

These lyrics remind me of the need to find balance in my practice; to balance formal qualification with critically reflective practice; to recognize the misery and suffering of the human condition, but also the beauty that lives within each individual and every different contribution. I hope that somehow I can inspire fellow educators to open the windows of their hearts and minds to the infinite possibilities that the future brings to us as we move between hybrid contexts and design culturally responsive pedagogies based on love, care and critical reflection. Thank you for reading.

## NOTES

1. The Nguni word *ubuntu* suggests that "I am because we are" (Nussbaum 2003). Ubuntu is something which means that my humanity is entangled in that of others:

   When we want to give high praise to someone we say, "Yu, u nobuntu"; "Hey, he or she has ubuntu." This means that they are generous, hospitable, friendly, caring and compassionate. They share what they have. It also means that my humanity is caught up, inextricably bound up, in theirs. We belong in a bundle of life. We say "a person is a person through other people". Tutu (1999, Ch 2)

   Ubuntu therefore foregrounds interconnectedness and "the responsibility to each other that flows from our connection" (Nussbaum 2003, p. 21). This is important for me as a teacher and a researcher concerned with ethical responsibility for it is "our connection" that prompts me to examine the ethical choices I make. In the spirit of *ubuntu*, I am because we are. This means that contributions from others in the literature as well as those with whom I encounter in person have shaped the emerging text, the autoethnographic product. I argued that autoethnography can be an ethical approach to practitioner-research, as it moves away from traditional power structures which objectify difference and exclude the relational ethics that flow from our interconnection.

2. *ladrões* (pl) / *ladrão* (s): I find this word very hard to translate. The precise word-to-word translation is simply "thief" or "thieves" but to me this does not quite sum up the cultural situatedness of the word *ladrão* which refers to street manifestations of violent, threatening behaviour from a person,

usually (but not always) male and abusing drugs like crack cocaine. In Brazil, *ladrões* often reside within *favela* communities marginalized from city centres (while some less obvious *ladrões* occupy well-paid positions in government, stealing public funds and neglecting public services) and often inaccessible to police. *Ladrões* sometimes wait and watch for a vulnerable target with obvious belongings like a handbag or a wedding ring which they can sell underground. I have seen *ladrões* stealing bags and cameras from people on the beach and I have been approached by a *ladrão* who attempted to rob me, but I had nothing of value only my life for which I am increasingly grateful.... My husband was carjacked at gunpoint by *ladrões*. I have witnessed two carjackings of the-car-in-front at gunpoint while stationary at a red traffic light in the last 12 months and escaped one myself, thanks to the quick-thinking of my husband. I say: Brazil is not for beginners.

3. The original fishing colony was on *Praia Mansa* which is no longer a public right of way.

## REFERENCES

Adichie, C. N. (2009, July). Chimamanda Ngozi Adichie: The danger of the single story [Video file]. Retrieved from https://www.ted.com/talks/chimamanda_adichie the_danger_of_a_single_story?language=en _.

Andreotti, V. (2006). Soft versus critical global citizenship education. *Policy and Practice: A Development Education Review.* (3). Retrieved from http://www.developmenteducationreview.com/issue3.

Andreotti, V. (2011). *Actionable postcolonial theory in education.* London, UK: Palgrave Macmillan.

Andreotti, V., & De Souza, L. M. T. M. (2008). *Learning to read the world through other eyes.* Derby, UK: Global Education.

Bevan, T., Fellner, E., & Thykier K. (Producers). (2014). *Trash* [DVD]. Available from http://www.amazon.co.uk/Trash-DVD-Rooney-Mara/dp/B00LSW77YG.

Biesta, G. J. J. (2006). *Beyond learning: Democratic education for a human future.* Boulder, CO: Paradigm Publishers.

Biesta, G. J. J. (2010). *Good education in an age of measurement: Ethics, politics, democracy.* Boulder, CO: Paradigm Publishers.

Blair, A. J. (2013). *Being in Brazil: An autoethnographic account of becoming ethically responsible as a practitioner-researcher in education.* (Unpublished doctoral dissertation thesis). University of Exeter, United Kingdom.

Boff, L. (2007). *Essential care: An ethics of human nature.* London, UK: Society for Promoting Christian Knowledge.

Boff, L. (2010, April 9). *Ética e Ecologia desafios do século XXI* [Video file]. Retrieved from http://www.youtube.com/watch?v=6YFTh2yEPlk.

Brookfield, S. D. (1995). *Becoming a critically reflective teacher*. San Francisco, CA: Jossey-Bass.

Carle, E. (1989). *The very hungry caterpillar*. Jefferson City, MO: Scholastic.

Corba Director, G. (2013). *Brazil: Forced to the streets* [Video file]. Available from http://www.aljazeera.com/programmes/letterfrommychild/2013/04/20134811918282936.html.

Curren, L. A. (2011, December 11). *Titan kids surfing trailer* [Video file]. Retrieved from http://www.youtube.com/watch?v=S2OvGBEVc3w.

Do Salgueiro, G. (2007). Janela da favela [Recorded by Ponto do Equilibrio]. On *Abre a Janela* [CD]. New York, NY: Warner Music Group Records.

Gilligan, C. (2011). *Joining the resistance*. Cambridge, UK: Polity Press.

Howard, T. C., & Terry, C. L. (2011). Culturally responsive pedagogy for African American students. *Teaching Education, 22*(4), 345–364.

IPOM. (2011, December 7). *IPOM Documentário Buca Dantas* [Video file]. Retrieved from http://www.youtube.com/watch?v=Zwrd9lzicJE.

Ladson-Billings, G. J. (1999). Just what is critical race theory and what's it doing in a nice field like education. In L. Parker, D. Deyhele, & S. Villenas (Eds.), *Race is…race isn't: Critical race theory and qualitative studies in education* (pp. 7–30). Boulder, CO: Westview Press.

Muncey, T. (2005). Doing autoethnography. *International Journal of Qualitative Methods, 4*(1), 69–86.

Nussbaum, B. (2003). Ubuntu: Reflections of a South African on our common humanity. *Reflections, 4*(4), 21–27.

Richardson, L., & St. Pierre, E. A. (2004). Writing: A method of inquiry. In N. Denzin & Y. Lincoln (Eds.), *Handbook of qualitative research* (3rd ed.). Thousand Oaks, CA: Sage

Sharp, J. (2008). *Geographies of postcolonialism*. London, UK: SAGE Publications.

Spivak, G. C. (1988). Can the Subaltern speak? In C. Nelson & L. Grossberg (Eds.), *Marxism and the interpretation of culture* (pp. 271–313). Urbana, IL: University of Illinois Press.

Spivak, G. C. (2004). Righting wrongs. *The South Atlantic Quarterly, 103*(2/3), 523–581.

Todd, S. (2008, March). *Facing humanity: The difficult task of cosmopolitan education*. Paper presented at the annual conference of the Philosophy of Education Society of Great Britain, Oxford, UK.

Tutu, D. (1999). *No future without forgiveness: A personal overview of South Africa's Truth and Reconciliation Commission* [Kindle version]. Retrieved from Amazon.co.uk

United Nations Human Settlements Programme (UN-HABITAT). (2012). *State of the world's cities 2012/2013: Prosperity of cities* (World Urban Forum ed.). Retrieved from http://unhabitat.org/books/prosperity-of-cities-state-of-the-worlds-cities-20122013/.

Vaughan, G. (2002). *The gift economy*. Synopsis of a paper presented at the Women's Worlds Conference at the University of Makerere, Uganda. Retrieved from http://www.gift-economy.com/articlesAndEssays/theGiftEconomy-article.pdf.

Whitehead, J. (2012). Educational research for social change with living educational theories. *Educational Research for Social Change (ERSC)*, *1*(1), 5–21. Retrieved from http://www.nmmu.ac.za/helpingteachers/ERSC%20VOL1%20NO1%20APRIL2012/Whitehead%20Vol%201%20No%201%20April%202012.pdf.

**Andrea Blair** at the time of writing this chapter, Andrea was working as the project coordinator at IPOM (Instituto Povo do Mar) in Fortaleza. She was leading a team of educators with whom she created a culture of ethical responsibility, love and respect in the most challenging of contexts. The people she met during her time in Brazil and the stories they gifted to her, call her back there on a regular basis as she gently moves away from the role she cultivated within IPOM to watch the local community embrace the pedagogy of unconditional love she created there with the children of *Titanzinho, Serviluz*. Andrea is now living and teaching in West Cornwall and spends her free time writing, practicing yoga and walking along cliff tops beside the ocean.

# PART III

# CHAPTER 6

# The Role of Song and Drum in Schools: A Response to Questions About Culturally Responsive Practice

*Anna-Leah King*

## INTRODUCTION

As a new teacher I found myself placed at inner city schools, first a high school then elementary school with a total school population of Aboriginal children. The schools I worked in also had drum and dance troupes. Assigned to be co-choreographer of the dance troupe I had a unique teaching portfolio that I embraced wholeheartedly. Knowing the drum since I was a child and being a part of powwow as a dancer for a time this was a familiar territory. At the high school, practice time was built into the program wherein drum and dance was titled "Cultural Arts" as a credit course. With regard to the elementary school, we had practice after school hours, twice a week for both drum and dance. We spent a lot of time performing for conferences and schools in the system. Sometimes the students were pulled out of class to perform, much to the chagrin of fellow colleagues, who often questioned the dance troupe as having any merit. In fact the troupe's excursions during school time became a bone of contention with some of our colleagues. I was a teacher myself and could not understand this

A.-L. King (✉)
Wikwemikong Unceded Reserve, Manitoulin Island, Ontario, Canada
e-mail: Anna-Leah.King@uregina.ca, Annaleah@ualberta.ca

© The Author(s) 2017
F. Pirbhai-Illich et al. (eds.), *Culturally Responsive Pedagogy*,
DOI 10.1007/978-3-319-46328-5_6

criticism. I felt we were giving students experiences that they would not have otherwise and exposure to a "bigger picture" of what's out there in the world. The students fit the role of an ambassador to the school. On a number of occasions the teachers asked questions such as:

1. Is song and drum really extracurricular?
2. Is that really music?
3. Are those words your singing?
4. Is that screaming?
5. Does this merit pulling students out of class?

One colleague took it upon herself to inquire whether I really considered song and dance as extracurricular activity. I am guessing she meant enhancing or extending the provincial curriculum in some way. I assured her drum and song has equal merit to other learnings. It was so much more than just an after-school practice for performance. This is the same colleague who did not think we were singing and did not equate drum and song with music.

The students were school ambassadors whether their status was clearly defined as such or not. They represented our school and the students knew this. Any acting out and they would no longer be a part of the troupe. We never had any difficulty with the students. In 10 years of practice and performance there was not a single incident.

The dance troupe allowed students to go outside the confines of the "inner city" and see the world. They toured north and south Saskatchewan and various cities in the United States. In La Loche, Saskatchewan, the community welcomed the students. The students got to fish in the creek. Local fresh fish then became our dinner for that evening. They were hosted by Sante Fe Fine Arts School and given an art workshop – a school they may consider for their future studies. The students participated in the Gathering of Nations Powwow in Albuquerque, New Mexico. Beyond the four square walls of the classroom setting, we provided learning by experience and travel that the students may have otherwise never experienced.

## TURNING TOWARD MY RESEARCH

The above writing is part of a reflective piece that called me to my current research. As an educator, I have taken my teaching and life experiences as an Aboriginal woman and more specifically an Anishnaabekwe to focus on the use of song and drum in schools. In particular I attempted to answer the questions posed to me in schools about my teaching practices; hence, the focus of my research is on working with the question "What is the significance of song and drum in schools?" from an Anishnaabekwe perspective. I chose to use a storied approach to research reflecting Anishnaabe ways of being and knowing as *traditional teachers* in two forms. The first is *debaajimowin* which are predominantly personal stories or narratives relative to the research question and secondly, *antasokaannan* which is a traditional or sacred story. These two kinds of stories are used to carry information and are rooted in our cultural way of teaching.

Stories are a functioning part of both the framework and methodology to present new and evolving stories of and for education. Within this evolving story, drum and song hold an exceptional history and cultural significance and are often the first cultural implementation in contemporary formal schools. I inquired into Anishnaabe stories, Elders' teachings, archival records, and autobiographical experiences throughout the inquiry. The analysis was guided by both an Anishnaabe perspective, as well as several key questions asked by Chief Justice Murray Sinclair (2014), questions that link identity and culture. Key recommendations to integrating song and drum in relation to formal schooling point to the necessity of being grounded in community and cultural ways of being and knowing.

As part of this research, I was inquiring into traditional practices from archives of recorded interviews with Anishnaabe and Cree Elders to understand better the cultural roots of drum and song. During my research I was increasingly attentive to the observation that traditional practice is still in place. The Elders who speak to this are aware of the erosion of language and therefore culture over time. Despite the fact that traditional practices still are in place, time is always a concern. As an Anishnaabe educator, I worked to engage students in traditional teachings. In the schools that I taught in with Aboriginal students, each school had a drum and dance troupe. As a co-choreographer, I worked 2 days per week in after school programing with these groups, and the students performed during school hours on occasion, as well as evenings and weekends. Through these experiences, the question about the significance of drum and song in schools became increasingly important.

Having worked in schools with only Aboriginal students, we always had Elders working with us in the schools or at the ceremonies. I learned a great deal from the Elders over time and in particular from Bowser Poochay and his wife Margaret Poochay, who took my daughter and I into their family and ceremonies. I have become fully aware of the drum's significance and place in ceremony and it is in reflection of the Elders' teachings and drawing from literature and archival records, that I search for the deeper meanings for drum and song that stem from ceremony.

## TRADITIONAL PRACTICE

Music has always been important to Anishnaabe people. It is an integral part of the culture and it is a focal point of ceremony. Music is the essence of traditional culture and has its purpose. For many cultures around the world it is of significance. Drum and dance in schools stems from a recognition of these traditional systems, systems that have always been. The instruments have their origin stories that are considered sacred, spoken in ceremony, and retold once again in ceremony.

It is important not to essentialize Aboriginal histories and the impacts of colonization; each community was affected in different ways and at different times. Therefore, there is no historical precedent for the evolvement of drum and song, nor is there a single version of why drum and song became completely eliminated from some communities. Nevertheless, there are oral histories still in place in the communities that need to be brought forward and shared with others. As Vennum's (1978) film *The Drummaker* reveals, the last drum maker from Lac Court Oreilles, Minnesota in the 1970's, laments that he has no one to teach the making of his last drum. The Elders in Western Canada see the erosion of cultural traditions around the drum today, primarily due to the erosion of language and understanding of sacred traditions and teachings relative to the drum. In another example during the time of transition from the colonial onslaught (Densmore 1979), the people of the Qu'Appelle Valley were predicting their Sundance songs would be gone in their lifetime with no one to pass them on to. Each community had varying experiences at the time of settler encroachment and in some communities, drum and song were completely eroded.

Yet in other communities, traditions have survived and ceremonies are still currently taking place in multiple areas across Canada. In some places, I have been told that Arapaho Elders from the USA came up to reteach about the sweat to Cree communities in the south of Western Canada. Our Anishnaabe prophesy states that we will go back along the trails of the Great Migration and look for the bundles that I interpret as what has been preserved in terms of language and ceremony. Ceremony transfers have already begun. New treaty is forming amongst the First peoples as we always did in the past. There is sharing of songs to relations who broke off from the original group and became separated over time, who are now making efforts to reunite in order to restore songs and ceremonies; the Dene and the Navajo are good examples.

In spite of great disruption to our ways through relocation, warring, starvation and residential schooling, many ceremonies, songs and stories have survived and have lived with the old people. The young have more awareness of the vital importance of preserving what we have. There are those who believe we only have remnants and the language and culture is dying. There are those who believe it can be preserved and it is worth making efforts to do so, including efforts through formal schooling. This effort was also prophesized by the Anishnaabe. In the time of the seventh fire the people will rise up and rejuvenate the language and culture. They will approach the Elders with questions and the Elders will wake up as if from a long sleep to bring the old knowledge forward and to answer questions they have been waiting for.

## Bɪᴅɪᴋᴜ Aʜᴍ Oᴏᴋ Nɪᴍᴋᴇᴇᴋ (Rᴜᴍʙʟɪɴɢ Tʜᴜɴᴅᴇʀ) – Tʜᴜɴᴅᴇʀ ᴀɴᴅ Hᴇᴀʟɪɴɢ

My research depicts a fragment of the Anishnaabe culture through pondering my research question: What is the significance of song and drum in schools? Song and drum is one small piece that holds major historical and cultural significance. In researching the traditional aspects of drum and song in Anishnaabe communities, Elders' teachings, archives, *debaajimowin*, and *antasokaannan* I have compiled a small body of knowledge that can be grown.

In reflecting on the work of the Truth and Reconciliation Commission (TRC), Chief Justice Sinclair (2014) stated that there is no quick solution to repairing the damage done by the genocidal mission of the Canadian government. The efforts toward reconciliation and healing we make today will take many generations to be fully realized. The relationship of First Nations, Inuit, and Métis people with non-Aboriginal peoples in Canada is the point of reconciliation wherein the highest standards need be set to create balance and harmony in this relationship. The TRC (2015c) has offered a set of significant and important principles in relation to education. "Reconciliation requires constructive action to address the ongoing legacies of colonialism that have had destructive impacts on Aboriginal peoples' education, cultures and languages, health, child welfare, the administration of justice, and economic opportunities and prosperity" (Truth and Reconciliation Commission of Canada 2015c, p. 3). The broad context for Aboriginal education sits here in light of the TRC's (2012) recommendations, the TRC's (2015c) principles, and the TRC's (2015b) calls to action.

In my research I had hoped to find *tebwewin* – truth and meaning around the drum and song of the Anishnaabe. I wanted to think about what can enhance the teaching of drum and song in schools – perhaps the questions I was asked pushed me to become more adamant about the importance of drum and song in formal education contexts. There is an exceptional amount of archival records that call for more archival research to be done. There is also a plethora of stories that accompany the drums coming to a community and the origin of song. Anishnaabe use a storied approach to learning and these stories compiled together is a place to begin for future educators and curriculum developers. To know the *antasokaannan* or sacred story enriches the understanding of drum and song and brings light to the traditional ties of cultural expression.

I believe that when the first thunders sound in the spring, they are telling of a time to begin ceremonies. It is a time for us to retreat to the land for prayer, fasting and ceremony, and maybe it is time for the education system to align with the natural order of things for us. If schools were responsive to these ways of being, they might close their doors at the first thunder and resume again in the fall. This way the students are back in the communities and with family and extended family to learn through ceremony and long immersion to *antasokaannan* and in the winter through *debaajimowin*. In this way our children become culturally grounded and are immersed in the language. When the weather cools, the students return to the schools to focus on reading and writing and a more self-directed learning program. The exact details would be worked out collectively with the community. This is just one possible scenario that is simpatico with Anishnaabe world-view and understandings of the cycle of the seasons.

I am cognizant that not everyone is a singer, beader, artist, or dancer. Our formal education system needs to provide for every budding talent. The children's gifts need to be recognized by parents, families, community members, and the students are taught accordingly. As an educator, I believe the singular most important thing we need to teach children in school is a love of learning, learning that engages children and is invested in families and communities. Everything else can be learned from that point. Our systems need to be based on teaching, coaching, mentoring, and guiding students in their learning relative to their home/community cultures and interests, and not the same old menu of the colonizers' story along with their recipes for competition. A design for schooling incorporating the Anishnaabe way would restore the focus on *Mino Bimadiziwin* – living the good life. Given new possibilities with the Truth and Reconciliation Commission of Canada (TRC) (2015b) calls to action, the question becomes, "How would we collectively envision this?" The instillation of drum and song is one way to begin to answer this question.

Drum and song are central to the culture and central to ceremony. Elders or cultural teachers are always willing to share the songs. They want the songs to continue. The drum and song are healing. In the words of Anishnaabe Elder Dave Courchene, "Who we are as a people is defined by our Seven Sacred Teachings[.] If our people are to be healed and get well again they will have to go back to the teachings that were given to them" (SagkeengCFS 2014, n.p.).

Healing is an important aspect of indigenous-based education (Cote-Meek 2010; Moeke-Pickering 2010). Many Elders have said that we can only heal by going back to our traditional teachings such as drum and song. Recapturing what has been lost allows us another opportunity for healing that is part of us. The prophesy of the seventh fire states that we will journey back along the trails to find the bundles that have been hidden. We will revive our culture and our language. The Elders will "wake up" from a long rest where their wisdom will once again be called upon. The possibilities for education are infinite. To set the framework around our value system housed by animal spirits as Elder Courchene's teachings will tell you, are a beautiful start; they include respect, love, courage, trust, humility, honesty, and wisdom (Sagkeeng CFS, 2014).

The TRC's work came to a close in Ottawa 2015, announcing principles to consider and sending a challenge out for a call to action. There has been a steady positive response but actions speak louder than words and only time will tell if actions follow. There is no question after thousands of testimonials about the detrimental impact of the residential schooling practice on First Nations peoples. My parents too were part of the children and families who attended residential school and I have and continue to see the intergenerational reverberations (Young 2005) of this experience. Understanding my early landscapes of learning within my family is important to me as it allows me to situate who I am in a larger context. It is the same context that also nurtures my interest in song and drum.

## RESIDENTIAL SCHOOLS

Part of Canada's dark history is the taking of aboriginal children from their families and placing them in residential schools in order "to take the Indian out of the child, and to assimilate them into Canada's 'white' mainstream" (Al Jazeera 2015, n.p.). The last of these schools closed as recently as 1996. The violence that occurred in residential schools includes sexual, physical, verbal, and emotional abuse (Truth and Reconciliation Commission of Canada, 2015a). Residential schools were a form of "cultural genocide": "the destruction of those structures and practices that allow the group to continue as a group" (TRC, 2015a, p. 1). While many never left the schools, they left this world while at these schools; it was a horrendous experience for all of the students who attended. Chief Justice Sinclair, the first Aboriginal Manitoba Court Judge, was the head of the TRC. Everyone in Canada needs to know that Chief Justice Sinclair recommends that school curriculum across Canada include this *dark* history. We are now in a good time where it at least feels like there could be positive change. Again, as an Anishnaabekwe teacher, I see this as a brilliant opportunity to evaluate our own efforts, to question that we have done and everything we could do, to honour the prophesy of the seventh fire and *pick up the bundles*, learn from them, and in essence to learn our traditional teachings, history, and worldview so that we can share our Anishnaabe perspective in classrooms.

Now is the time to bring forward all aspects of the culture and worldview that shape our being and to freely introduce traditional teachings of drum and song and its cultural grounding as a meaningful way of understanding. Drum and song is just one doorway to deeper truth – tebwewin. What is beautiful is that there are many ways.

## BIDIKU AHM OOK NIMKEEK (RUMBLING THUNDER) . . . MOVING FORWARD (AFTER THE STORM)

Thinking about song and drum in formal education calls for the consideration of the implications for education. As an educator I need to be cognizant of the traditional roots, and as Anishnaabe I need to pass forward this information. As a strongly grounded Anishnaabe educator I need students to know this. I have come to understand that one of the key aspects of this critical work is that it can only be achieved in the context of community, both within and outside of school communities.

Elders are an integral part of cultural teachings. While many of us seek cultural knowledge and guidance from them, we need to ensure that this respectful relationship continues. Elders need to be part of the envisioning process of what formal schooling can become in order to maintain our traditional understandings and practices of who we are and where we come from. Practices and policies that support these efforts need to reflect and value Anishnaabe worldviews. It is also critical that policies are in place to accommodate the need for community input in multiple capacities. In this way, the traditional understandings of drum and song and all aspects of language and culture can be ensured.

## Policy

I am drawing on my father's perspective on how policy is positioned from an Anishnaabe worldview.

### Naakonnigewinan *(The Rules)*

In contemporary times since the Indian Act and the treaties, the Band Council makes policies within the limited power granted to the Band Council by the Canadian law. Before the Canadian government enacted the Indian Act and before the treaties were signed, the Odawak lived by the Laws of the Orders (*Enendagwad*), and so it was meant to be. These laws, we believed, came from the Creator, not human beings.

*Enendagwad* set the framework of our lives. We were last in the universe, the most dependent. We recognized our limited knowledge and beseeched the Creator to give us direction for creating the policies by which we governed ourselves. The Creator gave us instructions on how to derive the policies. To develop the policies for living together, the Creator gave the Odawak a number of ways to ask – ceremonies, medicine, the Shaking Tent, the Sweat Lodge, the Sun Dance, prayers, etc. In developing policies for relations with other First Nations, where different nations agreed on ways on how to live together, our traditional governing structures were policy.

The Creator also gave us the Seven Grandfathers' and Grandmothers' teachings. They are not policies. They are values a person must learn to be able to follow the Creator's Laws. *Atsokanan* are the teaching tools to explain and enforce the Laws of the Orders, the Creator's instructions, and the values to live by. *Gwekwadissowin* which follows from the Law of the

Orders, results in teachings that inform what might constitute community policies as the community struggles to maintain life according to the Laws of the Orders. "One might say that Enendagwad – is the Creator's Policy and *Innowkohnigewinan* – is to fulfill the Creator's policy" (King, personal communication, 2015).

## Ihzhitchigewnan – *Direction*

The Law of Orders would be a starting place for establishing policy toward Indigenous or Anishnaabe education because it stems from an Anishnaabe worldview. It encompasses *atsokanannan*, the stories and the values of the people. Alongside this the principles of the Truth and Reconciliation Commission of Canada (TRC) (2015c) need to be considered. The Truth and Reconciliation Commission of Canada (TRC) (2015c) believes "reconciliation between Aboriginal and Non-Aboriginal Canada" (p. 3) can only be met by their established recommendations, principles, and call to order.

Reconciliation requires constructive action to address the ongoing legacies of colonialism that have had destructive impacts on Aboriginal peoples' education, cultures and languages, health, child welfare, the administration of justice, economic opportunities, and prosperity. Formal education today is no more successful for Anishnaabe people. The opportunity to centre Anishnaabe worldview and all First Nations worldviews in the curriculum, alongside language immersion, allows for cultural restoration and reconciling. Drum and song as the center of all ceremony is a natural teaching and learning focus for attaining these goals.

Through our collective efforts, it is our time now to remodel our formal education systems to ensure our language and culture is not lost, and cultural teachers and Elders are central to our efforts of teaching. Collective efforts with parents and grandparents, Elders, teachers and administrators are needed to set the direction in education for our children's future. Therefore, the communities must also be central, as song and drum are central to them. The drum and song will be alive and thriving as the central gathering place to our new positive world of teaching and the reconstruction of our Anishnaabe ways.

In this way we uphold the perspectives and understandings of Aboriginal Elders and Traditional Knowledge Keepers of the ethics, concepts, and practices of reconciliation; these are vital to long-term reconciliation.

I would add that these perspectives are needed in redesigning formal education where the centering of the Anishnaabe worldview requires drawing from the wisdom of *Gite Anishaabe* (Elders) and language speakers. These principles for forward movement are needed to support Aboriginal peoples' cultural revitalization and integration. To this end it is essential to place indigenous knowledge systems, oral histories, laws, protocols, and connections to the land into the center of the reconciliation process.

Currently, there is a great distance between formal education and pedagogies that are based on a connection to the land. On the land, Anishnaabemowin comes alive and so do the teachings inherent in the language. The land is the place of ceremony, song and drum. The land is our teacher with the ancient markers of the petroglyphs, the mountains, and the medicines. Our language is more closely tied to the land and the waterways. Connecting with our first teacher – *aki*, the earth – is essential to our efforts to revitalize our knowledge systems. *Kinamago* – all earth teaches us as we come to know in returning to the original teachings.

Educators will bring together Elders and wisdom keepers who will give guidance toward efforts in reconciling and reconstructing formal education as we know it. This effort of reconciling, Simpson (2011) has termed "*Aanji Maajitaawin*:...the art of starting over, to regenerate" (p. 22). She defines reconciliation as the process of regenerating values, political process, and philosophies. Connecting to the land, language, and culture would be integral to this. Further, Simpson (2011) leaves the term resurgence undefined, believing that this needs to be defined by Elders and communities in terms of what it means to them. This is the beginning place for formal educational redesign. Incorporating the principles generated by the Truth and Reconciliation Commission of Canada (TRC) (2015c), ensures a better working relationship and future for our children.

## FORMAL EDUCATION

From an Anishnaabe worldview, language and cultural understandings are where we can begin reassembling learning for our children. Language speakers need to be called upon to assist in the effort to revitalize indigenous languages. Cultural teachings would be an essential part of the curriculum and would include the field of drum and song. Formal education would be based on our Anishnaabe perspective, our history, our truth – *tebwewin*, and our language. From the natural laws and traditional laws that have always governed us we embrace and move forward. To include the history and acknowledgment of the disruptions is important; all cultures evolve and change and grow. To be cognizant of the past and reveal all truth – *tebwewin*, we will be stronger as a people; as people we will know who we are and where we come from. On this basis, together with the community, we can create a vision that will serve the needs of our children in education. Drum and song will be a central part of it.

The way forward with regard to formal education is to provide an indigenizing of the academies or school systems. Wilson coined the term *indigagogy* (Wilson, personal communication, 2012) which can be interpreted as to look at pedagogy and consider indigenizing all that could be set in place there. Formal education would be designed from our own creative minds and reflect the Elders' voices. The communities would also be invited and involved. The knowledges of the many Aboriginal teachers in the school systems, and their experiences in developing approaches that work in their classrooms are another vital contribution. In fact, I have already witnessed and experienced drum and song as the center for gathering and the center of ceremony in schools that served exclusively or primarily Aboriginal students. These schools are viewed as highly successful in terms of being open to creative and positive change.

Drum and song are only a part of the bigger picture for change and reconciliation, but in combination they are a powerful and crucial element. As the Elder Sakewew Tamowin (Sunrise) has shared, the drum is always at the center of any ceremony. He, like many Elders before him, uses the drum as a teacher. The Elders sing, interject with story and then go back to song again. It is a teaching instrument as much for song as it is for story. The songs are teaching us conceptual frameworks in the language imbued with spiritual meaning; as constructs drawn from our worldviews. "Songs are thought, sung out with the breath when people are moved by great forces and ordinary speech no longer suffices" (Kawagley 1995, p. 34).

## WHAT'S IN A SONG?

Song is the most powerful means to connect with spirit. It is a way of prayer. Our songs hold the knowledge. That is what the *Gite Anishnaabek* have told us. It may seem insignificant to an outsider of our culture; yet, it is very significant to us. We need the singers and the drummers to promulgate ceremony. The singers create the vision or pathway of ritual to the ceremony. A deeper level of meaning and significance can be revealed with the Elders leading ceremony with the schools. For students who are seeking to learn more on a deeper level the formal school setting can be the gateway to ceremony, should they choose this path.

A song is accessible to all ages. There are times when song and drum signal great promise. This is symbolic of great hope as the peoples in leadership positions invite Aboriginal people to the governing circle and promise to recognize the important work ahead.

There has always been a critique in academe that not all First Nations people are artists, singers, or dancers. This is true, but to eliminate the possibility in learning and to not provide students at least the opportunity to learn is a form of silencing and violence against them, continuing the harm and trauma so prevalent in residential schools. This is the opposite of the recommendations of the TRC (2012). Every opportunity needs to be provided for Anishnaabe, and other Aboriginal peoples to learn their language and culture, to find their place in it. Our drums and songs are still prevalent and realign us in multiple dancing circles country wide – our circle is symbolic of togetherness, support, ceremony, and the sacredness of life. Our peaceful protest, expressed in Idle No More across the country must have been a surprise to all those who witnessed. We acquired global support as people stood up, held up placards stating, "We support Idle No More" and posted them on social media for weeks in response to our cause.

## The Seventh Fire Prophecy

The seven fires of the Anishnaabe people relate to seven phases, epochs, or periods in time. The Anishnaabe Elders are predicting that we will soon enter the time of the prophecy of the eighth fire. Once the fire is lit we walk the pathway of spirituality.

> It is this time that the light skinned race will be given a choice between two roads. If they choose the right road, then the Seventh Fire will light the Eighth and final Fire, an eternal fire of peace, love, brotherhood and sisterhood. If the light skinned race makes the wrong choice of the roads, then the destruction which they brought with them in coming to this country will come back at them and cause much suffering and death to all the Earth's people. (The Seven Fires Prophecy n.d.)

Traditional Midewewin people, the Ojibwa, and people from other nations have interpreted the "two roads" that face the light-skinned race as the road to technology and materialism, and the other road to spiritualism. If peoples can join together in peace, harmony, brotherhood and sisterhood, then it will be possible for the eighth fire to be lit. Drum is for song. Our song is our prayer. As we move closer to the prophecy of the eighth fire it is our hope that our prayers will be answered.

## CONCLUSION

Is song and drum really extracurricular?
Is that really music?
Are those words your singing?
Is that screaming?
Does this merit, pulling students out of class?

In reflecting on my teaching experiences, these questions from colleagues that I was stymied by have become easier to both understand and to answer. I now understand that the questions are derived out of ignorance, from non-First Nations colleagues who have little understanding of the practice of song and drum in First Nations culture. The ignorance is indicative of a common pattern among white, European settlers who *see* the world in ways that make it possible to separate the past from the present and so to deny their own complicity in the violences that continue to be perpetrated against First Nations peoples (Cote-Meek 2014). The questions belittle First Nations culture. I have always been struck by what my non-First Nations colleagues feel justified in saying how they're interpreting something, without acknowledging that their interpretation comes from a particular location, and in ways that further alienation and racial divisiveness. I believe there is extraordinary merit to having a dance troupe to represent a First Nations school. The investment of time by the teachers and the students to finesse their dancing and learn the songs is worthwhile for many reasons. Learning the songs gives strength to the drum. The drum teachings are important for all the students to learn as we take care of the drum collectively. Although the powwows have been alive and well in urban areas for over 20 years and have always been open to the public, others have either not attended these, or not attended in a way that allowed them to understand the deeper significance. The deeper significance can only come through an engagement with and a facing up to the history of violence that is part of Canada's dark past. This is the work of the Truth and Reconciliation Commission.

The Truth and Reconciliation Commission of Canada (TRC) (2012) has made recommendations that are drawn from our stories of truth shared publically. This is a first step toward the healing process, and it requires a decolonizing of minds and structures at all levels in society, including education.

> [V]alidation of the collective history of oppression and colonization is an important part of the healing and decolonizing process. . . . These intergenerational wounds, or "soul wounds" (Duran and Duran 1995), will likely take longer than a single generation to heal, and the healing will need to occur on many levels and dimensions. (Cote-Meek 2014, p. 35)

If the current school system in Canada continues to uphold European, settler colonizer constructs and values, our First Nations students will continue to fail and feel this failure as violence and be traumatized by it. In light of the TRC's interim report (2012) and their calls to action (2015b), now is the time for a fundamental change in our way of schooling that will embrace traditional understandings and all original teachings, illustrated by my practices in song and drum given in this chapter. This is a call for centering indigenous worldviews in school curricula and pedagogies, and ensuring that Indigenous communities are also centered in this task. It is a counter-hegemonic, decolonization of education. It is *not* a call for replacement, but for a movement toward a new balance and a new coexistence of Anishnaabe alongside non-First Nations peoples. Education based on Anishnaabe teachings and language, answers the prophecy of the seventh fire wherein the culture and language will be revived and the people will be strong once again.

> We must forgive. There is no option[.]
>
> By forgiving we liberate, not only ourselves, but also our oppressor. By forgiving we open the door to those who desire forgiveness. It is not that we believe we are superior to those people who, because of their fear, blindness and isolation did not see us as we are, their brother and sister, their father and mother, their lover, their friend. Through forgiveness we allow the spirits of our ancestors to accomplish their mission, which began so many centuries ago on these very shores. (Dotsou 2000, p. 4)

## References

Cote-Meek, S. (2010). *Exploring the impact of ongoing colonial violence on Aboriginal students in the postsecondary classroom* (Doctoral dissertation, University of Toronto: Ontario Institute for Studies in Education). Retrieved from https://tspace.library.utoronto.ca/handle/1807/24729.

Cote-Meek, S. (2014). *Colonized classrooms: Racism, trauma and resistance in post-secondary education.* Black Point, NS: Fernwood Publishing.

Densmore, F. (1979). *Chippewa customs* (2nd ed.). St. Paul, MN: Minnesota Historical Society Press.

Dotsou, T. (2000, July 11). *The prophecy of the seven fires.* Retrieved from http://aboriginalliving.com/wp-content/uploads/2012/12/Fleming_Anishinaabe-Great-Migration1.pdf.

Duran, E., & Duran, B. (1995). *Native American postcolonial psychology.* Albany, NY: State University of New York Press.

Jazeera, A. (2015, June 3). Canada's dark history of abuse at residential schools. *Al Jazeera.* Retrieved from http://www.aljazeera.com.

Kawagley, A. O. (1995). *A Yupiaq worldview: A pathway to ecology and spirit.* Prospect Heights, IL: Waveland Press.

Moeke-Pickering, T. M. (2010). *Decolonisation as a social change framework and its impact on the development of Indigenous-based curricula for helping professionals in mainstream treaty education organisations* (Doctoral dissertation, University of Waikato). Retrieved from http://hdl.handle.net/10289/4148.

SagkeengCFS. (2014, May 16). *Our 7 Ojibway Teachings:* [Video file]. Retrieved from https://www.youtube.com/watch?v=sASjfNI_lD0.

Simpson, L. (2011). *Dancing on our turtle's back: Stories of Nishnaabeg re-creation, resurgence and new emergence.* Winnipeg, MB: Arbeiter Ring.

Sinclair, M. (2014, March 27–30). *Truth & Reconciliation Commission (TRC) of Canada: Alberta National Event.* Lecture presented at the Shaw Conference Centre, Edmonton. AB.

The Seven Fires Prophecy. (n.d.). Retrieved from http://www.anishinabe-history.com/history/seven-fires-prophecy.shtml.

Truth and Reconciliation Commission of Canada (TRC). (2012). *Truth and reconciliation commission of Canada: Interim report.* Retrieved from the Truth and Reconciliation Commission of Canada (TRC). website http://www.trc.ca/websites/trcinstitution/index.php?p=9.

Truth and Reconciliation Commission of Canada (TRC). (2015a). *Honouring the truth, reconciling for the future: Summary of the final report of the truth and reconciliation commission of Canada.* Retrieved from the Truth and Reconciliation Commission of Canada (TRC. website http://www.trc.ca/websites/trcinstitution/index.php?p=890.

Truth and Reconciliation Commission of Canada (TRC). (2015b). *Truth and reconciliation commission of Canada: Calls to action.* Retrieved from the Truth and Reconciliation Commission of Canada (TRC). website http://www.trc.ca/websites/trcinstitution/index.php?p=890.

Truth and Reconciliation Commission of Canada (TRC). (2015c). *What we have learned: Principles of truth and reconciliation.* Retrieved from the Truth and Reconciliation Commission of Canada (TRC). website http://www.trc.ca/websites/trcinstitution/index.php?p=890.

Vennum Director, T. (1978). *The drummaker [Film]*. University Park, PA: Produced by the Smithsonian Institution/Centre for Folklife Programs & Cultural Studies, Pennsylvania State University.

Young, M. (2005). *Pimatisiwin: Walking in a good way*. Winnipeg, MB: Pemmican Publications.

**Anna-Leah King** is Anishnaabekwe from Wikwemikong Unceded Reserve, Manitoulin Island, Ontario. She completed her doctoral degree from the University of Alberta in Policy Studies – Indigenous Peoples Education in 2016. She is a teacher who has worked for 13 years in urban schools with Aboriginal students. She has also worked as an Aboriginal Education consultant, where she was primarily a curriculum writer and researcher. She has worked at the University of Alberta as a postsecondary teacher, teaching assistant, and researcher.

# CHAPTER 7

# Using Māori Metaphors to Develop Culturally Responsive Pedagogy of Relations

*Iti Joyce*

## NEW ZEALAND CONTEXT

Epistemological racism, as explained by Scheurich and Young (1997), is embedded within the dominant Pākehā (New Zealanders of European descent) discourse within New Zealand (Bishop and Glynn 1999). It is a racism that has developed since the 1840 Treaty of Waitangi. Māori saw the treaty as a "charter for power sharing between Māori and the Crown" (Berryman 2008, p. 16), enabling them to participate as self-determining individuals in future decision-making. But from its very first moments, there were "difficulties of interpretation" (Orange 1987, p. 1). If Crown officials were aware of Māori understandings, they chose to ignore them and proceeded by addressing perceived Māori inadequacies through an education system developed within colonial epistemologies.

Contemporary Māori resistance to mainstream discourses has had little impact on the way Māori are viewed and represented in the New Zealand society. There are still disparities between Māori and Pākehā within a

I. Joyce (✉)
University of Waikato, Hamilton, New Zealand
e-mail: iti.joyce@wananga.ac.nz

© The Author(s) 2017
F. Pirbhai-Illich et al. (eds.), *Culturally Responsive Pedagogy*,
DOI 10.1007/978-3-319-46328-5_7

141

range of social indicators, with Māori being imprisoned well in excess of any other cultural group in New Zealand. Similarly, disparities between Māori and Pākehā exist within our mainstream education settings, particularly at the secondary level.

In the past decade, one response from the New Zealand's Ministry of Education to address educational disparities in secondary schools has been the implementation of a professional development and research project called Te Kotahitanga (unity). Te Kotahitanga is a school-wide reform that aims to improve the educational achievement of Māori students by supporting teachers to work in culturally appropriate and culturally responsive and relational ways. The professional development is an iterative cycle and recognises that changing teachers' theorizing and practice requires ongoing support. Participating schools are required to appoint a school-based facilitation team whose role is to implement a term-by-term cycle of in-school professional learning opportunities with teachers. Teachers are initially introduced to the idea of discursive repositioning (Bishop et al. 2003; Berryman 2011) where teachers are able to critically reflect on their own explanations for the historical disparities in educational achievement between Māori and non-Māori. For many teachers the possibility that their own explanations may be culturally located and that they may differ from those of Māori students and their whānau (family) is a revealing experience.

Te Kotahitanga works to change relationships of power and culture within mainstream education settings as a fundamental precursor to changing teacher pedagogy and subsequently Māori students' participation and achievement. Bishop, Berryman, Cavanagh, and Teddy (2007) state that "in order to change practice, we must investigate what constitutes appropriate metaphors to inform practice" (p. 9). Māori metaphors provide an alternative pedagogy where relationships and interactions are fundamental to the issue of power and control.

In Te Kotahitanga, the metaphors that are considered and understood are from the marginalized Indigenous group.

## Māori Metaphors

According to Pere (1994), "traditional Māori learning rested on the principle that every person is a learner from the time they are born (if not before) to the time they die" (p. 54). Traditional Māori practices in teaching and learning were valued and reciprocal. Learning was intergenerational and based on previous experiences and built on family members strengths. Skills and knowledge were developed and nurtured to benefit the collective.

The Māori metaphors that are used within Te Kotahitanga provide us with a picture of the sort of alternative educational relations and interactions that are possible, where educators draw upon an alternative culture than that previously dominant. As Bishop et al. (2007) suggest,

> Metaphorically a collective vision focusing on the need to address Māori students achievement, identifies the need for power over reciprocal decision making to be constituted within relationships and interactions constructed as if within a collective whānau (family) context. Whānau relationships would enact reciprocal and collaborative pedagogies in order to promote educational relationships between students, between pupils and teachers and between the home and the school as a means of promoting excellence in education (p. 14).

The metaphors are:

- whānaungatanga (extended family);
- wānanga (effective learning interactions); and
- tino rangatiratanga (self-determination).

These traditional principles and practices have applications for the teaching and learning of Māori students in mainstream classrooms.

Whānaungatanga – the metaphor which encapsulates the Māori worldview of whānau – represents the collective responsibility to assist and if necessary to intervene. There is an obligation for members to invest in the whānau group and determine individual and collective tino rangatiratanga (self-determination). In this way, one is interdependent, accountable and responsible to the whānau, just as the whānau maintains the same responsibilities back to the individual.

When using the metaphor of whānaungatanga in classroom contexts, relationships and interactions based on familial metaphors will be different if teachers were to think, theorize and practice in this way. Commitment, accountability and responsibility for the learning of others would underpin teaching practice that promotes self-determination. Developing relationships under the metaphor of whānaungatanga addresses the power and control issues and the metaphor of wānanga is reflected and demonstrated through communication that is interactive, dialogic and inclusive. These metaphors have been drawn together in Te Kotahitanga into an effective teaching profile.

## The Te Kotahitanga Effective Teaching Profile

The Te Kotahitanga Effective Teaching Profile (ETP) has been developed by researchers from the students narratives of experience, as "students expressed the types of relationships and interactions between themselves, and their teachers that both hindered their educational achievement and also promoted their advancement" (Bishop et al. 2003, p. 27).

Fundamental to the Te Kotahitanga ETP is the need for teachers to reject deficit theorizing as a means of explaining Māori students' educational participation and achievement. Deficit theorizing, in this context, is when the explanations given for Māori students' lack of achievement are focussed on things outside of the teachers' sphere of influence, such as the home conditions, the education system or the child himself. When the teacher focusses on the things that they do have control over, they are considered to have agency.

Teachers, who are agentically positioned, are then supported to be professionally committed and responsible to understand how to bring about change. Professional development supports teachers to show, in culturally appropriate and culturally responsive ways, that they:

- genuinely care and know their Māori students as culturally located (*Manaakitanga*);
- articulate high learning and behavioural expectations for their Māori students (*Mana Motuhake*);
- are organized and prepared with well-managed learning environments (*Whakapiringatanga*);
- engage in dialogic learning conversations with Māori students (*Wānanga*);
- facilitate and use a range of strategies that promote teaching and learning relationships (*Ako*);
- use evidence of Māori student achievement in formative and summative ways to promote, monitor and reflect on positive outcomes (*Kotahitanga*, Bishop et al. 2003).

The Te Kotahitanga ETP offers alternative Māori metaphors for teachers and educational leaders. These new metaphors disrupt the status quo as teachers work to develop new understandings to move their pedagogy forward, in their implementation of the Te Kotahitanga ETP. This is a complex challenging process, and one that is informed by changing views of relationships between teacher and learner.

## CULTURALLY RESPONSIVE PEDAGOGY OF RELATIONS

The Te Kotahitanga narratives of experience (Bishop and Berryman 2006) indicated a need to address how teachers think about Māori students and to develop an understanding of a culturally responsive pedagogy of relations which develops as teachers implement and increase their expertise with the Te Kotahitanga ETP.

The Te Kotahitanga ETP is the vehicle to operationalize teachers and school leaders embedding of a culturally responsive pedagogy of relations into the classroom and throughout the school. In Te Kotahitanga (Bishop et al. 2007), this culturally responsive pedagogy of relations is operationalized when the following five elements are all active and working interdependently:

1. **Power Is Shared within Non-Dominating Relationships of Interdependence**
   Within schools, power-sharing is fundamental to developing trust and respect. When teachers and educators develop these kinds of relationships with their students, they are able to engage in dialogic interactions that promote Māori students' self-determination over their own learning and sense making processes. When new learning is co-constructed, both teachers and students are more powerful. Interactions of this kind are fundamental to power-sharing relationships.

2. **Culture Counts**
   The Te Kotahitanga ETP supports teachers who are agentically positioned, to understand the important differences between culturally appropriate and culturally responsive, and to incorporate each effectively into their teaching. We all have our own cultures. Our culture is a means of learning and making sense of the world. We need new educational discourses that acknowledge our own culture as central to our teaching and learning experiences. We need the visible (culturally appropriate) aspects of culture. However, on their own they are tokenism. We also need the invisible (culturally responsive) aspects of culture so that we are able to make sense of our world from our own cultural understandings (Barnhardt 2005). By being

culturally responsive, students are able to use their own prior knowledge and experiences, or as Jerome Bruner (1996) calls it, their own "cultural tool kit" (p. 68) as the basis for developing new understandings.

3. **Learning Is Interactive and Dialogic and Spirals**
   Teachers who are agentically positioned are engaged in the ongoing co-construction of new knowledge, with their students within power-sharing relationships. In educational settings, many teachers over rely on traditional top-down pedagogical interactions that include instruction, monitoring and interactions based on whether students are following teacher's instructions or not. Through a culturally responsive pedagogy of relations, teachers are encouraged to include discursive interactions, involving Māori students' prior knowledge, in order for new knowledge to be co-constructed. These learning conversations promote dialogue and learning with and from others. Interactions such as these will engage students and teachers and transform classrooms from traditional transmission practices to new developing interactive and dialogic practices.

4. **Connectedness Is Fundamental to Relations**
   In Te Kotahitanga the aim of raising Māori students' participation and achievement, and our relationships with our learners, is what connects us to the vision. How teachers connect to the common vision is based on the relationships and interactions that they develop with students, staff and whānau from their school communities. The connectedness through relationships of care (both manaakitanga and mana motuhake) and the interactions teachers engage in with others are fundamental to effective teaching and learning.

5. **There Is a Common Vision of What Constitutes Excellence**
   New Zealand's mainstream schools need a common vision of what constitutes educational excellence. The aim of a collective vision is that it provides guidelines for what constitutes educational excellence in Māori education that connects with "Māori aspirations, politically, socially, economically and spiritually" (Smith 1992, p. 23). Te Kotahitanga has shown that this should incorporate the culture that Māori students bring to schools to make sense of their world. An agenda such as this will address the educational achievement and disparities of Māori students (Bishop et al. 2007). A socially just vision of what constitutes excellence might well be Māori students participating and achieving in education, as well as

non-Māori are achieving. This would be the closing of the educational gap and Māori students able to leave school with qualifications to enter the work force or a tertiary institution. Ka Hikitia promotes another vision of what constitutes educational excellence in their guiding principle of "Māori achieving education success as Māori" (Ministry of Education 2008, p. 1). While this might sound like *what constitutes excellence*, Te Kotahitanga has shown that these outcomes depend upon the discourses within which those who are interpreting education for Māori are positioned.

Developing a collective understanding of a culturally responsive pedagogy of relations requires the understanding that all aspects are inextricably linked. Together, they create a holistic metaphor for relationships and interactions within which no one element can be left out or modified without altering or disadvantaging the whole. This type of relational pedagogy challenges educators to create learning contexts that are responsive to the culture of the child as opposed to the culture of the teacher. This pedagogy asks that the prior knowledge that learners bring to the learning context is validated and accepted. Bishop et al. (2007) suggest that within a culturally responsive pedagogy of relations, the "learner's own culture is central to their learning and they are able to make meaning of new information and ideas by building on their own prior cultural experiences and understandings" (p. 34). As previously discussed, this allows for new knowledge to be constructed with teachers and addresses the issue of power imbalances in the classroom. These interactions can engage Māori students and their teachers, and transform classrooms from traditional pedagogies to new developing discursive interactive pedagogies. Importantly, with these pedagogies, non-Māori students can also engage.

## A Sample of Teachers and Māori Students' Experiences in Te Kotahitanga

### *The Teachers*

Four teachers were involved in this research and came from a diverse range of backgrounds and all four are experienced teachers. They represent a Māori male, a South African female, a Pākehā male and a Pākehā female. They teach a range of subject areas.

The teachers reflected on their positioning and their teaching practice previous to the Te Kotahitanga professional development. They talked about the relationships they had with Māori students. These were relationships based on manaakitanga (caring), but not so much relationships based on mana motuhake (high learning expectations).

Teacher C:   I don't think I was a strong deficit theoriser. I do think I felt that it was going to be really hard to get through to those Māori students who weren't getting any support from home or weren't able to bring their books and pens. But the reality is, I think we're always going to have that and through the programme, I kind of learnt ways to deal with some of that a little more.

Teacher B:   My feelings were that it was a problem, that it was probably home-based, that I really want to do something about it. My perception of them now is an appreciation that there is a cultural difference. As a white middle-class, middle-aged teacher I need to know that and be able to be more effective in bridging the gap.

Teacher D:   I had strong relationships with the kids, but they weren't relationships based on high expectations for learning, probably more about high expectations for behaviour.

Teacher C:   I think I really didn't believe that I could make that much of a change, but this year I've seen the change that we've been able to create as a group of teachers.

Teacher B:   Kids have just taken it on board and used it to maximise their involvement in learning and participation and just the rapport with all staff members.

They also talked about their interpretation of what good teaching practice was before they became involved with Te Kotahitanga.

Teacher A:   It [teaching] was pretty random, not bad, just random and no real pedagogy behind what I did. I just wrote a unit and did some fun activities because I thought they were fun. I never got taught how to teach the "what's and whys".

### The Te Kotahitanga Professional Development Cycle

The Te Kotahitanga professional development model is an iterative one. Everyone is part of a feedback loop wherein evidence informs practice. This relational framework is described by Bishop et al. (2010) as a "network of relationships" (p. 27) in which outputs (theorizing and explanations for outcomes) provide feedback and feed-forward to the learner.

The following diagram shows the four elements in the term-by-term Te Kotahitanga professional development cycle (Fig. 7.1).

*Teachers' Reflections on Their Experiences in Te Kotahitanga*
As a result of the term-by-term professional development cycle, teachers practice is observed and they participate in professional learning opportunities.

Teacher C: I've taken heaps of confidence from it to be honest. Someone coming into your room to observe your practice. I've had nothing but good feedback. I've got things I have to work on, and that's helped me examine my practice. When you look back it's told me that I'm going in the right direction and given me more confidence, given me direction and strength to push through stuff to follow those things that I guess I was doing tentatively.

Teacher B: For me, I felt I had to be the best teacher. I had to prove myself when I first came to this school. And I had to try and speak Māori because I was South African and I wanted to be the best teacher I could be. This programme has taught me that by sharing my strengths and by learning from [others], I don't want to say weaknesses, because I never felt I was weak in any area but it was always there and it showed that I had gaps in my teaching. By making other teachers around me better... I can be one of the best.

The narratives of experience and the professional development cycle support and challenge teachers to become agentic, to focus on their own job.

Teacher A: That's my job, to cause or effect change. That's what agency is and I've got the power. It's all me and it's no one else's job. I'm the professional and it's my job to make change and if I see areas that are negative, I can turn them into positives. The teacher has the greatest influence of what happens in the classroom. That's agency to me. So you can inflict change in relationships in learning and in expectations and outcomes... but it won't happen unless the teacher makes it happen. The teacher is the greatest influence.

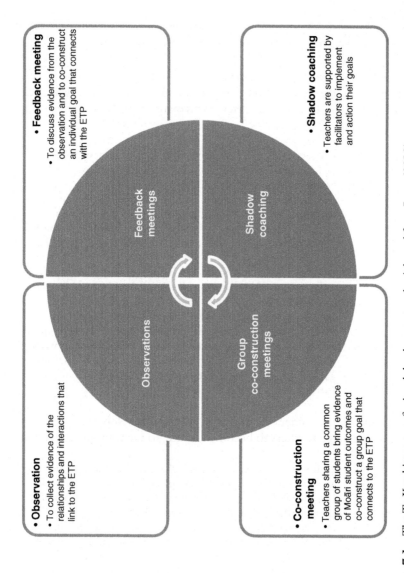

**Fig. 7.1** The Te Kotahitanga professional development cycle. Adapted from Joyce (2012)
Copyright 2012 by Chrisandra Itirana Joyce

Teachers reflected on the impact of being explicit with their learning and behavioural expectations (Mana motuhake), for Māori students.

Teacher D:   Mana Motuhake for both behaviour and learning in every lesson I think about it. I think, am I projecting my expectations... and I use the words every lesson about what I expect to be done. My kids just did a test and my expectation was that they get 80% and I put it out there because I have a Level 3 class and I'm also testing the Level 5 class and I wanted to see if that had an impact. I had no one fail. Everyone passed 50%, that was the pass rate, and all my kids [in Level 3 class] got in the 70s and 80s. Some of them got higher than the Level 4 and Level 5 kids.

Teacher B:   Reinforcing achievement and success. Acknowledging when they do well to reach their goals and if they haven't, still appreciating what they have managed to achieve. The target they have reached and going back to that and saying, "Hey remember when you did this or you did this last time so today what are you going to do, what are you going to remember to do?"

Teacher D:   I set high expectations and tell them every day even if I'm not teaching them that day. Sowing seeds of what they could possibly be.

Ako is a Māori metaphor and is an aspect within culturally responsive pedagogy of relations where learning is interactive and spirals. It means to learn as well as to teach (Pere 1994). Ako is a teaching and learning practice that is culturally specific and appropriate to Māori pedagogy (Bishop and Berryman 2006). Teachers expressed how this played out in their classrooms.

Teacher A:   Culturally responsive is important and that's about responding to the kids and what they want and how they use their voice, prior knowledge and AKO. I love saying to them, "You just taught me stuff," I love them knowing it's just as important.

Teacher D:   We do pre-tests to find out what the kids know. Every lesson it's, "who knows about this?" and if the kids go, "I don't know about that" I go, "what do you know then?" It's a deliberate thing and you let them figure it out, and you have a strong understanding of where to go to next.

These teachers were able to articulate that their relationships with Māori students were crucial for classroom teaching and learning interactions. The metaphor of *whānaungatanga* is central to these familial type relationships for Māori students. *Ako* enabled teachers to develop new pedagogies through their shared knowledge and understandings of a culturally responsive pedagogy of relations. *Wānanga* refers to effective teaching interactions. Professional learning conversations supported teachers to engage with evidence of Māori student academic achievement that focussed on Māori metaphor. The professional development cycle ensured the collective and individual responsibility supported teachers to work collaboratively and interdependently.

The Māori metaphors that emerged as important for these teachers participating in the Te Kotahitanga professional development resulted in their being challenged to move to a culturally responsive pedagogy of relations where whānaungatanga or familial type relationships were fundamental to classroom interactions. Ako played out with the sharing of knowledge and understandings being valued that led to the co-construction of new and different theorizing and practices. Wānanga is a proactive metaphor that ensured full participation of the professional development cycle, thus providing the space and the opportunities for professional learning conversations focussed on evidence from their Māori students that would subsequently improve the participation and achievement of these same students.

## The Students

The students are all Māori and represent the majority of the Māori students at this school. They all started this school as juniors. They were not doing particularly well academically or behaviourally, and their futures looked bleak.

### Students' Reflections on Teachers Prior to Te Kotahitanga

All four students recalled experiences prior to the implementation of Te Kotahitanga and provided examples of having negative feelings and poor behaviour.

Jane:      I hated my teachers in Year 9 and 10. I hated certain teachers; they'd pick on all the Māori kids. We didn't pay attention at all. We just did nothing.

Peter:    I had one last year with my English teacher, there was just nothing with her. There were no vibes, she had no interest in brown students, and she would just leave us.

Manu:    Year 9 we used to show off, get smart to our teachers, people laughed at me. Used to get impositions [referral to dean], staff would get peed off. I was getting into a lot of trouble...wasn't really listening to the teacher. Year 9 and 10 we were mischief. Pretty much got chucked in to the pool of Māori and Samoan. There was one Pākehā. There were about 30 of us.

Wiremu:    At the start of the year we were all naughty. I felt sorry for the teacher a little bit. We would never listen.

During the Te Kotahitanga professional development, teachers' and students' relationships became more positive. As Jane said:

Jane:    Now we have a routine...we do. It's all changed. Her attitude has changed and so has ours.

This was affirmed by one of the teachers:

Teacher B:    If you respect the students for who or what they are, likewise they give you that respect. Things are so much easier. The classroom management doesn't appear to be an issue. Participation levels are high. Students want to be there and they want to learn.

Then again by other students:

Wiremu:    We like teachers who are happy and not grumpy. And when we get something right, they're happy.

Manu:    She doesn't get mad at us if we do something wrong. She helps us with it. She'll come over and ask us if we're having problems with it.

Jane:    Teachers who have respect for us and will sometimes help you even if it doesn't have anything to do with school. They'll still help you. They'll give you advice.

And again by another teacher:

Teacher A:    I started seeing that it doesn't matter what's going on at home we can make a difference in the class and that's really exciting. It's like WOW, I'm just the teacher but I can have quite a significant impact on these students' lives.

### Students Reflections on Their Experiences with Te Kotahitanga Teachers

All four students talked about how their negative feelings and behaviour towards teachers changed. All four students clearly articulated that they became aware of their teachers participating in Te Kotahitanga. Their teachers cared about them and about their achievement. As teachers started to understand the concept of whānau, relationships with Māori students became more positive. Students talked about their engagement as a result of relationships with teachers.

| Jane: | Relationships with teachers, they're better with all students, welcoming us heaps. They've changed heaps. Teachers have changed towards the Māori kids since I've been here. |
|---|---|
| Wiremu: | Basically the teachers help us – help us do our work. If you do it wrong learn from your mistakes and learn from their examples of how to do it. Next time you do it better. |
| Jane: | If I didn't have those teachers, I still would've been like I was in Year 9. |
| Peter: | Mr A, I was a real dick to him at the beginning of the year. When it came to our boards I loved it. He pushed me so hard. He stayed an extra 30 minutes, just for me, to help me get my board done. Then I think back to how I was a dick to him, pretty rat shit. |
| Mamu: | Teachers treat the Māori good here. They know where we're coming from they give us an extra push. They take our crap as well. |
| Jane: | They [teachers] really want us to achieve our goals, which is really cool because you can be a real pain in the arse to them and you regret it because they're actually helping you. |

The students understood that the relationships had enabled teachers to develop a better understanding of who they were and how they could work with the students to achieve their goals. This facilitated a situation whereby students' experiences reflected this. Students talked about being motivated with learning and the benefits of being engaged.

| Manu: | They want you to achieve. They want you to do the best you can. He's only a teacher and I'm only a student but he still wants me to do well. He does that with the whole class. He pushes us. |
| Wiremu: | It's like a test. When you pass more tests, you get more credits. You feel good, you start to enjoy school. You're actually doing something good for once. You don't want to waste your time. |

Students talked about how their successes and achievement were influencing their confidence and self-esteem. They were comfortable in their own skin and achieving and succeeding as Māori was normal. They suggested that participation on their own terms brought their commitment. In these contexts students were able to be self-determining (tino rangatiratanga) and participate in power-sharing relationships (whānau) over the directions their learning would take.

Peter:      Self-drive, self-esteem, I do it because I enjoy it [Art]. It's something I can do. It relaxes me, something peaceful. I can see myself doing it for years.

Wiremu:   Māori careers they helped me in Year 10, being told what we needed to do, what we had to get to get to that place. They actually really helped me. Like maths, doing my work real good, but if I didn't do that kind of stuff I wouldn't actually get that career that I wanted.

Peter:      I'm getting there, working hard for my future, getting on the right track. Doing art, trying to pick up my game. My mates help me lots as well. That can be a real drive, passion, gives you an extra boost.

Wiremu:   Mr W pushes me. "If you do this and that, this is what you're gonna get." He always puts me in that position, like, "look at your future, this is going to help you big time. You don't want to end up involved in the wrong stuff." That's why you're working. And when you get tired, he'll say stuff that makes you want to work.

*Students Learning Outcomes While Working with Te Kotahitanga Teachers*
According to the New Zealand Qualification Authority (NZQA) website (n.d.), the National Certificate of Educational Achievement (NCEA) is the official secondary school qualification in New Zealand. It has three levels, corresponding to the levels within the National Qualifications Framework, and these are generally studied in each of the three final years of secondary schooling, Year 11 through Year 13 (Table 7.1).

Teachers had been participating in Te Kotahitanga for three years at the time that three of the students were sitting their first NCEA exams. A culturally responsive pedagogy of relations was operationalized in their classrooms, through their use of Māori metaphors in the Te Kotahitanga ETP. Teaching practice for these teachers and other teachers in the school were having a positive influence on Māori students' achievement.

**Table 7.1**   NCEA Results: Adapted from the school's management system

|        | NCEA Level 1 | NCEA Level 2 | University entrance | NCEA Level 3 |
|--------|--------------|--------------|---------------------|--------------|
| Peter  | 88 credits   | 87 credits   | Attained            | Art Design at Unitec |
| Manu   | 134 credits  | 111 credits  | Attained            | In Year 13   |
| Wiremu | 69 credits   | 80 credits   | Attained            | Forestry Apprenticeship |
| Jane   | 92 credits   | 72 credits   | Attained            | 60 credits. Second year at university |

*Note*: Adapted from Joyce (2012) Copyright 2012 by Chrisandra Itirana Joyce

*Māori Metaphors to Consider Students' Reflections and Learning Outcomes*
Māori students outcomes began to show more positive outcomes in classrooms when teachers were being encouraged and supported to change from traditional type pedagogies to more culturally responsive pedagogy of relations. Through Te Kotahitanga, teachers had developed more caring and learning relationships with Māori students and as a result Māori students' experiences were being transformed into positive educational outcomes. Students were clear that when teachers changed how they related and interacted in their classrooms, and created contexts for learning where Māori students' educational achievement could improve, then the self-determination of Māori students become central to classroom relationships and interactions.

## Alternative Teaching and Learning Metaphor

Māori students were aware of their teachers participating in Te Kotahitanga. They could see and feel the changes in teachers' pedagogy. Students knew that their teachers were committed to this relationship of mutual trust and respect that were based on whānau-type relationships. Knowing their teachers and their teachers knowing them was important for them. These relationships encouraged students to be confident as learners and be confident in who they were, as Māori. Māori students achieving education success was normal and Māori students were able to engage with their teachers in power sharing relationships and achieve on their own terms. The metaphor of tino rangatiratanga encapsulates this.

## Whānaungatanga (Extended Family)

Whānaungatanga involved the development of familial type relationships that were central for teachers and these Māori students. The experiences and theorising of these Māori students was in agreement with their teachers, knowing who their teachers were and that their teachers cared about who they were, was important to them. Although knowing each other was one thing, it was whānaungatanga that formed the basis of Māori students' developing confidence and self determination to succeed.

## Wānanga (Effective Learning Interactions)

For Māori students the metaphor of wānanga provided a safe place where they felt their prior knowledge and experiences were validated. They were able to participate in dialogic interactions with their teachers and other students and these contexts were inclusive and dynamic. Whānaungatanga establishes the contexts for these interactions to occur. Students were engaged in their learning as a result of a culturally responsive pedagogy of relations. The relationships they had built with their teachers encouraged them to be confident learners. As confident learners they were able to interact successfully with others. These effective interactions were focussed on learning. The results of these learning interactions are reflected in the increased academic results that students were achieving, particularly after three years when students were in Year 11.

## Tino Rangatiratanga (Self-Determination)

The word rangatiratanga comes from the word rangatira, which is most often translated as chief. Rangatiratanga refers to chieftainship, and the duties this responsibility holds, for example, authority, control and sovereignty. The word tino means very, full, total or absolute. Tino rangatiratanga means self-determination, total control, complete responsibility, full authority or absolute sovereignty. When learning is embedded and informed by the relationships of whānaungatanga, Māori students develop the confidence and competence to determine who they are and what they want to be. All of these students wanted to achieve academically and to succeed. Jane talked about how she felt that her teachers really wanted her to achieve her goals and how she believed this was what she was now going to do. Peter talked about how achievement had increased his self-drive and self-esteem. Manu talked about how he didn't want to finish school until he had attained NCEA Level 3. Wiremu talked about working towards the career that he wanted. In return, teachers were passionate in expressing and articulating how important it was to them, for these four Māori students, and for all Māori students to be successful, just as they would want of their own children.

Māori students' right to self-determination was exercised through the power sharing relationships they developed with their teachers. They tasted, experienced and enjoyed educational success.

## Emerging Metaphors for Māori Student Shifts

When Māori metaphors are implemented in educational settings Māori students and teachers can benefit from a new culturally responsive pedagogy of relations. When the concept of whānau is embedded in teaching practice, everything else grows from these familial relationships. Wānanga provides the settings for effective teaching and learning interactions. When Māori students' confidence and self-esteem develop from these relationships, they are able to define their right to tino rangatiratanga and succeed on their own terms.

It was through their teachers' understandings and applications of these metaphors and processes in practice that these Māori students finally began to enjoy education success.

## Teacher's Reflections of the Māori Students

Teachers talked about the changes they have seen in the four Māori students from Year 9 and 10 through to their senior years. They talk about the changes they have seen in Peter.

Teacher C:   I had Peter in Year 10. He was always on the outside looking in. When I see him around I have a bit of a kōrero (talk). He's more engaged in what he's doing. He's not like he used to be, always being compliant. He never engaged in eye contact, and I saw him the other day and he actually will look at you and you'll have a conversation.

Teacher A:   Last year he was one of the highest achieving students in Year 11. I think that was because he got heaps of praise. And he also did Te Reo (Māori language) Level 3.

They reflect on the changes they have seen in Wiremu.

Teacher B:   Wiremu and his mate came down to the PE [physical education] department the other day to have a long chat. He wouldn't have done that two years ago. I didn't feel at all that he was invading my space... and I thought that was something he wouldn't have done before.

Teacher D:   His Mum and Dad and all his mates didn't know he passed Level 1. He's the first in his family to have passed. His identity has changed. He's proud of himself.

Teacher A:   He became confident. He's the first person in his family to pass NCEA Level 1. First person in his family to pass NCEA Level 2. The only person in his family to get Level 1 and 2. And now he's got that apprenticeship.

Teacher C:   He's got leader written all over him.

Teachers reflect on the changes they have seen in Jane.

Teacher A:   I think [Jane], it's not just about being a good Māori student, it's about being a good student and being Māori. I think Jane should be Head Girl. When she was made Māori rep, I sort of thought is that tokenism just because she's Māori. She's more than that. Māori reps deserve a leadership position and not because they're Māori and we are looking for a Māori rep and who can we choose. She's been a good leader and she's Māori. She's not a leader because she's Māori.

Teacher B:   When she was in Year 10 she was a different kid. So shy, she wouldn't say boo!

Teachers talk about the changes they have seen in Manu.

Teacher A:   He's totally changed. He's got his literacy and numeracy. He's Year 13 next year. He knows he's powerful. That's what kids become. They become powerful about their learning. He came up to me and said, "Miss, I want to be in the Māori leadership group room. I want to be in there because you've got the high learning expectations." He'll tell me when he gets credits and he'll tell me when he passes. It's like he has pride and confidence. He's really confident. He says hello to every teacher. He knows every teacher. Everyone knows him. That's ownership of themselves and the school, and all these kids. This is their school. It's their destiny in how they achieve. He's become a kid who wants to be successful.

## Discussion and Conclusions

These teachers were supported to understand how the historical dominant discourses in New Zealand had impacted on Māori students' achievement, they were then able to reposition into positions that acknowledged a social justice and equity agenda. With new understandings and practices based on equity and Māori metaphor, they were more able to support Māori students to achieve more effectively.

When these two groups understood that family-like relationships were an example of whānaungatanga, where there was mutual trust and respect, everything else began to become more aligned. Their agency, vision and their commitment to ensuring Māori students' academic achievement followed.

These metaphors have all been incorporated into the poutama (stairway; Fig. 7.2). Teachers and Māori students' prior knowledge and cultural experiences are the starting points on either side of the figure. From this point forward the figure should then be read from the base up to the top and from side to side.

### Culturally Responsive Pedagogy of Relations

Figure 7.2 shows the Māori metaphors identified as important and the new understandings and practices that emerged when teachers' pedagogy started to become relational-based and both groups started listening to and learning from each other. The arrows indicate the discursive interdependent nature of this model. On the far left are Māori students' prior knowledge and cultural experiences. The metaphors that came with the arrival of Tāngata Whenua (ancestors) and that are still understood and practised by many Māori today emerge from this prior knowledge and cultural experiences. On the far right are the teachers' prior knowledge and cultural experiences then the new metaphors that began to be understood when these two groups stopped talking past each other and started learning together and from each other.

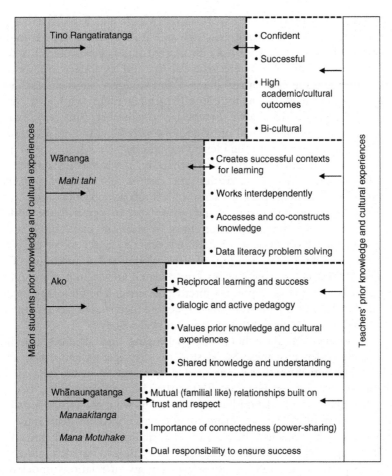

**Fig. 7.2** Culturally responsive pedagogy of relations poutama: using Māori metaphors to develop culturally responsive pedagogy of relations. Adapted from Joyce (2012)

Copyright 2012 by Chrisandra Itirana Joyce

The dotted ascending line coming diagonally up through the middle and forming the poutama indicates the interface or coming together of our separate cultural histories. Traditionally this has been a meeting space filled with misunderstandings and misinterpretation that have been seen as the collision of two differing worldviews (Metge and Kinloch 1978). In this school, however, through the new culturally responsive pedagogy of relations (Berryman et al. 2013) the dotted line is permeable. Knowing and understanding who we are gives validity and legitimacy in respecting and understanding each other. These Māori students and their teachers in this school are making this founding document their own reality. When we are engaging in alternative metaphors, to genuinely understand where both are positioned, this will bring about a truly bicultural understanding of one's own identity and the identity of others.

It is important to ensure that whatever particular pedagogies are employed and whatever activities are organized, classroom practices contribute to a young person's sense of self-efficacy and therefore, to the construction of positive identities and one's ability to cope with the world of school and in turn the global community (Wearmouth et al. 2009, p. 33). Teachers and Māori students treated each other as family members, where there were reciprocal relationships of responsibility and commitment. Their prior knowledge and experiences were validated and legitimated and contexts for learning created positive interdependence. The ultimate outcome being that Māori students were able to exercise their tino rangatiratanga and were able to take their rightful place in a global society.

The journey in this school was challenging and at times daunting. However, evidence of these Māori students participating and experiencing school differently from their parents and grandparents' generation has already begun to have an overwhelming effect in their home communities. Teachers are also taking these relationships and learnings from the classroom to the Māori community. They are maintaining their connections with these students and with others like them. The responsibility and commitment to the relationship is being maintained long after these students have left this school.

Perhaps with culturally responsive pedagogy of relations understood and modelled at the political and systemic levels, we will begin to see a more equitable partnership, based on mutual power-sharing relationships between Māori and non-Māori citizens, to take us further into the twenty-first century. People in this school have already begun that journey.

## References

Barnhardt, R. (2005). *Creating a place for indigenous knowledge in education: The Alaska native knowledge network*. Retrieved from http://ankn.uaf.edu/Curriculum/Articles/RayBarnhardt/PBE_ANKN_Chapter.html.

Berryman, M. (2008). *Repositioning within Indigenous discourses of transformation and self-determination*. (Unpublished doctoral dissertation). Hamilton, NZ: University of Waikato.

Berryman, M. (2011). *Discursive repositioning: Implications for leaders supporting teachers to work more effectively with Māori students*. Unpublished manuscript.

Berryman, M., SooHoo, S., & Nevin, A. (Eds.). (2013). *Culturally responsive methodologies*. Bedfordshire, UK: Emerald.

Bishop, R., & Berryman, M. (2006). *Culture speaks: Cultural relationships and classroom learning*. Wellington, NZ: Huia Publishers.

Bishop, R., & Glynn, T. (1999). *Culture counts: Changing power relations in education*. Palmerston North, NZ: Dunmore Press.

Bishop, R., Berryman, M., Tiakiwai, S., & Richardson, C. (2003). *Te Kotahitanga: Experiences of Year 9 and 10 Māori students in mainstream classrooms*. Wellington, NZ: Ministry of Education.

Bishop, R., Berryman, M., Cavanagh, T., & Teddy, L. (2007). *Te Kotahitanga: Phase 3 Whānaungatanga: Establishing a culturally responsive pedagogy of relations in mainstream secondary school classrooms*. Wellington, NZ: Ministry of Education.

Bishop, R., O'Sullivan, D., & Berryman, M. (2010). *Scaling up education reform: Addressing the politics of disparity*. Wellington, NZ: NCER Press.

Bruner, J. (1996). *The culture of education*. Cambridge, MA: Harvard University Press.

Joyce, C. I. (2012). *Relational responsive pedagogy: Teachers and Māori students listening and learning from each other* (Master's thesis, University of Waikato). Retrieved from http://hdl.handle.net/10289/7038.

Metge, J., & Kinloch, P. (1978). *Talking past each other: Problems of cross-cultural communication*. Wellington, NZ: Victoria University Press.

Ministry of Education. (2008). *Ka Hikitia: Managing for success Māori education strategy 2008–2012*. Wellington, NZ: Ministry of Education.

New Zealand Qualifications Authority (NZQA). n.d.. Secondary School and NCEA. Retrieved from www.nzqa.govt.nz/studying-in-new-zealand/secondary-school-and-ncea/.

Orange, C. (1987). *The Treaty of Waitangi*. Wellington, NZ: Bridget Williams Books.

Pere, R. R. (1994). *Ako: Concepts of Learning in the Māori Tradition*. Wellington, NZ: Te Kohanga Reo National Trust Board.

Scheurich, J., & Young, M. (1997). Colouring epistemologies: Are our research epistemologies racially based? *Educational Review, 26*(4), 4–16.

Smith, G. H. (1992). Research issues related to Māori education. In M. K. Hohepa & G. H. Smith (Eds.), *The issue of research and Māori* (Monograph No. 9, pp. 19–27). Auckland, NZ: Research Unit for Māori Education, University of Auckland.

Wearmouth, J., Berryman, M., & Glynn, T. (2009). *Inclusion through participation in communities of practice in schools*. Auckland, NZ: Dunmore Publishing Ltd.

**Iti Joyce** is a Māori mother of two tamarikii (children) and a grandmother of three mokopuna (grandchildren). Her primary and secondary schooling experiences were littered with academic failure, with many of her whānau (family and extended family) members also having the same experiences. As a teacher, she knew there was a major problem regarding Māori students' academic achievement, but was unsure how to address this issue. Te Kotahitanga was introduced and implemented in over fifty schools throughout New Zealand and Māori students' academic achievement was improving as a result of focussing on the Te Kotahitanga Effective Teaching Profile. Her current role is working alongside mainstream secondary schools and their school leaders to address practices that perpetuate the disparities between Māori and non-Māori students.

# CHAPTER 8

# Partnering Māori Whānau in Literacy Interventions

*Therese Ford*

## INTRODUCTION

Throughout the past two decades various sectors of New Zealand society have expressed concerns about the low educational achievement levels of Indigenous Māori students compared with non-Māori (Bishop et al. 2003; Bishop and Glynn 1999; Phillips et al. 2001). Addressing this disparity and raising the achievement of Māori students has, therefore, been a high priority and Brooking (2007) points out that the development of better partnerships between the homes of Māori students and schools has been seen by the Ministry of Education as an integral component of meeting this priority. Brooking (2007) explains:

> It has long been known that families have a significant effect on their children's achievement, and are their children's first teachers.... Schools traditionally have operated reasonably independently of families, some more so than others, but many are now trying to form closer links with their families and communities, so that both can work together more, for the good of the child in all respects, including learning and achievement.... Raising student achievement is a major focus of the Ministry's work, particularly for Māori and Pacific students, and it is believed that increased parental involvement could help address this. (p. 14)

T. Ford (✉)
University of Waikato, Hamilton, New Zealand
e-mail: tford@waikato.ac.nz

© The Author(s) 2017
F. Pirbhai-Illich et al. (eds.), *Culturally Responsive Pedagogy*,
DOI 10.1007/978-3-319-46328-5_8

165

More recently, the Ministry of Education (2013a) reiterated a major focus on raising the achievement of Māori students who are identified (alongside Pasifika students, special needs students and students from low socioeconomic areas) as being priority learners. Within The Māori Education Strategy – Ka Hikitia Accelerating Success (Ministry of Education 2013b) the drive to connect schools with their Māori parents, whānau (extended family) and community can be seen within the concept of *Productive Partnerships*, which is one of five guiding principles that underpin the strategy. A productive partnership is defined within Ka Hikitia as being a two-way, mutually respectful relationship that:

> starts with the understanding that Māori children and students are connected to whānau and should not be viewed or treated as separate, isolated or disconnected. Parents and whānau must be involved in conversations about their children and their learning. They need accessible, evidence-based information on how to support their children's learning and success. (Ministry of Education 2013b, p. 17)

The Minister of Education has also highlighted the focus on the secondary sector by articulating within the Statement of Intent 2013–2018 (Ministry of Education 2013a) the Better Public Services target that stipulates that 85% of 18-year-olds will achieve the National Certificate of Educational Achievement (NCEA) Level 2 or an equivalent qualification by the end of 2017. It is expected that 85% of Māori students in both English medium and Māori medium will achieve this target, and this presents a challenge for educators, given that the most recent national performance data indicates that in 2011 only 57% of Māori students achieved NCEA of an equivalent qualification compared with 74.3% for all students. Increasing the percentage of students who receive literacy and numeracy credits in Year 11 (prior to NCEA Level 2) is an associated goal that has been set by the Ministry, which indicates that they acknowledge that students need to be competent in these two areas if schools are to maximize the chances of achieving the target. Again only 67.3% of Māori students were achieving literacy and numeracy expectations in 2011 compared with 78.4% for all students (Ministry of Education 2013a). Hence we see within the current policy framework, very clear expectations that schools need to develop stronger partnerships with Māori whānau *and* accelerate the literacy and numeracy achievement of Māori students in order to achieve governmental targets and reduce disparities.

This chapter details four case studies that were based in mainstream secondary schools. The case studies were initiated by principals who were focussed on addressing the dual challenge of developing learning partnerships with Māori whānau and raising the literacy achievements of their Māori students. The chapter begins by contextualizing the research in relation to previous research. It then describes the varying levels to which principals and literacy coordinators engaged Māori whānau in the implementation of a reading–tutoring intervention, *Pause Prompt Praise*, and a writing intervention, *Responsive Written Feedback*, along with the outcomes of these interventions. The chapter concludes with a discussion about the outcomes that have emerged from the case studies and highlights the implications for schools seeking to partner with Māori whānau in order to accelerate literacy achievement and eliminate disparities between Māori and non-Māori students.

## HOME–SCHOOL PARTNERSHIPS IN NEW ZEALAND

Although as mentioned, productive partnerships have been emphasized in the most recent Māori education strategy, the notion of involving Māori whānau and communities in the education of children through home–school partnership initiatives is not a recent phenomenon in mainstream education. These initiatives have as their origins the Tomorrow's Schools reforms of 1989 (Wylie 1992). Subsequently, in the National Administration Guidelines of 1993, "clear and accurate communication and consultation with parents, whānau and families, and communities became a mandated expectation of schools" (Education Review Office 2008, p. 8).

Further evidence of the Ministry of Education's endeavours to increase Māori whānau and community participation in the education of students can be found within previously mentioned strategic statements (Ministry of Education 2013a, 2013b). Another important example is the New Zealand Curriculum (Ministry of Education 2007), which identifies community engagement as one of the foundation principles for making decisions, and emphasizes the need for the school's curriculum to connect with student's lives and engage "the support of families, whānau, and communities" (p. 9).

The Ministry of Education has been very clear, through the range of policies discussed above that they expect schools to connect with the Māori whānau and communities and develop relationships that will facilitate a situation where the Māori community and the school are partners.

Although this may be the aspiration, the Ministry also concedes that while school leaders and teachers know that it is important to engage with parents and whānau, the critical implication is that "many do not know how best to go about establishing learning partnerships" (Ministry of Education 2010, p. 28). However, within their *School Leadership and Student Outcomes: What Works and Why, Best Evidence Synthesis (BES)*, Robinson et al. (2009) go some way in addressing the challenge of home–school partnerships by referencing New Zealand research and providing examples of "how" these partnerships can be achieved.

Alton-Lee et al. (2009) conducted a synthesis and meta-analysis of 37 studies. The studies focussed on the effect of the following interventions: Structured Brainstorming (Whitehead 1998), Pause Prompt Praise (Glynn et al. 1979) and Responsive Written Feedback (Glynn et al. 1986). The latter two interventions were used in the project reported here. They required a greater level of partnership between the whānau and schools and thus represent how schools formed these educationally powerful connections. Alton-Lee et al. (2009) found that the interventions involving whānau/parents and teachers had a large impact on student achievement with a very high effect size of 1.81 – against an "average" effect size of 0.60 for a year of "excellent" teaching without any whānau intervention. A brief overview of the two interventions now follows.

## PAUSE PROMPT PRAISE

Pause Prompt Praise was developed by Auckland University in the late 1970s (Glynn et al. 1979). This reading–tutoring procedure was designed to be used by parents in the home with children who were experiencing reading difficulties, and during the original research the team worked intensively with a group of families, some of which were Māori.

The theoretical perspective that underpins Pause Prompt Praise "views proficient reading as learning to use all the sources of information within and around text to understand the particular message being conveyed" (Glynn and McNaughton 1985, p. 66). This approach is consistent with the principles of culturally responsive pedagogies, which emphasize the need for educators to develop relationships with learners that enable them to draw on their prior knowledge and experiences in order to make sense of new learning (Bishop et al. 2007). Successful tutoring of Pause Prompt Praise, therefore, requires tutors to develop relationships of care and trust with students and apply strategies that are specific and responsive to students' reading ability, or what Vygotsky (1978) refers to as their zone of proximal development. This includes selecting reading texts that connect with a student's life experiences and interests, which means that tutors need to really know and understand the world of the reader. Additionally, when engaging in the reading process, tutors encourage struggling readers, for example, to go beyond a phonetic focus on letters and letter–sound combinations and consider contextual information, and their prior knowledge and experience, in order to make sense of what they are reading.

Providing tutors with ongoing feedback and feed-forward on their tutoring practice is critical to the success of Pause Prompt Praise. These learning conversations affirm good practice and support tutors to improve and develop. Importantly they also represent an opportunity for tutors and coordinators to further develop relational trust, which in the case of whānau and community partnerships, serves to reinforce the school's commitment to both the partnership and the shared vision of accelerating students' reading achievement.

## RESPONSIVE WRITTEN FEEDBACK

Responsive Written Feedback originates from the work of Vargas (1978) and is a writing intervention that has been used successfully in New Zealand to improve the quantity and quality of students' writing (Glynn et al. 1986; Jerram et al. 1988; Vanstone 2008). Like Pause Prompt Praise, this intervention represents a culturally responsive pedagogical approach to literacy as it allows for the development of relationships by providing students with a process that facilitates social interaction, through a writing exchange or writing relationship, between a (less competent) student *writer* and a (more competent) *responder*. Writers are able to determine for themselves what they would like to write to their responders, which means that they can draw on their own prior knowledge, experiences and interests to develop their piece of writing. While it is important that the responder is more competent than the writer, the responder needs to focus on responding to the messages in the writer's writing, and refrain from providing evaluative or corrective feedback. This point particularly resonates with the culturally responsive principle of power-sharing (Bishop et al. 2007), as it supports the development of a non-dominating relationship between the writer and the responder, and positions the responder as the reader or audience. This does not mean, however, that responsive written feedback does not support the development of accurate spelling, grammar and correct structure. The responder optimizes the opportunity they have through their written response to demonstrate what correct spelling, grammar, punctuation and/or structure looks like, while at the same time they demonstrate to the writer (again through their response) that they understand and value the message the writing is conveying.

## WORKING WITH THE CASE STUDY SCHOOLS

The Ministry of Education expectations and the research reported in the previously-mentioned school leadership Best Evidence Synthesis (Robinson et al. 2009) stimulated interest in Pause Prompt Praise and Responsive Written Feedback for a group of principals who were part of a Ministry of Education-funded research and professional development project called Te Kotahitanga. Te Kotahitanga was a secondary school intervention research project that focussed on raising the achievement of Māori students and in 2011, I was part of the project team that facilitated professional development and supported senior leaders to develop educationally powerful connections with their Māori whānau and communities. Although the opportunity to work with me to implement Pause Prompt Praise and Responsive Written Feedback was provided to all 35 schools (who were engaged with the project at that time), four principals expressed a particularly strong desire to work with me and use the interventions to simultaneously improve home–school partnerships with their Māori whānau and the literacy achievement of their Māori students. In the next section I describe my own learning and reflections of the extent to which this happened in each of these case studies, and the outcomes of these endeavours.

### Case Study 1

The principal in Case Study 1 was interested in implementing Pause Prompt Praise and wanted to trial the procedure within the school, using adult teacher aides as tutors for a group of low progress readers. A specialist literacy teacher at the school was delegated responsibility for coordinating the procedure. The intention was to train the adult teacher aides who worked within the school and provide them with an opportunity to develop their tutoring practice during the final 3 months of the school year. It was envisaged that these teacher aides would then train

Māori whānau and community members at the beginning of the following year, to either become tutors within the in-school programme, and/or operationalize the procedure in their homes with their own children. Importantly, within the group of five teacher aides, two were Māori women who were parents of children who attended the school. Hence these women were the Māori whānau, and therefore members, of the very community the school was seeking to engage and develop partnerships with through this intervention.

The teacher aides engaged in the tutor training and each worked with two students from a group of 10 low progress readers. The teacher aides had two tutoring sessions per week with their students throughout a 10-week period and were provided with feedback and feed-forward around their tutoring practice. At the end of the 10-week period, diagnostic reading assessments indicated that over this 10-week period all students increased their chronological reading levels by at least 6 months, with the largest increase being a progression of 2 years.

Encouraged by this improvement and feeling confident that their tutoring practice had contributed to the students' success, the two Māori teacher aides talked to whānau and other members of the Māori community about becoming involved as tutors at the school so that a greater number of Māori students could receive the benefits of Pause Prompt Praise. However, the coordinator left the school to take up another position, and despite the improvement made by the students in the trial and the enthusiasm of the teacher aides, school leaders were unable to prioritize the reactivation of Pause Prompt Praise until August of the following year.

The newly appointed coordinator invited additional volunteers from the community to undertake training in Pause Prompt Praise and become tutors to work within the in-school programme. Although the school had a good response from the community, only seven community members were selected to join the teacher aides and become in-school tutors. The coordinator felt that seven in-school tutors was manageable. However, this greatly disappointed the Māori teacher aides, as whānau members that they had encouraged to become involved in Pause Prompt Praise were not part of the selected seven, and therefore did not receive the opportunity to undertake training.

While the in-school tutors received the initial training, this was not followed up with specific feedback on their practice. Furthermore, the school did not offer tutor training to the whānau of the students who were part of the in-school intervention until 2 months after the in-school programme had started and then again this initial training was not followed up by feedback on practice and further support. After 3 months, 18 of the 20 students completed the diagnostic reading assessments, which indicated that 10 students did not increase their chronological reading age. For the eight students who did progress, the increase in their chronological reading age ranged from 6 months to 3 years.

### Case Study 2

The principal designated coordinator in Case Study 2, who had been implementing Pause Prompt Praise as an in-school intervention for low progress readers for a number of years, found that the tutoring provided by two trained teachers' aides to be highly effective in accelerating reading achievement. While the in-school programme was operating successfully and the parents of students who were included in the programme were aware that their children were receiving support, the principal felt that the school had not optimized the opportunity to engage the whānau in a partnership around Pause Prompt Praise, and was keen to do this in an effort to improve home–school partnerships with their Māori community.

The coordinator enlisted the assistance of another specialist teacher to help facilitate the engagement processes and support whānau to implement the intervention in their homes. Whānau of students who received the in-school tutoring were invited to participate in a Pause Prompt Praise training session and representatives (parents, grandparents, aunts) from 19 whānau attended. These participants were very grateful to have the opportunity to learn how to support their children to develop reading strategies at home. Many of them talked about being concerned that their children had reading difficulties, while at the same time feeling helpless to address this without advice and support.

While the coordinator and the specialist teacher were encouraged by the enthusiasm demonstrated by the whānau who attended the training session, prioritizing time to provide whānau with feedback and support proved to be problematic and highlighted the implications of a lack of structures to support home–school partnerships. In some cases whānau declined any ongoing support, but by and large the processes that were in place to provide parents with feedback and feed-forward on their tutoring practice did not enable timely and regular conversations to happen between the home and school. Nevertheless, despite this breakdown in the feedback and communication cycle, all but one of the students from the whānau who attended the Pause Prompt Praise training hui (formal meeting) increased their chronological reading age over a period of two school terms (20 weeks). The improvement across the group ranged from between an increase of 1 year up to an improvement of 7 years.

## Case Study 3

The principal in Case Study 3 asked a teacher from within the English department to coordinate the implementation of Responsive Written Feedback. The coordinator wanted to initially locate the trial within the school and therefore trained senior school students (Year 13) to be the responders for a class of junior school students (Year 9). The senior school students were a class of mixed ethnicities and abilities. The intention was to expand the responder group to include members of the community in the following year.

In Case Study 3, the coordinator was surprised by how motivated the students in her junior school class were to both write to their responders each week and then read the messages their responders had written to them in response to their writing. While she noticed that both groups of students (writers and responders), were sharing many interesting perspectives and personal experiences within their writing, she worried that students might "just" focus in the exchange of information and not on what she determined to be "meaningful writing", so she decided to give the Year 9 boys a topic to focus their writing to the responders. By seeking to control this aspect of the intervention the teacher did compromise the non-dominating and participatory principles that underpin responsive written feedback. However, there were still some positive outcomes.

A comparative analysis was undertaken between the students' first piece of writing at the beginning of the responsive written feedback intervention and their tenth writing sample (after the 10-week exchange). Quantitative measures demonstrated that, across the Year 9 class, the students were writing more to their responders with increased accuracy and they were also using more challenging vocabulary. A qualitative analysis of the beginning sample and the final sample demonstrated moderate improvements in terms of audience appeal. The teacher conceded that this could possibly have been attributed to the fact that she set the writing topic rather than allowing the students to focus on what interested them in terms of the writing conversation. Overall the teacher was really pleased with the progress the students made. Despite recognizing the potential of this intervention to improve writing and engaging the community in the intervention, the school did not reactivate responsive written feedback the following year. Thus, their intentions to develop relationships with their community through this intervention were never fulfilled.

### Case Study 4

In Case Study 4, the Year 9 class of writers were a special education class that consisted of low progress readers and writers. The coordinator, who was also the English teacher of this class, struggled to engage these students in writing, many of whom would frequently refuse to write at all during their English lessons. As in Case Study 3, the teacher decided to use senior students as responders. For the first piece of writing, the coordinator encouraged the writers to write about themselves and effectively introduce who they were and what they enjoyed with their responders. When the writers received their responses, the teacher described giggling and shrieks of excitement as the writers read the responses and then shared what their responders had written with her and the other students. They were very enthusiastic about writing back to their responders and maintaining an ongoing writing conversation. They specifically asked to be given more than the specified ten-minute writing time and they also requested that they wanted more than one written exchange per week.

The coordinator was amazed and delighted that these previously reluctant writers were so keen to write that she did in fact allow the students to write for longer than ten min, and there were instances when some writers and responders exchanged more than one piece of writing in a week. Unfortunately, some of the responders (who were senior students) were unable to maintain this role as their commitments to their own studies prevented them from consistently responding to their writing partner.

Inconsistencies regarding time frames and the opportunities students received to write to responders compromised any quantitative data analysis that could have been carried out across the class. However, the coordinator did feel that her observations provided some qualitative evidence with regard to improvements in students' attitudes towards writing.

Feedback she received from some of the students reflected the position that they felt good that their responders answered questions that the writers posed, and they liked the fact that the responders shared similar experiences and thoughts. The coordinator felt that the affirmation that the writers received in the responses was a powerful motivator for them to keep writing, as it helped these students to recognize themselves as legitimate "writers" who could generate a piece of writing that was understood and then appreciated by others.

The coordinator in Case Study 4, unfortunately, left the school at the conclusion of the school year, and despite her positive feedback to the school leadership and her offer to help reinstitute Responsive Written Feedback, this did not happen. Again, as in the previously discussed cases, the intention of expanding the intervention to include other groups of student writers and community members as responders remained an intention that failed to become a reality. The next section discusses commonalities that are evident in all four of these case studies, and poses implications for home–school partnerships.

## DISCUSSION OF THE OUTCOMES

While the case studies above describe the implementation of two different literacy interventions in four separate case studies, the outcomes and implications for each case are very similar. As previously mentioned, all principals indicated that they wanted to implement either Pause Prompt Praise or Responsive Written Feedback in their schools primarily because these interventions represented how they could develop educationally powerful home–school partnerships, or more specifically, how they could develop these partnerships with their Māori whānau and communities to increase the academic achievement of the Maori students. The outcomes described in the case studies above have implications for principals and teachers, as well as Māori students, their whānau and their communities.

### Implications for Principals

Although it was principals who initiated the implementation of these literacy interventions as a means for developing home–school partnerships with their Māori communities, what happened in reality is that all responsibility for the implementation of the interventions was delegated to people who became coordinators. The delegation of responsibility for implementing the literacy interventions is not necessarily in itself problematic, as principals involved in the previous research (Alton-Lee et al. 2009; Glynn et al. 1979) demonstrated that they were able to develop effective learning partnerships with their Māori communities without being a coordinator or without becoming a reading tutor and/or a writing responder. Critically, however, they did remain involved and connected to the literacy intervention. Being involved in Pause Prompt Praise and Responsive Written Feedback enabled these principals to meet with and develop relationships of care and trust between themselves and their Māori whānau and communities. These relationships facilitated a situation whereby principals were able to better understand the aspirations of their Māori whānau and community to develop a shared vision for improved literacy achievement, which in turn engendered "a strong sense of collective responsibility. All those involved saw the initiative as urgent and important" (Alton-Lee et al. 2009, p. 232). Conversely, the principals in these case studies largely disengaged from the implementation process shortly after someone else accepted the responsibility for the coordinator's role. This disconnection meant that principals missed valuable opportunities to:

- invite whānau and community members to work in partnership with their schools;
- meet and speak with whānau and communities members who attended tutor training sessions to demonstrate their support for the whānau, the Māori students and the teachers who were facilitating the training;
- engage in conversations with whānau as the interventions progressed in order to gain their perspectives;
- celebrate student success with the community and jointly explore how they might consolidate and deepen their partnerships.

### Implications for Coordinators

Although in all four case studies the coordinators of the literacy interventions understood that the principals wanted to see partnerships with the Māori whānau and community emerge from these interventions, they largely focussed on exploring how the interventions could accelerate literacy achievement within the school. Two coordinators commented that spreading the interventions out into the Māori community would potentially mean an increase in their workload, and the prospect of this discouraged them from taking the "next step".

Case Study 2 was an exception, as they were already implementing Pause Prompt Praise as an in-school intervention. However, all of the coordinators framed the interventions as "trials" (they were either trialing the in-school intervention or trialing the training of whānau for a home–school intervention). The trial framework, consequently, provided coordinators with the opportunity to determine how the intervention was going to play out in each of their respective contexts.

The willingness of coordinators to share power was a critical consideration at this level of the literacy interventions. In Case Study 1, the coordinator limited the number of community volunteers that could undertake tutor training, despite the keen interest, and thus prevented the intervention from expanding into the community. Furthermore, the volunteers that did become tutors did not receive support to develop their tutoring practice. In Case Study 3, the coordinator was unable to let the students determine for themselves what they might like to write to their responders, and thus she controlled the writing exchanges and inhibited the writers' ability to freely respond to their responders. Common to all four case studies was the decision by coordinators to prioritize the in-school programme. By neglecting to support and grow the capacity of whānau and community members as reading tutors and/or responders, the coordinators effectively maintained power by keeping the expertise located within the parameters of the school. Furthermore, in case studies 1 and 4, when the coordinators left the school, there was insufficient capability left within the school to sustain the interventions.

### Implications for Māori Students, Whānau and Community

The data from this study indicate that the majority of the students across the case studies made positive gains, which included either an increase in chronological reading age, improvements in the quantity, accuracy and quality of writing and/or higher levels of engagement in writing. Māori whānau who engaged in the reading tutor training and tutored their children at home also reported feeling increased confidence in their ability to support their children and provide them with appropriate reading strategies in their home settings. However, without any feedback and feed-forward on their practice, some whānau worried about the integrity and more specifically the accuracy of their practice, and were conscious that they might have been using the wrong prompt at the wrong time. Some parents expressed that they would have really appreciated the opportunity to have feedback and feed-forward conversations, as this ongoing dialogue would have strengthened the sense of partnership between themselves and the schools.

## CONCLUSION

The elimination of achievement disparities between Māori and non-Māori students remains a priority for the Ministry of Education. This chapter has identified two central goals that are part of the wider policy framework that is focussed on addressing this situation. The development of productive partnerships with Māori whānau and communities and an increase in literacy achievement are two examples of "what" the Ministry expects the school leaders and teachers to do. Previous research has demonstrated that when schools and Māori whānau and communities develop partnerships, they can potentially significantly improve the literacy achievement of their Māori students, which is "why" these partnerships are so important (Ministry of Education 2013b). The literacy interventions Pause Prompt Praise and Responsive Written Feedback are examples of "how" these partnerships and subsequent improvements in literacy might be achieved. However, school leaders and teachers need to carefully consider the way in which these interventions are operationalized, if they want to maximize the potential for success. The small-scale case studies in this chapter offer some insight into this potential.

Principals and the coordinators in each case study felt satisfied that the interventions in their respective settings had resulted in positive outcomes for Māori students in terms of their engagement and achievement and the data would confirm that this was the case. Consequently, the school practitioners felt pleased that they had made some progress towards the goal of raising literacy achievement. However, given that the development and maintenance of the in-school intervention was prioritized in all case studies, to the detriment of the home and community intervention, the extent to which partnerships with whānau have been achieved is more difficult to quantify.

This raises questions therefore, about how much more improvement these Māori students might have made if principals had remained connected to the interventions and worked with the coordinators to initiate and maintain contact with whānau? A question around the sustainability of these interventions is also appropriate, especially if the school centres the responsibility for coordination and development with one person. In Case

Study 1, willing community volunteers did not make the selected seven who would have received the Pause Prompt Praise training, so it would be interesting to consider how many more Māori students might have had their achievement accelerated if these volunteers were given the opportunity to train. Another important question to ask in Case Study 1 is, what would the achievement of Māori students have looked like if the in-school tutors had received ongoing feedback and feed-forward on their practice? Similarly, we could ask what impact ongoing feedback and feed-forward support would have had if it had been prioritized for whānau and community members who were tutoring reading at home? In terms of Responsive Written Feedback we are left to contemplate what the quantity and quality of the writing would have been like if the teacher in Case Study 3, for example, had allowed the students to determine for themselves what they wanted to write to their responders. Additionally, we could ask, what might have happened if whānau and community members had actually been approached to be responders? Perhaps consideration of how these interventions played out, alongside the Ministry of Education's notion of a productive partnership being a two-way mutually respectful relationship, would also be a worthwhile exercise.

These questions provide critical points for reflection for the principals and coordinators in these case studies. Other school leaders and teachers who are contemplating "how" they might develop partnerships with Māori whānau to meet governmental targets of increasing literacy and numeracy credits in order to have 85% of their Māori students achieving NCEA Level 2 or an equivalent qualification might also consider the same questions. Similarly, these questions are relevant in other countries where educators are seeking to reduce disparities.

In terms of educational research, these unanswered questions ultimately represent an opportunity for further learning and investigation. The effective size increase of 1.81 in previous studies provides clear evidence that when schools do successfully partner with their Māori whānau they are much better positioned to significantly increase achievement than they would be if they tried to do this alone. Perhaps, therefore, the most critical question for future research is not how can schools develop learning partnerships with Māori whānau, but rather how serious schools are about partnering with Māori whānau to accelerate the literacy achievement of Māori students and crucially, how would they demonstrate this commitment?

# REFERENCES

Alton-Lee, A., Robinson, V., Hohepa, M., & Lloyd, C. (2009). Creating education-ally powerful connections with family, whānau, and communities. In V. Robinson, M. Hohepa, & C. Lloyd (Eds.), *School leadership and student outcomes: Identifying what works and why. Best evidence synthesis iteration BES* (pp. 142–170). Wellington, NZ: Ministry of Education.

Bishop, R., Berryman, M., Tiakiwai, S., & Richardson, C. (2003). *Te Kotahitanga: Experiences of Year 9 and 10 Māori students in mainstream classrooms.* Wellington, NZ: Ministry of Education.

Bishop, R., Berryman, M., Cavanagh, T., & Teddy, L. (2007). *Te Kotahitanga: Phase 3 Whanaungatanga: Establishing a culturally responsive pedagogy of relations in mainstream secondary school classrooms.* Wellington, NZ: Ministry of Education.

Bishop, R., & Glynn, T. (1999). *Culture counts: Changing power relations in education.* Palmerston North, NZ: Dunmore Press.

Brooking, K. (2007). Home-school partnerships. What are they really? *Set, 3,* Wellington NZ: New Zealand Council for Education Research.

Education Review Office. (2008, June). *Partners in learning: Schools' engagement with parents, whānau and communities.* Wellington, NZ: Education Review Office.

Glynn, T., McNaughton, S., Robinson, V., & Quinn, M. (1979). *Remedial reading at home: Helping you to help your child.* Wellington, NZ: New Zealand Council for Educational Research.

Glynn, T., & McNaughton, S. (1985). The Mangere home and school remedial reading procedures: Continuing research on their effectiveness. *New Zealand Journal of Psychology, 14,* 66–77.

Glynn, T., Jerram, H., & Tuck, B. (1986). Writing as an interactive process. *Behavioural Approaches with Children, 10*(4), 116–126.

Jerram, H., Glynn, T., & Tuck, B. (1988). Responding to the message: Providing a social context for children learning to write. *Educational Psychology: An International Journal of Experimental Educational Psychology, 8*(1–2), 31–40.

Ministry of Education. (2007). *The New Zealand curriculum.* Wellington, NZ: Ministry of Education. Retrieved from http://nzcurriculum.tki.org.nz/.

Ministry of Education. (2010). *Ngā Haeata Mātauranga, – The annual report on Māori education, 2007/08.* Wellington, NZ: Ministry of Education.

Ministry of Education. (2013a). *Ministry of education statement of intent 2013–2018.* Wellington, NZ: Ministry of Education. Retrieved from http://www.minedu.govt.nz/theMinistry/PublicationsAndResources/StatementOfIntent/~/media/MinEdu/Files/TheMinistry/2013SOI/StatementOfIntent2013.pdf.

Ministry of Education. (2013b). *Ka Hikitia – Accelerating success 2013–2017.* Wellington, NZ: Ministry of Education. Retrieved from http://www.minedu.govt.nz/theMinistry/PolicyandStrategy/~/media/MinEdu/Files/TheMinistry/KaHikitia/KaHikitiaAcceleratingSuccessEnglish.pdf.

Phillips, G., McNaughton, S., & MacDonald, S. (2001). *Picking up the pace: Effective literacy interventions for accelerated progress over the transition into decile one schools.* Auckland: Strengthening Education in Mangere and Otara, Report to the Ministry of Education. Wellington, NZ: Ministry of Education.

Robinson, V., Hohepa, M., & Lloyd, C. (2009). *School leadership and student outcomes: Identifying what works and why. Best evidence synthesis iteration (BES).* Wellington, NZ: Ministry of Education.

Vanstone, B. (2008). *Important Messages from Students' Responsive Writing: A bit of a holloboleoo.* (Unpublished master's thesis). University of Waikato, New Zealand.

Vargas, J. (1978). A behavioural approach to the teaching of composition. *Behaviour Analyst, 1*(1), 16–24.

Vygotsky, L. S. (1978). *Mind in society: The development of higher psychological processes.* Cambridge, MA: Harvard University Press.

Whitehead, D. (1998). *Catch them thinking and writing: A handbook of classroom strategies.* Arlington Heights, IL: Skylight Professional Development.

Wylie, C. (1992). *The impact of tomorrow's schools in primary schools and inter-mediates: 1991 survey report.* Wellington, NZ: NZCER. Retrieved from http://www.nzcer.org.nz/system/files/271.pdf.

**Therese Ford** is a Māori woman from the northern iwi (tribe) of Ngāi Takoto. With her two children attending mainstream schools, she represents Māori whānau (extended families) and community members who are willing and able to support schools in accelerating children's learning. Therese has a background in classroom teaching and senior leadership in both mainstream primary and secondary schools. While she understood that it was important to connect with Māori parents in order to improve the achievement of and eliminate disparities between Māori and non-Māori students, she and her colleagues were not always successful in engaging Māori whānau and community members in meaningful ways. These experiences, coupled with concerns about the achievement of Māori students in mainstream education, prompted her to pursue educational research. In her current role as a professional development service provider, she works with school leadership teams to support them in developing educationally powerful connections with Māori whānau and communities.

# PART IV

# CHAPTER 9

# What's At Stake in a High-Stakes Math Test? Analysis of Multimodal Challenges for Emergent English Bilingual Learners

*Theresa Austin*

## INTRODUCTION

While we live with multimodal literacies in all walks of life, contemporary schooling has traditionally favored only a limited number of modalities, in general verbal and written modalities in the main academic subject areas. With the advance of technologies in learning design, there is increased attention to how the use of multimodality impacts learning in culturally diverse settings. For emergent English bilingual learners, in particular, this multimodal orientation is significant because it holds both potential benefits and obstacles in its implementation. In this chapter, I argue that while multimodal literacies may hold benefits for all learners, these literacies are not culturally neutral and must be examined closely for assumptions that limit their potential use for learners from non-dominant cultural backgrounds. Drawing on tools for multimodal analysis from a critical discourse analysis perspective, assumptions are analyzed in the world of standardized testing through an examination of instructions or guidelines that were designed for math test proctors for the Partnership for

T. Austin (✉)
Department of Teacher Education and Curriculum Studies
University of Massachusetts College of Education, Boston, MA, USA
e-mail: theresaya@gmail.com, taustin@educ.umass.edu, austinty2@gmail.com

© The Author(s) 2017                                                     185
F. Pirbhai-Illich et al. (eds.), *Culturally Responsive Pedagogy*,
DOI 10.1007/978-3-319-46328-5_9

Assessment of Readiness for College and Careers (PARCC) math tests. While these instructions were designed so that proctors assure that testing conditions are the same for all learners, I analyzed these to reveal how they provide evidence that the required use of interrelated modalities increases the complexity of the items for emerging second-language learners (L2), often without necessarily revealing what the learner may know about the construct being tested. I point out how the resulting complexity may well impede such a learner from being able to demonstrate what s(he) knows and thereby potentially lead to errors of underestimation and overestimation of the learner's knowledge and skills. In this chapter I provide a brief explanation of the second-language learner and standardized testing movement in the United States, a description of the text and my procedures for analysis. Next I present my results with examples that represent several categories of potential areas of complexity. Furthermore, I include example items from prior test texts that also need to be considered in light of multimodal demands in testing. In closing, I discuss implications and raise questions that we as researchers and educators may take up to disrupt the flow continual disadvantaging of marginalized groups of learners.

## English as Additional Language Learners in the United States and Academic Performance on Standardized Tests

By several reports, in some school districts in the United States, students sit for as many as 91 days of testing in a 180-day typical academic school year (Florida). Emergent English bilingual learners, also known as learners of English as an additional language (EAL), may sit for even more. Since the passage of the Bush Administration's No Child Left Behind Act in 2001, and its continued implementation during the Obama administration, these tests increasingly have been relied upon to form part of the US attempt to identify and be accountable for this population's academic progress (Abedi 2002). The makers of these standardized tests go through painstaking effort to produce a defensible measurement instrument that can be used for large-scale assessments and decisions. While biases may exist in these tests, by the time they are released, the tests represent the test makers' best attempt to reduce these. Overtime these tests continue to be monitored for test takers' interactions with items that compromise the test results' ability to render a test takers' "true" score.

However, a continuing significant nagging problem is that these tests consistently produce lower scores for students who are designated as "English Language Learners" (this federal appellation applies to those whose home language is other than English and who enter schools without the level of English required for academic instruction; Hemphill and Vanneman 2011; Mahoney et al. 2009; Short and Fitzsimmons 2007). As early as 1999, the National Council on Measurement in Education in their publication entitled "Standards for Educational and Psychological Testing" stated that "the many psychoeducational tests have been developed for and normed with monolingual, English-speaking children are irrelevant for multilingual learners" (American Educational Research Association, American Psychological Association, & National Council of Measurement in Education [AERA, APA, & NCME] 1999, p. 7). Yet still it is not widely acknowledged that emerging second-language learners are being asked to perform in subject areas' knowledge and skills at the same level as their grade-level peers in ways that do not take into account their developing EAL. Public school districts subject them nonetheless to the demands of these tests, without necessarily preparing teachers adequately to critically interpret or use these scores.

Certainly there are also many external reasons why these learners attain lower scores, such as lack of prior instruction, lack of preparation for testing, and lack of appropriate accommodation in testing conditions (Abedi et al. 2006; Schafer Willner et al. 2008). Nonetheless, there are also test internal issues that merit further analysis. The tests themselves warrant scrutiny of their construct's domains, items, and response formats for their required use of multimodalities in assumed culturally neutral ways. Equally important objects for scrutiny are the instructions for administering the test, the preparation of such administrators and their understanding of accommodations, analysis, and interpretation of learner response patterns, and most importantly their resulting decision making. It can be argued that at every point along the production of a test, we need to be attentive to the cultural assumptions behind the use of modes and the complementarity of their use.

One internal indicator I focus on here is the text that prepares test proctors to administer the test and the subsequent potential effect on the EAL test taker. If we analyze the test guidelines for proctors, we can see how the ideal reader (proctor) must be well prepared multimodally in order to provide sufficient cues aurally, visually, and/or in writing to elicit the second-language test taker's performance.

I focus on a critical analysis of two areas of standardized testing: the instructions given to those who administer the audio segments of the tests, and then focus on multimodal test items themselves. These analyses are undertaken on a segment of the PARCC math tests, as they apply to EAL learners. In essence, the guidelines themselves are a text that demands the test administrator to be an "ideal performer" who must consistently and accurately solicit expectations for test takers to perform multimodally. We could say that test guidelines genre itself then is "doubly" multimodal for both the administrator and test taker as each is expected to produce results multimodally. Thus we need to review the level of complementarity between how the test construct is elicited multimodally and how the test taker is expected to perform in a corresponding manner.

By taking this approach, I make visible what is at stake in a subset of the multimodal literacies that are demanded of second-language learners in high-stakes testing. There appears to be an assumption by the test makers that the general multimodalities embedded in the tests are part of decodable information that can be recognized by the test taker. However, these multimodalities need to be deconstructed for EAL learners whose prior cultural and linguistic repertoires may not have been considered, and whose abilities within subject domains could be underrepresented without such a focus. I argue that the results of these analyses demonstrate the need to understand how multimodal items and aural instructions affect the ability of EAL learners to demonstrate what they know and can do.

Drawing on critical multimodal analyses (Kress and Van Leeuwen 2006), this chapter makes visible the multimodal assumptions in these instructions about visual–verbal synergy as well as aural–visual synergy. I argue for similar analyses to be conducted both of the prompts, and response formats of the items included in all high-stakes assessment systems. The current study points out several areas that need significant attention to help learners negotiate unfamiliar high-stakes multimodal texts.

POSITIONING THE RESEARCHER–TEACHER EDUCATION
IN THE CONTEXT OF THE GLOBAL SPREAD OF HIGH-STAKES
STANDARDIZED TESTING

I am a multilingual teacher educator and second-language researcher who has taken up the call to build a critical testing literacy (Austin and Ites 2012; Guillerme 2007; Shohamy 2014). Currently, while I face pressure to teach to the areas of teacher testing that will prepare aspiring teachers for professional licensure, there is even greater need to prepare all teachers to understand and navigate the obstacles in the path of second-language learners and students whose home language varieties differ from the dominant language. One of the biggest obstacles in second-language learners' academic progress is standardized testing that, in general, does not account for what these learners have accomplished, particularly in language arts, math, and science, but also in their family and community life. At the present time, second-language learners in the US K-12 public schools are also being held to standards that have been set in international standardized testing, Trends in International Mathematics and Science Study (TIMMS), as well as nationally set standards such as those set by the Common Core Curriculum through its assessment, World Instruction Assessment (WIDA).

One such standard is set by the PARCC. As of 2014, despite criticisms of these standards, over 40 of the 50 states in the United States have adopted Common Core Standards. This partnership has developed Model Content Frameworks, which have aligned standards, instruction, and assessment from the above-mentioned Common Core Initiative. Their alignment includes curriculum, materials, and PARCC assessments to fortify these discourses within public education, making them "norms" that govern instruction and monitoring of progress under new accountability regulations already in place in the No Child Left Behind (2001) and Race to the Top (2010) US federal initiatives. Increased deep thinking and high expectation for all learners form part of the promise. The use of this test will affect second-language learners' future and begs for further analysis of the demands placed on these learners. How can progress of second-language learners from diverse educational backgrounds and levels of English be fairly evaluated in their understanding of content and in progress toward becoming English users?

## Toward Culturally Responsive Tests – Recognizing Multimodal Challenges

Understanding Kress and van Leeuwen's (1998) account of multimodality that "[l]anguage always has to be realized through and comes in the company of, other semiotic modes" (p. 186) helps me explain how standardized tests are designed to make use of more than mere print-based text to elicit test taker responses. Royce (2007) points out that "[a] multimodal text (e.g., page or screen-based) is a text where the modes utilized 'work together' in various ways to produce comprehensible meanings – there is a synergy in their combined meanings" (p. 374). This can be seen in the relations of these modalities to shaping ideational meanings, interpersonal meanings, context, and coherent textual meanings.

The study of multimodal literacies recognizes the complementarity of modes in the production of meaning in texts. When two or more modes co-occur, they constitute new potential meanings that need to be interpreted and often reproduced by learners to demonstrate their understanding. In order to make sense, learners draw on their background knowledge and past experiences which are always culturally situated. For example, at the interpersonal level, beginning L2 learners may not be culturally prepared to interact in the roles designed by the test makers. Thus the L2 learners' verbal or written response may suffer from coherence or cohesion on the textual level because they may not be familiar with a visual prompt to meaningfully draw on its represented information. Particularly in a testing context, the culturally diverse learner would then be cut off from meaning-making resources, which could penalize them if they are at beginning stages of language development. In this way, the interaction of visual and language modes in the test items need to be examined for their level of complementarity and for how L2 learners use these resource options. With this analysis we can see if, at the ideational level, the combined modalities offer L2 test takers a sufficient range of information for conceptualizing and responding to the targeted item. At a minimum with the results of the analysis a test's affordances for these learners could be augmented to create a more culturally responsive test.

## Preparing Test Administrators – Invisible/Inaudible Multimodal Issues in Aural Testing Prompts for Math

Aside from the test construction itself, preparing people to properly administer an oral exam is a critical to obtaining an accurate sample representing what learners understand and can do in the subject matter being tested. Rigorous training attempts to ensure that standardized conditions for administering a test do not vary significantly because variations in administering the oral sections have potential to alter the test takers' responses. However standardized conditions are often in reality a greater challenge than is generally recognized, particularly in terms of meeting optimal conditions for second-language learners. It is here that the variance caused in actual conditions can adversely affect second-language learners who are at the most vulnerable and earliest stages of developing their comprehension of multimodal test items. The PARCC Math Assessment is leading the current wave of standardized testing in the United States. It is promoted as rigorously aligned with the Common Core Standards. At the time of writing, 13 states and the District of Columbia have joined together to support the development and use of these assessments. For research purposes, I obtained a copy of the manual for preparing testers to administer the PARCC Math Assessment Audio Guidelines Version 3.0 (PARCC 2014). This 84-page-long document is one of many documents describing the rigorous processes undertaken to develop these assessments that are available for public scrutiny. Due to the need to maintain test security these most likely are not the actual or most current guidelines, but they do provide a window to examine potential multimodal issues in administering such tests.

This particular document provides instructions on how test administrators are expected to provide oral instructions as the test takers interact with test items. The web-published version includes a Change History Log, indicating that it has undergone at least three revisions across four dates, in which items have been revised or deleted by particular authors. The guidelines include instructions for the test administrator to describe the following items: visuals and the symbols, numbers and expressions/equations/operations, and diagrams/figures and keys that are included in the tests. The guidelines (PARCC 2014) also provide a classification of the embedded codes used to describe items for text speech. The codings reveal the three levels of all items with visual elements, for example: "[1] is not construct-relevant and can be eliminated"; "[2] is construct-relevant and can be represented using accompanying textual description"; and "[3] is construct-relevant and can be represented using accompanying textual description together with a tactile representation or physical manipulative" (p. 7). Explicit instructions for the test administrator's reading of each section of items included in the guidelines are necessary because the aural "reading" is needed to guide the test taker and must not inadvertently provide cues to the answer being sought nor vary greatly in the details of the instructions. More importantly, notice that each instruction exists because there is variance in orally rendering each item. These guidelines provide an example of the item, then provide instructions, and finally present an application of how to read each.

I selected this document precisely because it provides an opportunity to analyze how training of a test administrator is alerted to the multimodal challenges to represent the tasks, but moreover to point out how these might impact L2 learners listening in these tasks and working with the items. Since the test taker needs to use the audio section to focus attention on the item in order to understand the question, the relationship between this prompt and the item ideally should guide the test taker to perform the anticipated processes in order to produce the response that best represents the test taker's knowledge and skill.

Since I theorize that second-language learners at beginning stages of English development and new to learning math concepts will predictably perform differently from the second-language learners at beginning stages of English development and who are already familiar with and understand the math concepts being tested, I envision the former population as I conduct this analysis of these guidelines to identify items that could potentially cause them confusion or misinterpretation of the oral instructions and written language and symbols used together in math items. In reviewing this document I used three features of these test items: ideational, interpersonal, and textual. Ideational are meanings that are

> concerned with the identification of participants (who, or what is involved in any activity), the activity (the processes in terms of what action is taking place, events, state, types of behavior), the circumstances (where, who with, by what means the activities are taking place), and the attributes (the qualities and characteristics of the participants). (Royce 2007, p. 375)

The interpersonal level of a test consists of how the designers address their viewers/readers, express degrees of involvement, and exert degrees of power relations through forms of address (questions, commands, statements, etc.) and attitude (necessary/unnecessary, possible/impossible, true or false, etc.). The textual level is how the designers make use of combined modalities to produce coherent meanings. In examining these three levels of the test items described in the guidelines for proctors, I found several types of potentially problematic issues for L2 learners (interpersonal) at the beginning stages of aural comprehension.

## A Critical Analysis of Instructions for Math Test Proctors

In the following paragraphs, I discuss two categories: (1) orally representing written math symbols and (2) polyphonic items/repetition of cues/coordination of modes and provide corresponding examples.

Imagine listening to an oral passage on a math test that uses symbols and having to select a correct answer afterward. In the guidelines (PARCC 2014), the administrators are challenged to orally perform this task that requires the second-language learner to see a symbol in a number of items but listen to the word that is being represented. This task is made more difficult if abbreviations are used. On the ideational level, the test item's use of abbreviation would expect the second-language learner to recognize and understand the symbol representing abbreviation as well as the word corresponding to the abbreviation. However, they are repetitions of each other only if the test taker knows/recognizes the abbreviation visually and understands the corresponding orally rendered item. The use of abbreviations in math is one category that merits attention because it is integral to showing and representing math knowledge. In the guidelines (PARCC 2014), two examples of how items included in the visual and symbols section are displayed for use in the test below:

**Abbreviations** (ft., km)
Example 1
3ft.

Example 2
What is the correct abbreviation for kilometer?
A: kl
B: K
C: km
D: klm

### Audio Guideline
Present abbreviations by speaking the whole word the abbreviation represents.

If the item measures the ability to identify the meaning of the abbreviation, then read the abbreviation letter by letter.

If speaking the abbreviation violates the construct being measured, then read letter by letter.

If the item has measurements that are all uppercase or lowercase, then it is not necessary to reference the cases.

**Application of Audio Guideline**
Example 1
Three feet

Example 2
What is the correct abbreviation for kilometer?
A: kl
B: K
C: km
D: klm
(PARCC 2014, pp. 14–15)

As you can see here, the guidelines (PARCC 2014) specify when the test proctor must read the text of the item as a whole word or letter-by-letter or when the texts vary visually in use of upper/lowercase. However, this particular example overlooks the role of punctuation as a visual cue. Note that in the first example, feet is abbreviated as "ft." Yet in subsequent abbreviations punctuation is not evident in any of the choices for "correct abbreviation." While punctuation here may be considered a minor visual cue that can be corrected through subsequent editing of the multiple choice responses, attention to such details is important. In other abbreviations, such as in measurement where the marks $''$, $'$, and $cm^2$ indicate meaningful measurements of inches, feet, and square centimeters, should these be missing all learners could be affected. Other patterns of aural/ visual text issues that involve symbols appear in this version of the guidelines (PARCC 2014) may be even more problematic to second-language learners who are expected to listen to the prompt and map what they are hearing to the symbols. One item belonging to this category is illustrated later.

A second category of potentially problematic items are those that have multiple oral renditions for the same written symbol. An illustrative example consists of those items with a negative number ($-x$) versus the symbol representing the operation of subtraction symbol ($-$). However, the oral reading of parenthesis in math varies more dramatically across test items of probability and multiplication. In probability items, the test proctor is instructed to read the parenthesis as "*of*", for example: "P(orange) $= 1/6$" is rendered as "P of orange is one sixth" (PARCC 2014, p. 31). The word probability is abbreviated to the notation only mentioning the letter "p." In contrast in the multiplication items, the tester is asked to

Read the multiplication symbol as "times" when it appears in a math item.

When a number, symbol, or another set of parentheses appears before a set of parentheses, read the number or symbol as is and "open parenthesis" before what is within the parentheses. When multiple sets of parentheses appear consecutively, read as "open parenthesis and closed parenthesis."

If there are two variables or a variable and a number consecutively, do not read "times" to represent implied multiplication. (PARCC 2014, p. 32)

## Expressions/Equations/Operations

**Multiplication**
Example 1
$$3 \times 5 = X$$

Example 2
$$xy + 4x = 10$$

Example 3
$$(3 + x)(y - 2)$$
(PARCC 2014, p. 32)

These are only two examples where items using multiple oral readings of the same symbol may cause confusion for emerging learners of English. There are also potential problems when visuals and written text are supposed to be used in a complementary manner to respond to a test item.

## A Critical Analysis of Visuals and Language in Multimodal Math Test Items: Cultural Issues in Interpreting Multimodal Math Test Items – Visuals and Language Use

When language tests are designed to elicit "receptive skills" such as reading and listening comprehension, they inevitably require cultural knowledge of context to make sense. Reading and listening call on the test takers to use their knowledge of sociocultural expectations for the use of language in relation to its nonlinguistic context and knowledge of how utterances and functions of these utterances are organized to create coherent communication. Specifically test takers must attend to a stimulus provided by a text or illustration, interpret meanings that they expect that test makers want, and register appropriately their responses in formats that are provided. For example, a typical listening comprehension test item may require a test taker to listen to a short narrative, and understand main points and details before answering by reading to select an appropriate multiple choice answer before accurately bubbling-in the corresponding answer on a response protocol or computerized form. For newcomers to such standardized testing, becoming accustomed to juggling so many performances requiring attention becomes a taxing short-term memory task aside from knowing how to solve the problem and answer within the requirements of the mode – narrative, visual, and/or orally. For those in the early stages of second-language development who know how to resolve the item but do not have skill in providing the required short answer narrative genre and appropriate accompanying visual may well be misidentified as not knowledgeable by the requirement to perform multimodally. If asked to respond orally, they may be able to explain their processes and their visual in their stronger language. However if asked in a language they are still in the beginning stages, their explanation may underrepresent their math knowledge, herein raising the questions about where the items are actually measuring the targeted constructs' math knowledge or math literacy development (ability to use their second language in math literate ways).

Moreover when test makers construct standardized subject matter tests, second-language learners are required to draw on visual, aural, and oral and written modes to interpret communication, leaving language almost as neutral or taken for granted. Yet the learner's coherent interpreting and producing of meaning depends upon multiple representations simultaneously in a cultural context. For example, problems occur for second-language learners when too much or too little information is conveyed by a single modality. Trumbull and Solano-Flores (2011a) point out that the language and cultural demands placed on learners becoming bilingual through English as a second language may obscure what they can actually demonstrate in subject matter. Here multimodality of an assessment item is also a factor that can distract students attention rather than focus their perception and support understanding of the text and the task it presents (see Fig. 9.1).

You are going to make jello for 12 people.

| Ingredients | Price per unit |
|---|---|
| fruit | $2.00 total |
| 2 cups of hot water | from the sink |
| 2 cans of juice | $1.50 per can |
| 2 packages of jello | $1.00 per package |

Water
Heat the water for 3 minutes

With the information above, find the total price of the ingredients. You can use pictures, numbers, and/or words.

Explain how you used the information above to find the total price of the ingredients.

**Fig. 9.1** The language demands of mathematics assessments. Taken from E. Trumbell and G. Solano-Flores (2011b)

In this figure, interpreting meaning can be problematic – as it may produce an additional source of cultural bias because this item requires at a minimum two steps in cognitive tasks. One is to discern the relevant information in understanding what information counts in this "hide-and-seek" problem. Information such as "Heat the water for three minutes" and the number of people for the recipe required the second-language learner using valuable time for reading but were irrelevant for the task. In addition, the first question asks the price but the figure only lists costs for three items. The cost for heating water is assumed to be not important to include. It provides a linguistic element that must be understood in relation to the graph and illustrations that is "per" in order to answer correctly. In addition, the prompt makes use of the phrase "Find the total price," which is also repeated in the label listed in the graphic as "total." Potentially this repetition creates a confusing need to find the word "total" in contrast to the word "sum."

The second task has been created to understand the test takers' processes to "calculate the sum." While this explanation can be done multimodally by drawing each ingredient and labeling the costs, it can also be accomplished through the use of numbers and a formula. Neither is excluded but one may be preferred over another. The learner must discern which ways are more highly valued than others.

What does this indicate? In the standardized testing field, rather than illustrating or clarifying a relationship between text and visual, this test item uses multimodality as a distractor and, moreover, treats this as normal. Distractors are common in multiple choice testing formats when only one answer is correct, and the other options are distractors. Therefore, in a typical math word problem, extraneous information may be communicated in a text that the learner must disregard to answer correctly. In this use of a visual there is a deliberate effort to distract, which reflects a reasoning process that is valued in the field of constructing multiple choice standardized testing. For a learner not prepared to deal with visuals meant to mislead and the need to discern this fact and thereby ignore that visual data, this can be confounding to say the least. In essence, this poses a type of hidden cultural bias that is part of a wider field of cultural production and use of multimodality that is dangerous for a learner prepared to display math knowledge and unprepared to deal with this "tricky" visual.

How many of these types of items cause even second-language learners who are "good" at math to be evaluated as "weak" at math? Some would argue that test-taking skills might be needed to prepare learners for the expectations in these cultural traps. While this may help, many test-taking skill lessons focus on vocabulary skill building (Robison 2010), largely ignoring cultural expectations regarding the relation between the visual and text modalities. In other words, they presume multimodal interpretation is shared in standardized testing. Others argue for removing these types of items as they are construct irrelevant, meaning they elicit responses that are not relevant to the underlying knowledge/performance that the item is attempting to test. Since all items will have cultural bias to some degree, it would be important to monitor which visuals and text combinations present the most difficulty to second-language learners of diverse linguistic and cultural backgrounds.

Another issue occurs when the text accompanying the visual is too limited to indicate the focus of the tested item. Ostensibly this strategy in test item construction is to lessen the linguistic load of the math problem for the second-language learner, an effort that has many advocates (Abedi et al. 2001). Yet, this tact also presents problems when viewed from the perspective of questioning how this type of multimodal representation affects the learner's ability to interpret what is expected. Many have critiqued the cultural assumptions that standardized test creators fail to consider (Emihovich 1994; Trumbull and Solano-Flores 2011b) but few have identified the multimodal nature in test items that has potential to cause confusion and thereby weakens the reliability of the questioning format's ability to assess the test taker's abilities to use mathematical thinking. Note the figures in the following item (Fig. 9.2) and the sparsity of procedural text, an interpersonal feature that could be improved.

The issues raised in this item (Fig. 9.2) include procedural language that is absent. In addition, the logic assumes that a second-language learner knows this, as this knowledge is required to answer the item. However, the test maker relies on the learner interpreting the figures without this guidance. While many test reviewers do attempt to examine tests for bias in responses to items and in terms of specific language used, the level of appropriateness of the language for guiding the intermodal (verbal–visual) interpretation of the figure, thus the test item, needs to be also scrutinized. In the instructions for test administrators, this intermodality link is not made explicit. In fact, scrutiny of such items often escapes bias reviews as visuals are taken to be explicit cues. Scrutiny of the relation between the ideational affordances maybe a case of taken for grantedness in assuming all logic is culture free (O'Connor 2006). Hence, again the conditions are not clear for gaining an accurate measure of the second-language learners response to the mathematical construct being tested.

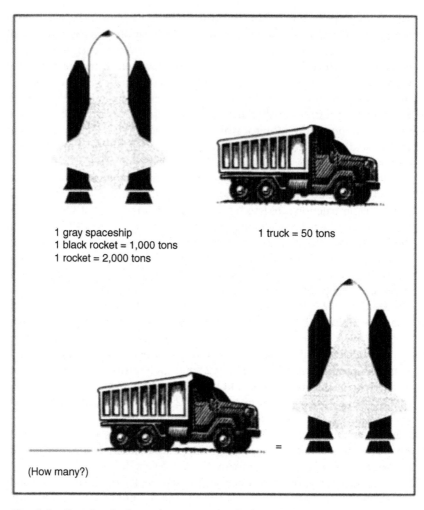

**Fig. 9.2**   Sample of a formative assessment (Mihai 2010)

Some test designers would argue that assumptions about shared interpretation have to be made. Others would argue that problematic assumptions need to be identified in a dynamic fashion by providing students support to help complete the task. This would allow testers a way to determine which prompts help test takers display their knowledge.

Thus by examining the expectations of the test items using the ideational, interpersonal, and textual meanings that are assumed, these elements of cultural bias are made visible. Such an analysis can be applied to other aspects of standardized tests to uncover problematic validity issues in the test domains, items, and response formats.

## CONCLUSION

Discourses concerning the "new basics" underlie and reinforce global standards that are implemented through standardized testing in mathematics and reading such as the Programme for International Student Assessment which is a triennial international survey that takes place across national borders conducted under the auspices of the Organization for Economic Co-operation and Development. Concurrently, the spread of English as a language of wider communication during this time of globalization continues to fuel the demands for testing regimes such as the Test of English as a Foreign Language (TOEFL), Graduate Record Examination (GRE), S.A.T™, and so on. The reading of both discourses of new basics as well as the actual spread of culturally influenced multimodal tests create unusually demanding material conditions that are particularly problematic for underserved students and those who seek to educate and assess them in culturally sustainable ways. Paris and Alim (2014) define culturally sustaining pedagogies' goal as one that "seeks to perpetuate and foster – to sustain – linguistic, literate, and cultural pluralism as part of the democratic project of schooling and as a needed response to demographic and social change" (p. 88). Culturally sustaining pedagogies ask us to not simply value our current communities' assets, rather also to be concerned about assessing the critical skills, knowledges, and ways of being needed for success in evolving meaningful participation and contribution both in the present and future. Past research has alerted us to the major role language plays in testing (Abedi and Lord 2001; Garcia et al. 2010; Fairbairn and Fox 2009) but attention to developing learners critical multimodal understandings of tests must be developed as well.

This chapter highlights the institutionalized practices of standardized testing that not only neglect culturally and linguistically diverse learners but also jeopardize their access to higher education and to becoming productive contributors in their communities. Throughout the examples shown in these guidelines for proctors as well as in the item design, there are assumptions about multimodality being understood and produced in the context of testing, which highlights culturally situated performances required to demonstrate certain knowledge. While the particular items may have been addressed by the time this chapter is published, most likely the multimodal issues will not have been adequately addressed. I have shown how the use of multimodalities in math test items requires a much closer scrutiny of the test makers' cultural assumptions about logical correspondences between modalities. Considering this, if the ideal reader (proctor) must be so well prepared to administer the test, how much more must be done to prepare the EAL learner to sit for these types of items? Because the test constructs are represented multimodally, test takers who are second-language learners need to be better prepared for these expected performances to interpret and produce their responses using multimodality. Furthermore, if standardized testing will always need to examine this aspect, why not disrupt this orientation to envision other means to capture the student's processes for answering an item rather than just right or wrong responses. Bavali et al. (2011) support dynamic assessment by gathering this type of information as it would be more productive in assessing both the item and the child's zone of proximal development. In essence this accumulated information would be useful to

> modify learners' performance level in order to enable the mediators not only to understand individual learners' current level of abilities but to predict (assess) their unassisted potential future abilities based on their present performance in assisted (instructed) completion task settings. (p. 896)

Inevitably such information would reveal the test's cultural assumptions and the learners' level of knowledge used to respond to the item.

Given the spread of high-stakes testing, from the very initial test development stage in the testing world these items merit piloting to provide test makers of a better understanding of how these multimodalities affect second-language learners' meaning making in specific subject areas. In a globalized world, why not begin with linguistic and cultural diversity as a starting point for each context of testing? How do the text and visuals impact students display of what they know and how well they can use this knowledge? For example, in one study on the use of diagrams in quadratic functions, how learners created their diagrams provided additional information to researchers about the processes evidencing their mathematical thinking (Lobato et al. 2014). Under what contexts are particular concepts represented better in multimodal forms over written texts? With the increasing presence of computerized testing, these questions will become even more significant. Under what contexts are there concepts that require less written text and more detail in the graphics in the prompts in order to assess second-language learners?

In classrooms, teachers can play an important role in ascertaining and developing second-language learners production and comprehension of multimodal texts, even beyond performances in the genres of testing. If teachers can take up the perspective of assessment as "inquiry" into the modalities needed (language and literacy) in different text types, second-language learners can be socialized into ways of critically interpreting and producing texts. The "tricky" parts of tests can be unpacked and scrutinized as a social practice. Using multimodal analysis as part of the pedagogy helps students understand forms of representing knowledge and even better how to make use of these to create knowledge through using multimodal communication skills, collaboration, problem solving, and creative thinking.

Furthermore, researchers collaborating with teachers can help document these learner engagements in activities that learners production and comprehension of multimodal texts are evidenced. Consequently, these activities can then be used for generating situated evidence that captures second-language learners development and progress in much more valid and reliable ways than bubble-in assessments. The performances of all those involved, the test designers, the testing proctors, teachers, and the students together produce the results we end up with. To hold only teachers and students accountable would be ethically misguided in an era of globalization.

## References

Abedi, J., Hofstetter, C., Baker, E., & Lord, C. (2001). *NAEP mathematics performance and test accommodations: Interactions with student language background.* Technical Report No. 536. Retrieved from National Center for Research on Evaluation Standards, & Student Testing. Website http://www.cse.ucla.edu/products/Reports/TR536.pdf.

Abedi, J. (2002). Standardized achievement tests and English Language Learners: Psychometrics issues. *Educational Assessment, 8*(3), 231–257.

Abedi, J., Courtney, M., Leon, S., Kao, J., & Azzam, T. (2006). *English Language Learners and math achievement: A study of opportunity to learn and language accommodation.* Technical Report No. 702. Los Angeles, CA: CRESST/UCLA. Retrieved from ERIC. Website http://eric.ed.gov/?id=ED495848.

Abedi, J., & Lord, C. (2001). The language factor in mathematics tests. *Applied Measurement in Education, 14*(3), 219–234.

American Educational Research Association, American Psychological Association, & National Council of Measurement in Education (AERA, APA, & NCME). (1999). *Standards for educational and psychological testing.* (2nd ed.). Washington, DC: American Education Research Association (AERA).

Austin, T., & Ites, E. (2012). Testing/assessing literacies: How do educators build useful knowledge about second language development? *Languages and Linguistics, 29*(30), 181–210.

Bavali, M., Yamini, M., & Sadighi, F. (2011). Dynamic assessment in perspective: Demarcating dynamic and non-dynamic boundaries. *Journal of Language Teaching and Research, 2*(4), 895–902. doi:10.4304/jltr.2.4.895-902.

Emihovich, C. (1994). The language of testing: An ethnographic-sociolinguistic perspective on standardized tests. In K. Holland, D. Bloome, & J. Solsken (Eds.), *Alternative perspectives in assessing children's language and literacy* (pp. 33–54). Norwood, NJ: Ablex.

Fairbairn, S. B., & Fox, J. (2009). Inclusive achievement testing for linguistically and culturally diverse test takers: Essential considerations for test developers and decision makers. *National Council on Measurement in Education. Educational Measurement: Issues and Practice, 28*(1), 10–24. doi:10.1111/j.1745-3992.2009.01133.x.

Garcia, E., Lawton, K., & Diniz De Figuereido, E. H. (2010). *Assessment of young English language learners in Arizona: Questioning the validity of the state measures of English proficiency.* Los Angeles, CA: The Civil Rights Project, University of California.

Guilherme, M. (2007). English as a global language and education for cosmopolitan citizenship. *Language and Intercultural Communication, 7*(1), 72–90.

Hemphill, F. C., & Vanneman A. (2011). *Achievement gap: How Hispanic and White students in public schools perform in mathematics and reading on the national assessment of educational progress.* National Center for Educational Statistics. Retrieved from http://nces.ed.gov/nationsreportcard/pdf/studies/2011459.pdf website.

Kress, G., & Van Leeuwen T. (1998). Front pages: (The critical) analysis of newspaper layout. In A. Bell & P. Garrett (Eds.), *Approaches to media discourse* (pp. 186–219). Oxford, UK: Blackwell.

Kress, G., & Van Leeuwen T. (2006). *Reading images: The grammar of visual design.* (2nd ed.). London: Routledge.

Lobato, J., Hohensee C., & Diamond J. M. (2014). What can we learn by comparing students' diagram-construction processes with the mathematical conceptions inferred from their explanations with completed diagrams? *Mathematics Education Research Journal, 26*(3), 607–634.

Mahoney, K., Haladyna, T., & MacSwan, J. (2009). The need for multiple measures in reclassification decisions: A validity study of the Stanford English Language Proficiency Test. In T. G. Wiley, J. S. Lee, & R. Rumberger (Eds.), *The education of language minority immigrants in the United States* (pp. 240–262). Bristol, UK: Multilingual Matters.

Mihai, F.M. (2010). *Assessing English language learners in the content areas: A research into practice guide for educator*. Ann Arbor, MI: The University of Michigan Press.

O'Connor, M. C. (2006). The implicit discourse genres of standardized testing: What verbal analogy items require of test takers. In J. Cook Gumperz (Ed.), *The social construction of literacy* (2nd ed.., pp. 264–287). Cambridge, UK: Cambridge University Press.

Paris, J., & Alim, H. S. (2014). What are we seeking to sustain through culturally sustaining pedagogy? A loving critique forward. *Harvard Educational Review*, *84*(1), 85–100.

Partnership for Assessment of Readiness For College and Careers (PARCC). (2014). PARCC Accessibility Features and Accommodations Manual. Appendix J: PARCC Mathematics Audio Guidelines Version 3.0. Retrieved from http://www.jcboe.org/boe2015/images/PARCCCCSS/PARCC%20appendix-j-math-audio.pdf.

Robison, S. (2010). Teaching math to English learners-myths and methods. In E. N. Whelan Ariza (Ed.), *Not for ESOL teachers. What every classroom teacher needs to know about the linguistically, culturally, and ethnically diverse student* (pp. 127–139). Boston, MA: Pearson, Allyn & Bacon.

Royce, T. (2007). Multimodal communicative competence in second language contexts. In T. Royce & W. Bowcher (Eds.), *New directions in the analysis of multimodal discourse* (pp. 361–390). Mahwah, NJ: Lawrence Erlbaum Associates.

Schafer Willner, L., Rivera, C., & Acosta, B. (2008). *Descriptive study of state assessment policies for accommodating English language learners*. Oregon Department of Education. Retrieved from website www.ode.state.or.us/wma/teachlearn/commoncore/descriptivestudyell.pdf.

Shohamy, E. 2014). *The power of tests: A critical perspective on the uses of language tests*. ([Kindle version]. Retrieved from Amazon.com.

Short, D. J., & Fitzsimmons, S. (2007). *Double the work: Challenges and solutions to acquiring language and academic literacy for adolescent English language learners – A report to Carnegie Corporation of New York*. Retrieved from Carnegie Corporation of New York website: https://www.carnegie.org/media/filer_public/bd/d8/bdd80ac7-fb48-4b97-b082-df8c49320acb/ccny_report_2007_double.pdf.

Trumbull, E., & Solano-Flores, G. (2011a). The role of language in assessment. In M. R. Basterra, E. Trumbull, & G. Solano-Flores (Eds.), *Cultural validity in assessment: Addressing linguistic and cultural diversity* (pp. 22–45). New York: Routledge.

Trumbull, E., & Solano-Flores, G. (2011b). Addressing the language demands of mathematics assessments: Using a language framework and field-based research findings. In M. R. Basterra, E. Trumbull, & G. Solano-Flores (Eds.), *Cultural validity in assessment: Addressing linguistic and cultural diversity* (pp. 218–253). New York: Routledge.

**Theresa Austin** As a professor of language, literacy, and culture at the University of Massachusetts College of Education: Department of Teacher Education and Curriculum Studies, Theresa teaches courses that explore the impact that becoming multilingual has on individuals and their community, teachers, and institution administrators. This exploration leads to curricular planning as well as policies that are designed to be more culturally nurturing and sustaining across race, class, and gender. In particular, as a critical ethnographer of L2 language and literacy contexts, Theresa collaborates with teachers, L2 learners, and administrators to examine how assessments can better function to increase learning. Theresa also volunteers in numerous local, national, and international projects to increase culturally and linguistically diverse population's access to meaningful education that furthers realization of their aspirations. Her publications can be found in journals such as *Modern Language Journal, Languages and Linguistics, Journal of Latinos and Education* and in numerous book chapters.

# CHAPTER 10

# Spoken Language and Literacy Assessments: Are They Linked?

## *Ann Daly*

### INTRODUCTION

The chapter begins with an overview of the modes of spoken and written language through a critical analysis of the ways in which a lens of cultural difference, rooted in a system of colonialism, replicates discourses of deficit theorizing. It is argued that a reframing of cultural difference, from the perspectives of marginalized Indigenous communities in Australia, is required before assessment practices can become culturally responsive. Current dominant practices in scaffolding language development are then considered before moving on to the research studies themselves.

### CONTEXT

In New South Wales (NSW), the majority of Indigenous students do not speak their Aboriginal language, but instead speak a dialect of English known as Aboriginal English. This can be traced to the "cultural effects of colonialism" (Pennycook 1998, p. 25) in which the systemic racial exclusions of the White Australian policies from the 1850s, the Victorian Aboriginal Protection Act of 1869, and the New South Wales Aborigines

A. Daly (✉)
University of New England, Armidale, NSW, Australia
e-mail: ann.daly@det.nsw.edu.au

© The Author(s) 2017
F. Pirbhai-Illich et al. (eds.), *Culturally Responsive Pedagogy*,
DOI 10.1007/978-3-319-46328-5_10

Protection Act from 1909 to 1969 were felt by Indigenous people, many of whom were forced to live in missions and where Indigenous children who were considered to be "fair-skinned" enough to pass as white were taken from their families, brought up to take on white ways of being, and forbidden to use their own language. Missions were set up by the British government in the 1830s in order to *protect* Aborigines and to provide them "with religious instruction and education" (AIATSIS 2016a, n.p.). This was seen as a duty of the British government at the time, reflecting colonial paternalistic attitudes toward the Indigenous population. The categorization of Australian Aborigines as inferior was part of the colonizers justification for the demand "that Aborigines accept a destiny as an imitation of the colonizer" (AIATSIS 2016b, n.p.) and the speaking of Aboriginal English, a *dialect* of English, today needs to be viewed in this context.

## OVERVIEW OF SPOKEN AND WRITTEN LANGUAGE

In discussing the different modes of language, a paradigm will be introduced in which cultural difference is viewed as being not only about racial difference, but also about differences stemming from the home environment and vernacular language (spoken dialects such as Aboriginal English) in contrast to the school environment and academic language (standard English dialect). These cultural and linguistic differences often compound the effects of cultural differences stemming from other sources in culturally diverse societies. In order to compare Aboriginal English and standard English it is important to define these concepts. Diana Eades (1993) defines Aboriginal English as "the name given to dialects of English which are spoken by Aboriginal people and which differ from standard Australian English in systematic ways" (p. 2). Strevens (1982) defines standard English as "a particular dialect of English, being the only non-localised dialect, of global currency without significant variation, universally accepted as the appropriate educational target in teaching English, which may be spoken with an unrestricted choice of accent" (p. 2). In the binarized categorization that is a continuing legacy of colonialism, Aboriginal ways of speaking English have been judged against this criterion of standard English, identifying a "heavy Aboriginal English [that] is spoken mainly in more remote areas...while light varieties of Aboriginal English...[is found] mainly in metropolitan, urban and rural areas" (Eades 1993, p. 2), such as the majority of NSW. Eades (1993) also points out that there is often specific regional variation in word meanings between Aboriginal communities and there are also some English words used with different meanings in Aboriginal English, for example, *deadly* means *really good* in Aboriginal English. Additionally, Eades (1993) identifies differences in pragmatics or how language is used in sociocultural contexts, for example, the direct question and answer format which "is so central to western notions of how to teach children... doesn't appear to be characteristic of interactions between Aboriginal people and their babies" (p. 4). In terms of the written language of school education texts, most children's texts in primary school use standard English. Texts for young children tend to reflect spoken language containing mostly simple or compound sentences with independent clauses, whereas complex sentences are more prevalent in texts for the upper primary years of schooling. Secondary education uses written texts that are more academic and lexically dense.

Bernstein (1974), in a binary classification that continues to influence literacy teaching and assessment today, identified differences between the vernacular language used by highly educated people (elaborated codes) and the vernacular language of less educated people (restricted codes). Elaborated codes are closer to written English language than restricted codes and are more likely to include explanatory language which relies on the use of dependent clauses beginning with conjunctions such as *because, when, if... then, after,* and *before.* In contrast, restricted language codes are more likely to be conversational, using limited vocabulary and the simple grammar of independent clauses strung together with coordinating conjunctions such as *and, but, or.* Children learn language from the models provided by their parents or caregivers (foster parents, grandparents, guardians, or other caregivers) and their language can continue to be developed with support from other adults. In a critique of Bernstein's work, Jones (2013) argues that, setting aside the contention by many linguists that codes even exist, "the 'codes' are *defined* through a relationship of relative deficiency; 'deficit' is *inherent* to the model" (p. 165), and that this dichotomy is both colonial and racist, merely "replacing 'the older dichotomy *civilized/primitive*'" (Gee 1994,167–168). However, Bernstein saw the different codes as stemming from a difference in power between the working class and managerial class, not between races.

## THE ROLE OF SCAFFOLDING IN LANGUAGE DEVELOPMENT

Vygotsky (1962) describes the gap between a child's actual development and his or her potential development when learning is assisted as the Zone of Proximal Development (p. 187). The form of assistance Vygotsky intended was by teachers explicitly directing a child's learning and the term *scaffolding* has since been used as a metaphor to capture the nature of this support and guidance in learning.

It seems that talk about written texts, which is scaffolded by teachers or other adults, might improve students' comprehension of those texts. Brian Gray and David Rose have long promoted such an approach for Indigenous and other students who are behind in literacy achievement, through "scaffolding literacy" (Rose et al. 1999) and now "Accelerated Literacy" (Wills et al. 2006; Gray 2007) and "Reading to Learn" (Rose 2010).

## The Importance of Spoken Language to Reading Comprehension

Axford (2007), who uses a scaffolding literacy approach in tutoring programs, claims that "'Learning to be literate' is, by its very nature, dialogical: it is about entering the human conversation as a reflective participant" (p. 33), and she notes the importance of recognizing author intention and communication in relation to reading and writing. This is particularly important when students come from different cultures and may have a different expectation of the text than that intended by the author. An important aspect of the Accelerated Literacy teaching sequence is that students have conversations with the teacher about a text using the literate language of the text and this dialogue scaffolds their spoken language. Dialogue helps students to comprehend texts by "bridging between formal and colloquial language ... [so they] talk their way to comprehension" (Lemke 1989, p. 140). Dialogue is also important to assist students to bridge different cultural understandings.

As students develop more complexity in their spoken language the use of more adverbial clauses is an important stage in learning to link related ideas within and between sentences to make explanatory inferences. It seems logical that, when students use spoken language to reflect on the meanings in texts and how texts are structured to achieve those meanings, the students are connecting from their vernacular language repertoire to the meanings and structures in formal written English language. At the same time as they are becoming more familiar with complex linguistic structures in literate texts, they are building their field of knowledge about culturally unfamiliar concepts.

It is important to establish whether there is a relationship between spoken language complexity and comprehension of written language because most prior research studies comparing reading and oral language have not considered syntax and have focused on the number of spoken words rather than the complexity of vocabulary. Accordingly, the third research study reported in this chapter analyzed the complexity in both spoken and written modes (interview transcripts and reading texts), ensuring a focus on syntax, particularly the dependent clauses used in elaborated language codes.

## RESEARCH STUDY ONE

The Indigenous educator who was consulted on the research project confirmed that the communities included in the research sample spoke a light version of Aboriginal English. The study found that many grammar items in the language section of the *Basic Skills Tests* (BST; New South Wales Department of Education and Training [NSWDET] 1998a) and the *Trial Writing Assessment* (NSWDET 1998b) were more difficult for the Indigenous students than for the non-Indigenous students in Year 3 and/or Year 5 and most of these items were typical of the features of Aboriginal English identified by Eades (1995), Mulhausler and Rose (1996), or Malcolm and Koscielecki (1997) in their research with the Aboriginal community at La Perouse. Examples of items that were more difficult for Indigenous students included their ability to recognize

- incorrect use of the preposition *of* where "at" is required in "at least";
- incorrect use of the verb *pressing* where "press" is required in a text;
- incorrect use of the article *a* where "an" is required to precede a vowel;
- Standard Australian English (SAE) use of articles in a written description;
- SAE use of correct sentence pattern when writing sun safety instructions;
- SAE use of prepositions when writing sun safety instructions; and
- SAE use of modality when writing instructions.

Other grammatical items that were equally more difficult for the Indigenous students and for students from non-English-speaking backgrounds than for other students included the use of subject–verb agreement in writing instructions for Year 3 students, use of the correct tense in writing instructions for Year 3 and Year 5 students, and knowing when to use conjunctions when writing a description text for Year 5 students.

## RESEARCH STUDY TWO

The second research study was concerned with establishing whether there were significantly different responses by Indigenous students to reading items in the *BSTs* (NSWDET 1998a) and if so, whether these differences were related to bias in the content of the texts, or the questions that the students were required to read to make the responses. The study found that there were as many questions biased in favor of students who spoke Aboriginal English as there were questions biased against them.

### *Questions Biased in Favor of Indigenous Students*

The test questions that more Indigenous students than non-Indigenous students answered successfully in the Year 3 sample came from the narrative texts, *Flying Fish* and *Captain Johnno*. The *Flying Fish* text is an extract out of a myth from Papua New Guinea, which explains how the sea and flying fish were released from a tree. This text is similar in style and tone to an Aboriginal Dreaming story, which could be why a greater proportion of Indigenous students than of non-Indigenous students were able to identify the main idea. The *Captain Johnno* extract was about an Italian fisherman who is trying to convey his love of the sea through the smell and sound from within a shell. For this text, more Year 3 Indigenous students were able to answer a question about the meaning of "aroma." It could be that Indigenous students are more familiar with the natural environment, and that they had place knowledge to infer the sense of smell from the words "breathed in the aroma of the sea."

In a reading assessment text titled *Magpie Island*, Year 5 Indigenous students were able to answer the comprehension questions more accurately than non-Indigenous students. A larger proportion of Indigenous students could discern which event was imagined and could identify the main idea up to the time when Magpie "felt a surge of hope." In another text about the environment, called *Clean Up Our Beaches* (an argument in the form of a short letter), more Indigenous students than non-Indigenous students identified "environment" as the word "it" referred to in the sentence, "It should be protected by all of us."

In another item, the Year 5 Indigenous students were more able to identify the most important thing to remember when performing a trick with eggs. This question concerned the text *Sink or Swim*, which is ostensibly a set of instructions about how to perform a magic trick. The Indigenous students might have related well to a text about "how to perform" since storytelling and performance are important aspects of Aboriginal culture, just as they are in African American cultures in the United States as noted by Heath (1982) and Gee (1990).

### Questions Biased Against Indigenous Students

In the *Sink or Swim* text, in response to the question, "Why does the egg float?" nearly 20% of Indigenous students chose, "It is a magic trick" and nearly 12% of Indigenous students chose "One egg is labeled 'swim.'" This is a procedural text and although it positions the reader as someone learning how to perform a trick, there is a hidden agenda in that the text is really a science experiment about how objects can float better in saltwater than plain water.

The author has written in this manner in order to entertain and get the interest of children who might otherwise be uninterested in science. The Aboriginal educator who was consulted about this research project considered that, for Indigenous students, performance would have more cultural importance than scientific experiments, so the incorrect responses to the multiple choice question would have seemed plausible answers to them. The author's voice is also very authoritative and the strong claims about the performance, together with the fact that the text is within an official test, give a tone of certainty and authority that could have backed up the students' own culturally based perception of the text as a performance rather than a scientific procedure.

Another reading assessment text, *Captain Johnno*, also had one question that was challenging for the Year 5 Indigenous students. This was a question that asked students why Johnno changed the volume on his hearing aid. There were several plausible distractors, but Indigenous students would have been especially disadvantaged by the use of the word, "volume" which would not be commonly used in Aboriginal English and therefore not connected to sound. However, the word volume would be used in Year 5 mathematics classes in connection to measurement of space. If the word was not connected to sound, it is likely that students would make a direct connection to the text which stated, "turned the volume up until it made a painful screech" and thus choose the incorrect option "to make some noise" (by connection to the word "screech") or "to stop the sound" (by connection to the word "painful"). The Aboriginal educator who was consulted could see no other cultural bias in the text that referred to "my sea" and "my waves" in the same way that Aboriginal people talk about "my country."

The other two questions that fewer Year 5 Indigenous students answered correctly were questions about the text, *Marlene Stewart and Her Memories.* This text is about a Ngarrindjeri woman who worked in Indigenous education in South Australia. It comes from a South Australian government booklet for teachers of Aboriginal students. It is a recount in the first person but it does not use Aboriginal English and does not have the tone of spoken English, except by the use of the pronouns "I" and "we." Additionally, the line drawing of Marlene does not clearly show that she is Aboriginal and students in NSW might be unaware that Ngarrindjeri is the name of an Aboriginal group in South Australia. According to the Aboriginal educator who was consulted, one of the questions that was more difficult concerned the meaning of the words, "looked forward to," is not an expression generally used in Aboriginal English. It was therefore not surprising that 39.5% of the Indigenous students chose incorrect responses derived from the term "looked forward": "had good eyesight," "could see the future," or "viewed from the front." As Marlene's destination, the Coorong in South Australia is not shown in any way to be an exciting place, and it would be difficult for students to infer that the words meant "felt excited" other than by the reference to holidays. The second question about this text that fewer Indigenous students were able to answer correctly was, "How did the children get the fishing lines?" Although 75% of Indigenous students chose the correct answer that "they made them with string or nylon," 18.4% chose "they took them off the jetty." This could have been a misreading of the question as "Where did they get the fishing (or fish in)?" since the word "lines" was returned onto the next line and the words in the text say "fishing off the jetty." Alternatively the students might have thought the fishermen got the string and nylon "off the jetty" especially since the words "get" and "made" are not synonymous and students might have been looking for a literal answer to the question. Since it is likely that some Indigenous students could have been economically disadvantaged it would be more plausible for them to give an answer about finding the nylon on the jetty, than buying it in the shop, to make the fishing lines.

The text, *Facts about Authors Who Love the Sea*, had two questions that Year 3 Indigenous students found challenging. The text consisted of four fact files about authors. None of the authors were of Australian Indigenous ancestry and some of the language would have been unfamiliar but the most alienating aspect was probably that the fact file had a heading and list format. There was a lot of information scattered across two pages that needed to be traced through headings, picture icons, and a key, and this factual genre is not typical of Aboriginal discourse patterns. Incorrect answers about a "birthdate" suggested that Indigenous students might have been just locating a date and not connecting it to the subheading. The term "birthdate" is also formal terminology, whereas students who speak Aboriginal English would be more familiar with "birthday," "date born," or just "born."

## METHODS FOR RESEARCH STUDY THREE

Data was gathered using mixed methods. Test scores from participants in the *BSTs* (NSWDET 2005a, 2005b) were analyzed for variance "across 59 Year 3 students and 52 Year 5 students," and against categories of gender, "Aboriginal, non-Aboriginal, metropolitan, provincial and remote students" (Daly 2008, p. 7). "[A]nalyses sought correlations between the percentage of reading items answered correctly... [according to the test core criteria] and the complexity of students' oral grammar and vocabulary" (Daly 2008, p. 7). Interviews were conducted with students using the tests as a form of stimulated recall whereby "complexity of grammar...was determined by the percentage of dependent clauses spoken out of the total number of clauses uttered. The complexity of vocabulary...was determined by the number of non-core words... [and] the number of classification shifts" used during the conversation (Daly 2008, p. 7).

## RESEARCH STUDY THREE

The third research study concerned the *BSTs* (NSWDET 2005a, 2005b) for Year 3 and Year 5 students (8- and 10-year-olds). These reading comprehension texts included images with them. Previous articles (Daly and Unsworth 2011; Unsworth and Chan 2008) have discussed findings from the research project in relation to the construction of intermodal meaning in texts, the complexity of language in the texts, students reading strategies, and how these factors might affect reading comprehension. The aspect of the research study to be discussed here concerns a different aspect of the research relating to the students reading comprehension and the degree of complexity in spoken language used by students during interviews about the texts (Daly 2015).

## Context

In 2006, the year following the BST (NSWDET 2005a, 2005b), 110 students in Year 4 and Year 6, then around 9 and 11 years old, were interviewed about the meaning of the reading comprehension texts after answering the test questions assessing their comprehension of image-text relations in the reading stimulus. After noticing that students with low comprehension spoke with restricted language, it was decided to analyze both the texts and transcripts of the "think aloud" part of the research interviews to see if there was a connection between students reading comprehension and their spoken language complexity, that is, in both syntax (grammatical structure) and semantics (vocabulary).

One text, *Tobwabba Art Gallery*, which contained two Aboriginal artworks with an accompanying descriptive text, had two questions requiring understanding of similar image-text relations based on the different parts of the text. Both questions required students to make connections to the written text in order to identify a part of the image. A question about the text, answered correctly by 44% of students in the state, involved understanding a structurally complex SAE sentence. Another question, which involved understanding a simple sentence, was correctly answered by 66% of students in the state.

The difficult question required students to identify which abstract shape in the painting represented a net, by understanding the following complex sentence involving three dependent clauses (/), ellipsis of words, and three instances of the passive voice (underlined):

> *The sailfish is believed to to be a cunning fish/ able to feed amongst the various fish traps and nets/ shown by the dark areas/, without being caught.*

In contrast, the question assessing complementarity of meaning between words and image required students to identify the grass in a stylized picture by understanding the following simple sentence:

> *The kangaroos are feeding on the fresh grass after the rain.*

For this question, 66% of students selected the correct answer (a green area beneath kangaroos at the top of the picture representing grass) despite having a visually plausible incorrect option (water weed low in the picture) chosen by 27% of students.

The number and percentage of dependent clauses was used as the measure of grammatical complexity, and as words can be simple or more advanced, relative lexical complexity in language was assessed by the instances of noncore words (Carter 1987, p. 33). Core words are generally seen to be the most basic or simple word choice. The test used for core and noncore words utilized substitution words, for example, "eat" is a basic or core word but "dine" is less common, the test being that "*dine* entails *eat* but *eat* does not entail *dine*" (Carter 1987, p. 35).

Pearson correlations were conducted on the test items across all students and differentiated across Indigenous and non-Indigenous students separately. The correlations were significant ($p < 0.01$) for both Year 4 and Year 6 students across the variables of the combined grammatical and lexical complexity of spoken language, the number of correct answers to all reading questions in the *BST* (NSWDET 2005a, 2005b), and in the posttest during the interview.

Further analysis was conducted across the older cohort of students, who provided more data, which enabled a separate analysis of complexity in grammar and vocabulary and separate analyses for Indigenous and non-Indigenous students. Pearson correlations were conducted across the percentage of dependent clauses, the number of noncore words used by the students in Year 6 interviews and their reading scores in the Year 5 and Year 7 reading tests. The correlations were significant ($p < 0.01$) for all students (see Table 10.1), for Indigenous students (see Table 10.2) and for non-Indigenous students (see Table 10.3). Non-standard English, such as Aboriginal English, was also considered; however, no significant correlation was evident between any of these variables and the use of non-standard English.

Few examples of non-standard English dialects such as Aboriginal English were found in the interview transcripts and where they were found there were only one or two instances, with the exception of one Year 3 student who had five instances of non-standard verb form (the use of "seen" for "saw" and "done" for "did"). Since this student scored in the top 21% of students for reading comprehension and he used 17 dependent clauses out of a total of 103 clauses, it is clear that dialectal differences in word choice did not impact on this student's ability to use grammatically complex spoken language or comprehend written text. He was apparently capable of code switching between Aboriginal English and SAE.

**Table 10.1** All Year 6 students (Pearson correlation for all Year 6 among % correct BST and ELLA scores and number of noncore words, nonstandard grammar, and % of dependent clauses used in interviews (Daly 2011, p. 168))

| All Year 6 | | % correct BST Year 5 | % correct ELLA Year 7 | Year 6 % dependent clauses | Year 6 noncore words | Year 6 nonstandard grammar |
|---|---|---|---|---|---|---|
| % correct BST Year 5 | Pearson correlation | 1 | 0.881(**) | 0.689(**) | 0.581(**) | -0.327(*) |
| | Sig. (two-tailed) | | 0.000 | 0.000 | 0.000 | 0.018 |
| | N | 52 | 47 | 52 | 52 | 52 |
| % correct ELLA Year 7 | Pearson correlation | 0.881(**) | 1 | 0.694(**) | 0.612(**) | -0.295(*) |
| | Sig. (two-tailed) | 0.000 | | 0.000 | 0.000 | 0.044 |
| | N | 47 | 47 | 47 | 47 | 47 |
| Year 6 % dependent Clauses | Pearson correlation | 0.689(**) | 0.694(**) | 1 | 0.656(**) | -0.175 |
| | Sig. (two-tailed) | 0.000 | 0.000 | | 0.000 | 0.215 |
| | N | 52 | 47 | 52 | 52 | 52 |
| Year 6 noncore words | Pearson correlation | 0.581(**) | 0.612(**) | 0.656(**) | 1 | -0.192 |
| | Sig. (two-tailed) | 0.000 | 0.000 | 0.000 | | 0.174 |
| | N | 52 | 47 | 52 | 52 | 52 |
| Year 6 nonstandard grammar | Pearson correlation | -0.327(*) | -0.295(*) | -0.175 | -0.192 | 1 |
| | Sig. (two-tailed) | 0.018 | 0.044 | 0.215 | 0.174 | |
| | N | 52 | 47 | 52 | 52 | 52 |

*Correlation is significant at the 0.05 level (two-tailed)
**Correlation is significant at the 0.01 level (two-tailed)

**Table 10.2** Year 6 Indigenous students (Pearson correlation for Year 6 Indigenous students among % correct BST and ELLA scores and number of noncore words, nonstandard grammar, and % of dependent clauses used in interviews (Daly 2011, p. 169))

| Year 6 Indigenous | | % correct 05 | % correct 07 | % dependent clauses | Noncore words | Nonstandard grammar |
|---|---|---|---|---|---|---|
| % correct 05 | Pearson correlation | 1 | 0.865(**) | 0.705(**) | 0.632(**) | −0.327 |
| | Sig. (two-tailed) | | 0.000 | 0.000 | 0.001 | 0.119 |
| | N | 24 | 22 | 24 | 24 | 24 |
| % correct 07 | Pearson correlation | 0.865(**) | 1 | 0.653(**) | 0.630(**) | −0.314 |
| | Sig. (two-tailed) | 0.000 | | 0.001 | 0.002 | 0.155 |
| | N | 22 | 22 | 22 | 22 | 22 |
| % dependent clauses | Pearson correlation | 0.705(**) | 0.653(**) | 1 | 0.704(**) | −0.290 |
| | Sig. (two-tailed) | 0.000 | 0.001 | | 0.000 | 0.169 |
| | N | 24 | 22 | 24 | 24 | 24 |
| Noncore words | Pearson correlation | 0.632(**) | 0.630(**) | 0.704(**) | 1 | −0.353 |
| | Sig. (two-tailed) | 0.001 | 0.002 | 0.000 | | 0.091 |
| | N | 24 | 22 | 24 | 24 | 24 |
| Nonstandard grammar | Pearson correlation | −0.327 | −0.314 | −0.290 | −0.353 | 1 |
| | Sig. (2-tailed) | 0.119 | 0.155 | 0.169 | 0.091 | |
| | N | 24 | 22 | 24 | 24 | 24 |

*Correlation is significant at the 0.05 level (two-tailed)
**Correlation is significant at the 0.01 level (two-tailed)

**Table 10.3** Year 6 non-Indigenous students (Pearson correlation for Year 6 non-Indigenous students among % correct BST and ELLA scores and number of noncore words, nonstandard grammar, and % of dependent clauses used in interviews (Daly 2011, p. 170))

| Year 6 non-Indigenous | | % correct 05 | % correct 07 | % dependent clauses | Noncore words | Nonstandard grammar |
|---|---|---|---|---|---|---|
| % correct 05 | Pearson correlation | 1 | 0.901(**) | 0.690(**) | 0.545(**) | -0.305 |
| | Sig. (two-tailed) | | 0.000 | 0.000 | 0.003 | 0.115 |
| | N | 28 | 25 | 28 | 28 | 28 |
| % correct 07 | Pearson correlation | 0.901(**) | 1 | 0.728(**) | 0.633(**) | -0.237 |
| | Sig. (two-tailed) | 0.000 | | 0.000 | 0.001 | 0.253 |
| | N | 25 | 25 | 25 | 25 | 25 |
| % Dependent clauses | Pearson correlation | 0.690(**) | 0.728(**) | 1 | 0.610(**) | -0.022 |
| | Sig. (two-tailed) | 0.000 | 0.000 | | 0.001 | 0.912 |
| | N | 28 | 25 | 28 | 28 | 28 |
| Noncore words | Pearson correlation | 0.545(**) | 0.633(**) | 0.610(**) | 1 | -0.058 |
| | Sig. (two-tailed) | 0.003 | 0.001 | 0.001 | | 0.770 |
| | N | 28 | 25 | 28 | 28 | 28 |
| Nonstandard grammar | Pearson correlation | -0.305 | -0.237 | -0.022 | -0.058 | 1 |
| | Sig. (two-tailed) | 0.115 | 0.253 | 0.912 | 0.770 | |
| | N | 28 | 25 | 28 | 28 | 28 |

*Correlation is significant at the 0.05 level (two-tailed)
**Correlation is significant at the 0.01 level (two-tailed)

## Cultural Differences in Responses to Assessment Questions

A closer inspection of the student transcripts showed a range of complexity used by Indigenous and non-Indigenous students as well as cultural differences in the way students understood some of the texts. Examples of complexity in spoken language will be considered first.

The student with the highest percentage of dependent clauses (33%) was a Year 6 metropolitan male Indigenous student with a reading score in the top band for the Year 5 BST (NSWDET 2005b). The following excerpts from his interview provide examples of explanatory inferences using adverbial, relative, embedded, and nonfinite clauses.

*Indigenous student:*   *... a float that moves up and down [relative embedded]*
      *to move the larger, longer one [non-finite].*
*Indigenous student:*   *Because if you go around the place [adverbial]*
      *it takes longer*
      *where if you just go straight [adverbial]*
      *it takes much less time.*
*Indigenous student:*   *They are colours*
      *that have been used through the generations [relative].*

This student also had more complex vocabulary than any other student, using 19 noncore words, which included, *coordinates, capsized, indication, generations, hieroglyphs, evaporated, ochre,* and *distinguish.* These findings are a reminder of the ability of Indigenous students despite the gap in mean performance across the state.

All of the eight students who did not use dependent clauses had low BST reading scores. These students were non-Indigenous or Indigenous and from metropolitan areas or from provincial and remote areas. Many other students with low reading scores used only one or two dependent clauses. Even though they used fewer complex grammatical structures, some of these students made a large number of statements. Therefore, a lack of understanding of the verbal text did not limit their vocal output.

In response to the text, *Animal Records,* many of the inferences by Year 4 students concerned comparisons of size in the photographs and mathematical concepts in a symbolic image representing a length scale (see Fig. 10.1). For example, the Year 4 non-Indigenous provincial student who made the most inferences about the image said, *"It's got people linking*

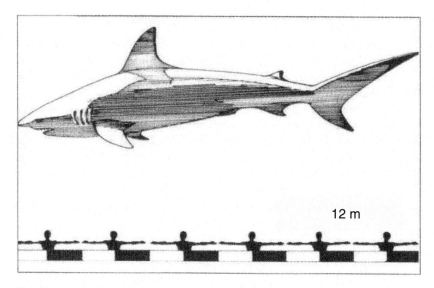

**Fig. 10.1**   Scale image from the "Water Animal Records" text

Scale image from the "Water Animal Records" text in the Year 3 *Basic Skills Test* (NSWDET 2005a). Taken from "Aboriginal and rural students' comprehension and talk about image-language relations in reading tests" by A. Daly (2011), Doctoral dissertation, University of New England Armidale, p. 280. Retrieved from http://e-publications.une.edu.au/1959. 11/10929. Copyright 2011 by Ann Daly

*arms making like a ruler, compared to the great white shark"* and she could identify that each arm span represented 2 m.

Both Indigenous and non-Indigenous students with low reading scores made similar numbers of correct and incorrect inferences about the scale image in *Water Animal Records*. For example, an Indigenous student in a provincial school said, *"It's got a wall there, like a little wall back at the pool,"* while a non-Indigenous student in a remote school responded to the scale image with linked arms as follows:

| | |
|---|---|
| *Non-Indigenous student:* | *It's showing us how long the shark is on a cinema screen.* |
| *Interviewer:* | *How did you know it's on a cinema screen?* |
| *Non-Indigenous student:* | *'Cause there's people sitting down in the chairs.* |

It can be seen from these incorrect inferences that both Indigenous and non-Indigenous students can be disadvantaged by texts that might be out of their field of knowledge and experience such as the technical mathematical scale with symbolic images of arm spans. Consequently, these students have instead connected the image to their own fields of experience.

Sometimes it was the wording of a question that was interpreted differently by students, for example, a question about the map in the Year 5 text *Mapping Islands* was more difficult than expected because 20% of students interpreted "shortest way" in the question as shortest time, not shortest distance, leading to an incorrect answer being chosen. Some students also identified valid safety issues as reasons for choosing "along the track" instead of "through the trees," saying that people should take the path as they might get lost if they go through the trees. A student in a wheelchair naturally selected the path rather than the shorter distance through the trees.

In answer to the difficult question about the text, *Tobwabba Art Gallery*, which required understanding of a complex sentence, all of the metropolitan non-Indigenous students with low BST reading scores chose an incorrect response. The non-Indigenous students with low BST reading scores did not understand the complex sentences in the text, as evidenced in this example:

| | |
|---|---|
| *Interviewer:* | *So what's that second paragraph about?* |
| *Non-Indigenous female:* | *A cunning fish, that eats like I think, that, a fish that destroys like other fish's lives and ruins things.* |

This student seems to be relating the beginning (*The sailfish is believed to be a cunning fish*) and end of the paragraph (*This art highlights the use of long lines and nets that are destroying our coastal fish*) without understanding the connections between the dependent clauses in the middle. However, two Year 6 metropolitan Indigenous students with low BST reading scores (a male and a female) selected the correct response. The male student said he found the answer in the verbal text but the female student only referred to the picture saying, "It's trapped." It seems possible that the cultural relevance of this text may be why these students were able to understand it better than non-Indigenous students who had similar BST reading scores.

It can be seen from most of the examples here that non-Indigenous students with low reading scores found many of the texts and questions to be as unfamiliar and difficult to understand as the Indigenous students did. This was particularly true of factual texts where the structure was more complex, or the format less familiar, and the language and images more technical, suggesting that the students with lower reading scores might be less familiar with factual genres.

### Discussion About the Sample Results and State Data

The significant correlations for Indigenous and for non-Indigenous students in the third research study indicate that for both of these groups there was a relationship between their reading comprehension and the amount of complexity in their spoken language. There was also a similar range of reading scores between the Indigenous and non-Indigenous students. It is therefore important to ask why similar patterns were found in this research despite a large gap in performance between Indigenous and non-Indigenous students across the state of NSW.

First, the selection of similar numbers of Indigenous and non-Indigenous students with a range of reading achievement meant that the sample was not representative of the whole state, where Indigenous students are less than 5% of the student population. Second, the Index of Community Socio-Educational Advantage (ICSEA) values, which became available after the research was conducted, showed that the sample schools in the third study were mostly close to the average, whereas across the state there is a concentration of Indigenous students in schools with below average ICSEA values. ICSEA is a measure based on Australian Bureau of Statistics figures for student characteristics such as parents' educational background and occupation and school characteristics such as location.

It has been found in the National Assessment Program in Literacy and Numeracy (NAPLAN) that "mean scores are higher for students whose parents have higher levels of education" (Australian Curriculum, Assessment and Reporting Authority 2013, pp. 64, 128, 192, 256). Census data reveal that Indigenous children are more than twice as likely to have parents who left school early (Scougall 2008). Therefore, the wider population differences between Indigenous and non-Indigenous students could be due to generational differences in education levels stemming from generations of disadvantage due to discriminatory policies and other consequences of colonization.

When considering that the higher reading scores relied on inferential comprehension of more complex written text, the correlations between reading comprehension scores and spoken language complexity suggest that developing complexity in spoken language could play a role in developing inferential comprehension of complex written English text.

In the current situation where national tests in reading and writing have led to an earlier focus on these skills, sometimes at the expense of speaking and listening, it is important to remember that oral language is the foundation on which literacy is built (Hay and Fielding-Barnsley 2009, p. 158). The findings from the third research study are a timely reminder for teachers of the need to recognize that students from a variety of backgrounds could have a range of complexity in their spoken language. The findings also highlight the need for teachers to consider a focus on strategies to develop students' spoken language through talk about text.

From the sample of students in the third research study, it is clear that both Indigenous and non-Indigenous students have the capacity to achieve high reading scores and to develop complexity in their spoken language. The significant correlations between the degree of complexity in spoken language and reading scores support Brian Gray's (1990) claim that "it is doubtful if children can produce and understand written texts in any depth unless they can orally produce texts of that type themselves" (p. 113).

## WHY IS COMPLEXITY IN SPOKEN LANGUAGE RELEVANT TO READING COMPREHENSION?

Formal written language is difficult for young students to comprehend because it is so different from the spoken language that children use to make sense of the world. Lemke (1989) contends that when we read we need to translate "the patterns of written language into those of spoken language. Spoken language is the medium through which we reason to ourselves and talk our way through problems to answers" (p. 136).

It is useful to consider the difference in purpose between spoken and written language. Dialogue usually focuses on simplifying meaning so that the listener can understand, while formal language (whether written or an oral presentation) is usually concerned with conveying complexity of meaning.

The relevance of structural complexity in spoken language to reading has been largely ignored by many researchers because they have focused on the more obvious effect of vocabulary knowledge on cognitive development. However, students must develop both aspects of their spoken language. Once students are familiar with the structure of language, they find it creates connections and cues, which help them to access meaning, thus making the texts easier to understand.

Even the factual multimodal texts in the BST (NSWDET 2005a, 2005b) with their nonlinear structures were more difficult for Indigenous students and this does not auger well for other non-narrative factual texts in online environments. In their current form, the language structures of national literacy tests favor non-Indigenous students because there is a greater likelihood that the test language structures are congruent with the language structures into which they have been socialized from childhood.

## SOCIOCULTURAL DIFFERENCES IN LANGUAGE DEVELOPMENT

Culture influences the way children learn language. This has been clearly shown by the eight Aboriginal Ways of Learning[1] (links to the land, links to community, nonverbal communication, nonlinear learning, deconstructing and reconstructing meaning, story sharing, using learning maps, and using symbols and images) for students in Western NSW (Wagga Network of Schools, New South Wales Department of Education [n.d.]), which has been developed in conjunction with Aboriginal elders from Western NSW (Yunkaporta 2009). For example, it highlights Indigenous approaches to learning through strategies such as narrative storytelling and deconstruction of language (working from whole to part) rather than through rote learning of words and phrase building (working from part to whole text).

Hasan and Williams (1996) point out that "children from different segments of the society come to school speaking differently: their literacy development will take different forms" (p. 394). This is a natural result of acquiring language through scaffolding and/or modeling by family and local community members. If the family and community group do not speak formal English, then it follows that their children will not be familiar with the terms and structures of formal English. Hasan and Williams (1996) explain the educational consequences as follows:

> specialized contexts of education are somewhat remote from the contexts of everyday living so that it is rather doubtful that the ability to engage in educational discourses could develop naturally without experience of the

educational processes...Members of the dominating classes do engage more often, than do those of the dominated ones, in practices of saying and meaning which are closer in their discursive properties to educational discourses. (p. 394)

Within a similar context in the United States, Heath (1982) points out not only the importance of talk in learning to read, but also the need to be responsive to the cultural context in which that talk takes place:

Close analyses of how mainstream school-oriented children come to learn from books at home suggest that such children learn not only how to take meaning from books, but also how to talk about it. In doing the latter, they repeatedly practice routines which parallel those of classroom interaction. (p. 56)

## CONCLUDING COMMENTS

The difference between spoken language and elaborated written language will be greater where students come from a background where a restricted language code is used. Bernstein (1974) contends that restricted and elaborated language codes are used by different groups of people according to their social position. As argued at the beginning of the chapter, since the effects of colonization have left most Indigenous people in a position of social disadvantage, the majority of Indigenous students in Australia have lost their own language and been forced to take on Aboriginal English, which Bernstein (1974) would refer to as using a *restricted code*. However, it is dangerous to infer from this that use of Australian Aboriginal English automatically restricts Indigenous students from developing elaborated language codes. The contention is that Indigenous students are doubly disadvantaged because first, the sociocultural context within which national and state-wide reading tests have been developed are more closely aligned with non-Indigenous language structures; and second, teachers (who are also predominantly non-Indigenous) require additional training in culturally responsive ways of assisting Indigenous students to switch between the language codes of home and school.

Gee (2008) warns that the specialized forms of language and interactions at school can lack resonance with a child's vernacular cultural ways, "thereby raising the child's affective filter and ensuring that school-based input" (p. 101) is not actually taken in. It is crucial that teachers do not correct or undervalue the home/vernacular language. Using culturally responsive approaches, teachers can assist students to move between home/vernacular language and academic language for relevant purposes so that they have the capacity to comprehend and use the complex language of mainstream school texts in relevant contexts and also continue to use their home dialect and feel it is valued within the community.

## NOTE

1. For detailed information about each of the *8 Aboriginal Ways of Learning*, including visual representations, see Yunkaporta (2009). *Aboriginal pedagogies at the cultural interface: Draft report for DET on Indigenous research project conducted by Jason Yunkaporta, Education Consultant, in Western NSW Region schools, 2007–2009.* Retrieved from Wagga Network of Schools (n.d.). Aboriginal pedagogy research review website: https://8ways.wikis paces.com/file/view/draft+report.doc.

## REFERENCES

Australian Curriculum, Assessment and Reporting Authority. (2013). *National Assessment Program in Literacy and Numeracy (NAPLAN) achievement in reading, persuasive writing, language conventions and numeracy: National report for 2013.* Retrieved from http://www.nap.edu.au/verve/_resources/naplan_2013_national_report.pdf.

Australian Institute of Aboriginal and Torres Strait Islander Studies (AIATSIS). (2016a). Remembering the mission days: Stories from the aborigines' inland missions. Retrieved from http://aiatsis.gov.au/exhibitions/remembering-mis sion-days.

Australian Institute of Aboriginal and Torres Strait Islander Studies (AIATSIS). (2016b). Mission days. Retrieved from http://aiatsis.gov.au/explore/arti cles/mission-days.

Axford, B. (2007). Parents and their children working together: A scaffolding literacy case study. *Australian Journal of Language and Literacy, 30*(1), 21–39.

Bernstein, B. (1974). *Class, codes and control: Theoretical studies towards a sociology of language.* (2nd revised ed. Vol. 1). London: Routledge & Kegan Paul.

Carter, R. (1987). *Vocabulary: Applied linguistic perspectives.* London: Allen & Unwin.

Daly, A. (2008, July). *The oral resources of readers.* Paper presented at the National Conference for Teachers of English and Literacy, Adelaide, AUS. Retrieved from: http://www.englishliteracyconference.com.au/files/docu ments/Daly-Oral%20resources%20of%20readers.pdf.

Daly, A. (2011). *Aboriginal and rural students' comprehension and talk about image-language relations in reading tests* (Doctoral dissertation, University of New England Armidale). Retrieved from http://e-publications.une.edu.au/1959.11/10929.

Daly, A. (2015). Relating students' spoken language and reading comprehension. *Australian Journal of Language and Literacy, 38*(3), 193–204.

Daly, A., & Unsworth, L. (2011). Analysis and comprehension of multimodal texts. *Australian Journal of Language and Literacy, 34*(1), 61–80.

Eades, D. (1993). Aboriginal English, *PEN number 93*. Newtown, NSW: Primary English Teaching Association.

Eades, D. (1995). *Aboriginal English*. North Sydney, AUS: Board of Studies NSW.

Gee, J. (1990). *Social linguistics and literacies: Ideology in discourses*. Brighton, UK: Falmer Press.

Gee, J. (1994). Orality and literacy: From the savage mind to ways with words. In J. Maybin (Ed.), *Language and literacy in social practice* (pp. 168–192). Clevedon, UK: Multilingual Matters.

Gee, J. (2008). A sociocultural perspective on opportunity to learn. In P. Moss, D. Pullin, J. Gee, E. Haertel, & L. Young (Eds.), *Assessment, equity, and opportunity to learn* (pp. 76–108). New York: Cambridge University Press.

Gray, B. (1990). Natural language learning in aboriginal classrooms: Reflections on teaching and learning style for empowerment in English. In C. Walton & W. Eggington (Eds.), *Language: Maintenance, power and education in Australian aboriginal contexts* (pp. 102–139). Darwin, NT: Northern Territory University Press.

Gray, B. (2007). *Accelerating the literacy development of indigenous students*. Darwin, NT: Charles Darwin University Press.

Hasan, R., & Williams, G. (Eds.). (1996). *Literacy in society*. London: Addison Wesley.

Hay, I., & Fielding-Barnsley, R. (2009). Competencies that underpin children's transition into early literacy. *Australian Journal of Language and Literacy, 32*(2), 148–162.

Heath, S. (1982). What no bedtime story means: Narratives at home and school. *Language in Society, 11*(1), 49–78.

Jones, P. E. (2013). Bernstein's 'codes' and the linguistics of 'deficit'. *Language and Education, 27*(2), 161–179.

Lemke, J. L. (1989). Making text talk. *Theory into Practice, 28*(2), 136–141.

Malcolm, I., & Koscielecki, M. (1997). *Aboriginality and English: Report to the Australian research council*. Mount Lawley, Western Australia: Centre for Applied Language Research, Edith Cowan University.

Muhlhausler, P., & Rose, D. (1996). *Desert schools*. Darwin, AUS: Northern Territory University Press.

New South Wales Department of Education and Training (NSWDET). (1998a). *Basic skills tests 1998*. Sydney, AUS: NSW Department of Education and Training.

New South Wales Department of Education and Training. (NSWDET). (1998b). *Trial writing assessment 1998*. Sydney, AUS: NSW Department of Education and Training.

New South Wales Department of Education and Training (NSWDET). (2005a). *Year 3 basic skills test 2005*. Sydney, AUS: NSW Department of Education and Training.

New South Wales Department of Education and Training (NSWDET). (2005b). *Year 5 basic skills test 2005*. Sydney, AUS: NSW Department of Education and Training.

Pennycook, A. (1998). *English and the discourses of colonialism*. London, UK: Routledge.

Rose, D. (2010). *Reading to learn: Accelerating learning and closing the gap. Teacher training books and DVDs*. Sydney, AUS: Reading to learn. http://www.readingtolearn.com.au.

Rose, D., Gray, B., & Cowey, W. (1999). Scaffolding reading and writing for Indigenous children in school. In P. Wignell (Ed.), *Double power: English literacy and indigenous education* (pp. 23–60). Melbourne, AUS: The National Languages & Literacy Institute of Australia (NLLIA.

Scougall, J. (2008). *Lessons learnt about strengthening indigenous families and communities*. Occasional Paper No. 19 Retrieved from Australian Government: Department of Social Services. website https://www.dss.gov.au/sites/default/files/documents/op19.pdf.

Strevens, P. (1982 ). *What is Standard English?* (Occasional Paper No. 23). Singapore: SEAMEO Regional Language Centre.

Unsworth, L., & Chan, E. (2008). Assessing integrative reading of images and text in group reading comprehension tests. *Curriculum Perspectives, 28*(3), 71–76.

Vygotsky, L. (1962). *Thought and language*. Cambridge, MA: The MIT Press.

Wagga Network of Schools, New South Wales Department of Education. (n.d.). Home: 8 aboriginal ways of learning. Retrieved from http://8ways.wikispaces.com.

Wills, S., Lawrence, C., & Gray, B. (2006, July 8th–11th). *In the Zone: Moving from discomfort to confidence and improving literacy*. Paper presented at 2006 ALEA & AATE National Conference: Voices, Visions, Vibes, Darwin, NT, Australia. Published on CD-ROM.

Yunkaporta, T. (2009). *Aboriginal pedagogies at the cultural interface: Draft report for DET on Indigenous research project conducted by Jason Yunkaporta, Education Consultant, in Western NSW Region schools, 2007–2009*. Retrieved from Wagga Network of Schools. (n.d.). Aboriginal pedagogy research review website: https://8ways.wikispaces.com/Aboriginal+pedagogy+research+review.

**Dr. Ann Daly** taught in primary schools for 10 years and worked in literacy assessment for 10 years. She has since then conducted research in schools and evaluations of education programs in the state of NSW in Australia. In her MA in language and literacy, Ann's research comparing the writing results of students who did and did not use Aboriginal English in a state-wide test found that the average scores of speakers of Aboriginal English were lower on criteria that tested features of standard Australian English grammar that were different in the Aboriginal English dialect. In her PhD research, Ann compared and found a correlation between Aboriginal and non-Aboriginal students' complexity in their spoken language and comprehension of multimodal texts.

# PART V

# CHAPTER 11

# Beyond Culturally Responsive Pedagogy: Decolonizing Teacher Education

*Fran Martin, Fatima Pirbhai-Illich and Shauneen Pete*

## INTRODUCTION

This book is a project in criticality. In the introductory chapter, we set out an argument supporting what we identify as the need for teacher education to be decolonized. This was, in part, in response to our growing concern that culturally responsive pedagogy (CRP) as practiced in education was not having the desired effect. Drawing on our varying experiences of working with pre-service and in-service teachers, we have had many opportunities to reflect on two things. First, multicultural education and CRP, as taken up by white educators, often focuses on surface features and the needs of the "Other". This is a focus based on narrow understandings of culture, on deficit dispositions towards difference, and on the teacher self as an agent in changing the Other (e.g. minoritized students' academic achievement, and life chances). Second, our attempts to connect CRP to the more fundamental issue of white privilege (embodied in education systems, curricula, school structures, and the teaching profession), as a

F. Martin (✉)
University of Exeter, Exeter, United Kingdom
e-mail: Fran.Martin@exeter.ac.uk

F. Pirbhai-Illich · S. Pete
University of Regina, Regina, Saskatchewan, Canada
e-mail: Fatima.Pirbhai-Illich@uregina.ca; Shauneen.Pete@uregina.ca

© The Author(s) 2017                                                            235
F. Pirbhai-Illich et al. (eds.), *Culturally Responsive Pedagogy*,
DOI 10.1007/978-3-319-46328-5_11

means of decolonizing what we perceive to be the key barriers to success-ful implementation of CRP, is often met with resistance.

In this concluding chapter, we wish to make the case that CRP/relevant teaching is never going to be effective in the ways in which Gloria Ladson-Billings (1992, 1995) and Geneva Gay (2002, 2013) originally intended because it does not speak to mainstream educators in ways that are intelligible to them – much is "lost in translation". In the chapters of this book we see some of the reasons why CRP may not be intelligible and these are grouped together as four interconnected, ideas, or issues: CRP, by its very name, encourages a focus on the Other, albeit from a positive rather than deficit position; this enables teachers (who are, as established in Chapter 1, predominantly white European/European settler) to avoid facing their own whiteness and white privilege; it does not address the "epistemic blindness" (Andreotti 2016, p. 104) of whiteness and Eurocentric worldviews; and finally, it focuses on changing individual teachers' practices and does not address systemic and structural inequalities inherent in education systems which are a direct product of the colonial world system (Grosfoguel 2011).

In Chapter 1 we set out the reasons for calling the current world system "colonial" and showed how it is a totalizing system that has affected every aspect of society. We showed how Indigenous studies and research on minoritized students (Gillborn 2010) bring much needed perspectives to our understanding of the pervasive effect of colonialism over time, not least the ontological and epistemic violences that were perpetrated and which continue to be felt as collective trauma today (Cote-Meek 2014). We proposed that nothing short of radical change is needed, change that works at macro- and micro-levels from policies to practices, and whole systems to classroom relationships. This change is a transformative process of decolonization – a decolonization of minds (Dascal 2009) and, by default, a decolonization of the colonial world system:

> Decolonization, if it is to be successful as a reaction against such a deep, powerful, and long lasting colonization of the mind, cannot but be itself as radical as its opponent. It must, therefore, eradicate not only its surface manifestations and the concomitant "colonial system", but its epistemic roots as well. (Dascal 2009, p. 316)

For us, this means confronting whiteness and white privilege – turning the gaze 180 degrees towards those whose assumed normalcy and neutrality support their narratives of "doing good" while hiding from themselves their complicities in ontological and epistemological violences. In proposing this shift, we are cognizant of the danger that whites who reflect on their own whiteness may "centre the analysis on themselves and make the object of whiteness studies (the oppressive nature of white supremacy) more about the subjectivity of white people" (Preston 2013, p. 2). We agree that this is a very real danger *if* the decolonizing project is taken on by only whites, or only people of colour, or only Indigenous peoples. If the metaphor of a war is used, then the places of war are situated in the mind (the battleground), while the spaces in which the "fighting" is done are the third spaces between cultures, with the tools (the weapons) of intercultural communication and dialogue. In addition, "Since different knowledge practices take place on different spatial scales and according to different durations and rhythms, inter-subjectivity [between different knowledge systems] entails also the disposition to know and act in different scales (inter-scalarity) and articulate different durations (inter-temporality)" (De Sousa Santos 2007, p. 14).

Centring narratives of the marginalized, Indigenous, and people of colour is essential to the initial process of conscience and consciousness-raising among white, mainstream populations. This requires *critical* inter-culturality, which we discuss below.

## CRITICAL INTERCULTURALITY

The field of intercultural communication and understanding in the West is dominated by research in the United States (Bennett 1993; Bennett and Bennett 2004; Hammer et al. 2003; Deardorff 2006) and the United Kingdom (Byram 1997; Byram and Parmenter 2012). The work in the United States is a response to increasing globalization and the need for greater intercultural sensitivity and competence in, for example, commerce and education. In the United Kingdom, the research has been driven by the field of foreign language acquisition and an understanding that during their study abroad semesters, language students need to be interculturally competent. In both regions, although the emphasis is on individuals' levels of competence and sensitivity, this is framed within a neoliberal discourse of commodification and a culture of pragmatism (Gorski 2008) in the focus on categorization, assessment, and judgement on the one hand, and on the value ascribed to successful intercultural competence on the other. Bennett's (1993) work, built on by Hammer et al. (2003) and Deardorff (2006), created a developmental model of intercultural sensitivity in which individuals could be assessed against six categories from ethnocentrism to ethnorelativism, with movement from one category to the next being seen to be evolutionary/developmental. Byram's (1997) work focused on the knowledge, skills, and values necessary for successful intercultural *communicative* competence, bringing the role of language to the fore. Therefore, while there is a discourse of individual competence and sensitivity, these attributes are measured against categories and sets of competences with the assumption that it is (a) desirable to measure such things (i.e. to make judgements in order to assign people to categories) and (b) possible to do so. The second area of concern is that the value ascribed to successful intercultural competence within the west is, ironically, often couched within an ethnocentric discourse itself. Two examples serve to illustrate this point: first, that interculturalism as a dimension of international understanding is about securing a new form of imperialism in the World, for economic advantage (Kabir 2011, p. 47); second, in the context of international students studying in a Finnish university, intercultural competence centres on offering advice to international students that enables them to fit in – i.e. to take on Finnish ways of being (Dervin and Layne 2013).

In accordance with Dervin and Layne (2013), we view this as a further example of abyssal thinking and the pervasive effects of the colonial world system. De Sousa Santos (2007) shows how, with abyssal thinking, the debates about what counts as valid knowledge – objective and scientific versus existential and philosophical – are based on visible differences on one side of the abyss, while being ignorant and thus rendering invisible what is on the other side of the abyss. We interpret this, in the context of interculturality, as a debate over the differences in *perspective* about whether the emphasis becomes intercultural communication/intercultural competence/intercultural sensitivity/intercultural understanding/intercultural education. These perspectives may be informed from different knowledge communities, but their validity as acceptable forms of knowledge is not questioned. In other words, while the tensions between the various perspectives are visible in academic debate, this

> visibility is premised upon the invisibility of forms of knowledge that cannot be fitted into any of these ways of knowing. I mean popular, lay, plebeian, peasant, or [I]ndigenous knowledges on the other side of the line. They vanish as relevant or commensurable knowledges because they are beyond truth and falsehood. (De Sousa Santos 2007, p. 2)

Today as then, both the creation and the negation of the other side of the line is constitutive of hegemonic principles and practices. Today as then, the impossibility of co-presence between the two sides of the line runs supreme. Today as then, the legal and political civility on this side of the line is premised upon the existence of utter incivility on the other side of the line. (De Sousa Santos 2007, pp. 4–5)

If, as we contend, intercultural studies are inscribed with abyssal thinking, it needs to move not into a mode of anti-abyssal thinking (which would continue to be derived from abyssal lines), but into a mode of post-abyssal thinking which

> involves a radical break with modern Western ways of thinking and acting... to think in non-derivative terms means to think from the perspective of the other side of the line, precisely because the other side of the line has been the realm of the unthinkable in Western modernity. (De Sousa Santos 2007, p. 11)

We support this view as our own experiences testify to the ways in which white Europeans and European settlers appropriate knowledges (Grosfoguel 2011) from the other and create history in ways that erase the histories of others, leading to the disappearance of knowledge that is inconvenient (see Dussel 2012 for a discussion of Muslim culture in Spain prior to the "conquest" of America), and the construction of knowledge that is more convenient, for example, the "knowledge" that has been created about Muslims as a homogenized, fundamentalist group since 9/11 (Kabir 2011).

A post-abyssal interculturality would therefore need to be founded on ontologies and epistemologies that are unthinkable; a *critical* interculturality that requires centring the knowledges of southern, Indigenous, and other marginalized peoples by those communities and their allies, and which then is negotiated interculturally. It also requires the creation of spaces for interaction and dialogue that address "structural inequalities, unequal power relations and discrimination" (James 2008, p. 13).

In the remainder of this chapter we connect the themes that have emerged in Chapters 2–10 to our own intercultural experiences. Our aim is to make explicit the process of connecting the authors' practices in CRP to the theories introduced in Chapter 1, and how the interplay between the two enabled us to extend theory and to consider the

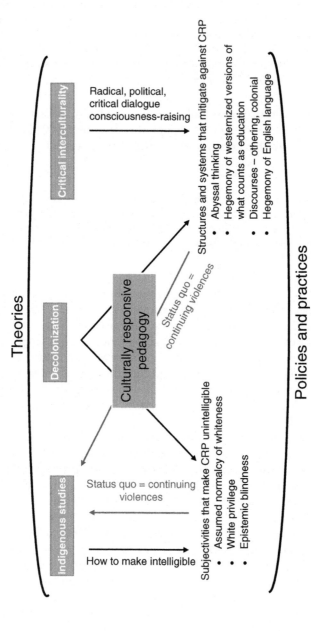

**Fig. 11.1** Theorizing issues in policies and practices that mitigate against CRP

Copyright 2016 by Martin & Pirbhai-Illich

implications for teacher education. In the weaving of theory with practice we pay particular attention to the ways in which our colleagues attempted to create spaces for post-abyssal thinking, and the barriers to this that they identified. We have structured this discussion under two headings: structures and systems that mitigate against CRP, and subjectivities that make CRP unintelligible (Fig. 11.1).

## STRUCTURES AND SYSTEMS THAT MITIGATE AGAINST CRP

Four themes were consistently identified creating barriers to the learning of marginalized students in the chapters – although not necessarily using the same language: (1) abyssal (or colonial) thinking; (2) the hegemony of westernized versions of what counts as education; (3) discourses of marginalization and othering; and (4) the hegemony of the English language. These macro-level issues are examples of the divisive effect of the colonial world system and serve as the context for the issues in practices discussed in the section that follows.

Macro-level issues require macro-level solutions and, as argued above, nothing short of radical change to current education systems will suffice. Education policy, schools, and national curricula are three areas written through with hegemonic discourses and we focus on these as potential spaces for radical change.

All of the chapters in Sections 2–4 provide evidence of the damning effect of abyssal thinking and how it has created a hegemony of what counts as education, of how education policy, schools, and curricula are centred on White European and European settler ways of being and knowing, and of how this marginalizes and erases alternative ways of being and knowing: "a massive epistemicide has been under way for the past five centuries, whereby an immense wealth of cognitive experiences has been wasted" (De Sousa Santos 2007, p. 16). The use of English as "world language" is a prime example of the processes by which those who gain most from abyssal thinking retain their hegemonic position. These processes are evident at all phases from primary (Ford, Austin, and Daly) and secondary (King and Joyce) to higher education (Jabbar and Mirza; Pete; and Tinker Sachs et al.), in curricula (King and Joyce) and assessment materials (Austin and Daly), and in partnerships with communities (Blair and Ford).

What is illuminating is that, even in those chapters that focus more explicitly on structures and systems that support abyssal thinking, their solutions have focused on partial rather than systemic change. For example, Jabbar and Mirzar (Chapter 2) argue for epistemological change, "mainstream academic knowledge needs to become more responsive in the creation and production of knowledge", but then focus on individual teacher choices about pedagogy and curriculum rather than radical changes at faculty/university level; equally, Austin (Chapter 9) and Daly (Chapter 10) suggest changes in the cultural contexts for math and literacy assessments, but do not query that English is the language in which assessments are conducted. We do not criticize the authors, but highlight this as an issue that is facing us all – that the hegemony of neoliberal, colonial, westernized ways of doing education has become so dominant that it is difficult to imagine "other possible worlds" (Andreotti 2016, p. 105).

Between two fundamentally different positions, such as western knowledge and Indigenous knowledge, "there are those who defend that there are not one but many philosophies and believe that mutual dialogue and enrichment is possible. They are the ones who often have to confront the problems of incommensurability, incompatibility, or reciprocal unintelligibility" (De Sousa Santos 2007, p. 16). However, De Sousa Santos (2007) goes on to argue that this does not mean that communication is impossible. Communication may lead to "unsuspected forms of complementarity" depending on "the use of adequate procedures of intercultural translation" (De Sousa Santos 2007, p. 16). This chimes with our own discussions about the risk in suggesting radical changes to systems, that the messages are unintelligible to precisely those audiences for whom they are intended. In one conversation, we spoke of the challenge of expecting white pre-service teachers to care for others – that this is not something that can be forced on them. We also agreed that it is not that they do not care, but that they care in ways that are *laden with color blindness, and laden with not taking on difficult topics.* In addition to this, we gave examples of how their pre-service teachers often avoid listening to the voices of the marginalized students in their classrooms because they can't relate to the stories of poverty, hunger and trauma.

An ethics of care is taken up by Blair in Chapter 5 where she discusses her own position in relation to the Brazilian street children with whom she is working. Hers is a reflexive moral standpoint, but there is an assumption that it is possible to care in the ways she outlines that we trouble here. What it means to care has been the subject of discussion in many fields (Gilligan 1982; Held 2005; Noddings 2003) and theorized within the western academy largely from feminist, and philosophical/ethical perspectives in the contexts of motherhood, international relations, and political theory. For the purposes of this discussion we focus on how "care" is construed from different ontological and epistemological positions, and from particular ideological perspectives. Ontologically and epistemologically, notions of care are just as subject to the effects of abyssal thinking as any other area of life. De Sousa Santos (2007) argues that, in the colonial world system that is capitalism, there has been a withdrawal of the state "from social regulation.... as public services are privatized" (p. 7). The result is that services delivered by non-state actors are free of some of the regulations that constrained the state – not least that services could become a commercial enterprise. Even in those companies that are not commercial (e.g. International Non-Governmental Organizations [INGOs]), they are still subject to a value for money discourse. In effect, the constitutional state is being "replaced by privatized, depoliticized contractual obligations under which the weaker party is more or less at the mercy of the stronger one" (De Sousa Santos 2007, p. 7).

The dual ideologies of neoliberalism and liberalism coexist in this structure, evident in the commodification of care on the one hand, and the increase in charitable activities on the other. The place of charity in society brings with it a discourse of deficit, pity, and paternalism with regard to the recipients, and a discourse of benevolence, self-worth, and exceptionalism (Andreotti 2016) with regard to the donors/caregivers. The rise of charitable fundraising through, for example, television and social media platforms has created a discourse of what it means to care that is so pervasive that it makes it hard to imagine other modes of care, and when those other modes call into question the modes that charities and individuals are heavily invested in, they become unintelligible. This presents a challenge to educators such as the authors in this book, because their work requires "the softening of edges if one wants to be effective in inviting people into conversations where their self-image and world views will likely not be affirmed", and a recognition that "pedagogical possibilities are circumscribed by constraints of intelligibility, educational desires and investments, institutional mandates and availability and attention of learners" (Andreotti 2016, p. 107).

If we return to the example of Blair, she is married to a Brazilian who is part of a group who established the charity for street children, and so she is heavily invested in needing to unpack her white privilege and westernized modes of care. This is not the case for those who are heavily invested in the privileges afforded to them by westernized education systems. Care features strongly in the reasons that teachers give for entering into the profession. The pre-service teachers we work with, when first confronted with knowledge that calls their view of care into question, they don't want to believe it. Fatima has discussed the notion of "innocent racism" in an earlier paper (Pirbhai-Illich et al. 2011, p. 28), while others have referred to it as the "luxury of ignorance" (Howard 2007, p. 6). This ignorance is sanctioned by the current world order, the colonial world system. But if the continuing cycle of ontological and epistemological violence (Fanon 1967) from one generation to the next is to be disrupted, sanctioned ignorance is no longer an option. We go beyond this to argue that through the K-12 and higher education systems there is *pedagogical* violence that is being perpetrated against marginalized students, because the teaching approaches that are used, the way in which classrooms are set up, how the days are structured, who is seen to be the holder of knowledge, and the pedagogies that flow from that are also colonial.

These hegemonic, violent ways of "doing school" have to be disrupted, and it is that disruption that Tinker Sachs et al. (Chapter 4), King (Chapter 6), and Ford (Chapter 8) aim to achieve through the expansion of what counts as a classroom space and an education pedagogy. Through partnerships with community groups (Chapters 4 and 8), what counts as *knowledge* is opened up; through educating in the community, *where* education might take place is opened up; and through using Indigenous approaches of song and drum with young people, what counts as *pedagogy* is opened up. They achieve differing levels of success, but we argue that they are extending understandings of CRP and moving towards something that might be post-abyssal.

Another form of correction to violence is in the centring of other languages as a direct challenge to the hegemony of English, such as the use of Māori metaphors by Joyce (Chapter 7). In discussing how cognitive experiences lost through colonialism might be recuperated, De Sousa Santos (2007) proposes an ecology of knowledges which necessarily require "intercultural translation" (p. 16) in order to relate to each other. "Embedded in different Western and non–Western cultures, such experiences use not only different languages but also different categories, symbolic universes, and aspirations for a better life" (De Sousa Santos 2007, p. 16). It is with this in mind that we have discussed at length what term we might use to encompass what we see as being beyond CRP, a radical post-abyssal pedagogy that moves us towards decolonization, indigeneity, and critical interculturalism. We discussed concepts from other cultures, such as "Ubuntu" from South Africa, "manacihitowin" from the Cree people, and "Ujamaa" from Tanzania. But none seem to cover all of the elements that we are now proposing should be used to extend CRP. So although all the authors in this book have used the term CRP, we believe that this no longer describes what is being done through their practices. As discussed earlier, the term culturally responsive is commonly interpreted from a mainstream, multicultural perspective, as teachers needing to be responsive to the cultures of *others* while continuing to be ignorant of their own culture and how it is bound up with white privilege and superiority. It is to the issue of whiteness and the "epistemic blindness" (Andreotti 2016, p. 104) that comes with it that we now turn.

## Subjectivities That Make CRP Unintelligible

In my practice as an educator and educational researcher in this area, the greatest challenge I face is indeed one of intelligibility. (Andreotti 2016, p. 105)

A single theme dominates the chapters in their identification of barriers to successful implementation of CRP, that of whiteness and white privilege. Despite the availability of well-known tools such as that by Peggy McIntosh (1988) on unearned privilege which raises white students' awareness of the privileges afforded to them on a daily basis that are invisible to them, the issue of whiteness continues to have a profound impact on people of colour, diaspora populations, and Indigenous peoples. Without addressing the issue of whiteness, education will continue to produce future citizens who (if they are also white) may continue to be ignorant of their whiteness and racism, and who (if they are marginalized) continue to be othered.

Lund and Carr (2013) identify the following problems associated with whiteness: that it is racist, that it carries an assumed normalcy as *the* way of being leading to deficit theorizing about difference, that it carries with it a superiority and certainty leading to blindness to other ways of being, and that it is individualistic and that it reaps unearned privileges. Our experiences of working with white pre-service teachers testify to this

(Pirbhai-Illich et al. 2011; Pete, Chapter 3). The assumed normalcy of whiteness and white culture renders it invisible to them and makes it possible for them to say,

"This is irrelevant to me", "I may have classes where most of my kids will just be like me, so why should I need to learn how to be culturally responsive?" And if we are saying being culturally responsive is to be <u>inter</u>cultural, then they'll say, "But I don't have any culture to be intercultural with." (Pirbhai-Illich, Pete, & Martin, editors' discussion, May 2016)

The issue of being cultureless is one thing, but the impact of this on minoritized and marginalized groups is, as we have argued, violent and traumatic. The work for pre-service and in-service teachers of decolonizing their ways of being and doing is an absolute necessity. This is a responsibility held by teachers (Chapters 5–8) and teacher educators (Chapters 2–4, 9, 10).

It is our contention that the majority of teachers have been socialized into a teacher ontology that is written through with colonialism. This conclusion is inescapable if one subscribes to the view that we are in a colonial world system. It is therefore essential to do the work of decolonizing the mind (Thiong'o 1986), and it means facing the discomfort of truths that white people have been protected from. We described this earlier as turning the gaze 180 degrees. CRP, in the way in which it has been taken up, encourages teachers to move from deficit theorizing to working with, and honouring their students' cultural funds of knowledge. This needs to be turned 180 towards members of the dominant group who have to examine the deficits that they carry for themselves, deficits that *"are evident in their discomfort, their anger, guilt and shame"* (Pirbhai-Illich, Pete, & Martin, editors' discussion, May 2016).

There is no shortage of examples of anger, guilt, and shame in the book. For example, Blair talks about her own guilt and anxiety in relation to the poverty she experiences in Brazil, which moves to a fear of reproducing coloniality in her relations with the street children – a move that only happens through her openness to new knowledges, to questioning her identity and to letting go of old investments through a process of "hyper-self-reflexivity" (Andreotti 2011, p. 17). Tinker Sachs et al., and Joyce, in their chapters, discuss how they worked with teachers in decolonial ways and the challenges faced by those teachers as they became aware of their subjectivities and positionalities – and in both chapters there are examples of teachers' self-denials. These denials are vividly brought to life in the opening of King's chapter, expressed often as direct hostility to the "otherness" of song and drum that has been brought into their school. The teachers in King's chapter are examples of those who do not wish to develop another way of relating to difference other than the one they have been socialized into.

The denial of possibilities of other ways to be as teachers, and that other knowledges have a place in the curriculum is connected to the barrier of what we call "teacher ontology". Pre-service teachers do not come to teacher education programs devoid of knowledge of what it means to be a teacher. They have, in effect, served an apprenticeship through their years as school students themselves (Martin 2008).

> Thus, they enter teacher education already knowing and believing a great deal about the field, and assuming they know a lot about teaching (Richert 1991). According to Lampert and Ball (1998), student teachers, therefore, believe that what they need to learn during their teacher education is what to do, not to think or reflect on what they are seeing or hearing.... as the classroom is a well-known arena, it is difficult for prospective teachers to consider alternative visions and ways of teaching. (Moen 2006, 65)

Again, it is an issue of unintelligibility. Pre-service teachers are not disposed to question what it means to be a teacher in the same way they might if they were entering a less known profession (Moen 2006). Laid onto this is the problem of socialized colonial identity, which they are also not disposed to question. It is for this reason that we propose that there is no other way forward than to disrupt whiteness and white dominance, colonialism, and all that goes with it. This presents a huge challenge for teacher education and we do not underestimate the task.

## BEYOND CRP: DECOLONIZING TEACHER EDUCATION

In this final section we offer some thoughts on the processes that for us show potential to move beyond CRP towards a radical, decolonizing pedagogy in teacher education. We repeat that *this book is a project in criticality* and therefore we are not going to provide a set of principles, a blueprint, or a recipe to follow. To propose something that is already formed in such a way would be to fall foul of the essentializing, totalizing discourses that we critique. As evidenced in the preceding chapters, there is no one way of going beyond CRP towards something that is decolonial.

> Any…movement is going to be necessarily unique to each area, to its nations, to the colonial encounters in its territory, because context with colonialism has not been all alike, and these diverse histories and experiences would need to be addressed. Decolonising these spaces…is also not a linear and tidy process. Rather, as in the case of making universities responsive to Indigenous peoples, women, minorities, or diverse knowledge systems, the sites of struggle for recognition, acceptance, and integration were going to require collaborative, interdisciplinary, participatory, and Indigenous research methodologies to decolonize educational institutions. (Battiste 2013, p. 111)

Every teacher educator, teacher, and class of students will be unique, and the solutions that are found for those situations will need to be co-created to suit the specificity of their contexts. *And* solutions will also need to place the contexts into the broader sociopolitical and historical forces that have influenced them. What we *do* have is an agenda – one of decolonizing teacher education (Tables 11.1 and 11.2). In this agenda we do not negate CRP and the pedagogies associated with it; we argue that given that the majority of teachers in the West are from white, mainstream backgrounds, unless a decolonization of minds written through with whiteness is done first then CRP is seriously undermined. In this agenda, we also do not set out clear goals and objectives; it is an agenda based on a "logic of emergence" (Osberg 2008, p.144) in that we do not have a clear end point – this will emerge because it is currently unimaginable (Andreotti 2016). Our agenda has a pedagogical dimension and addresses the teacher education system as a whole. Colonialism is a process, not an act (De Sousa Santos 2007) so we also need to decolonize the structures, knowledge systems, and institutional processes that support the status quo. This includes working with teacher educators, administrators, relevant government bodies, funding bodies, librarians, and so on, to critically examine the content of teacher education (curricular, resources) and the processes (procedures, pedagogies, assessment practices) by which teachers are prepared to enter the profession.

At the macro-level we identified four key, interconnected, themes each of which brings a series of issues that need to be addressed through this decolonial project: (1) abyssal thinking – which divides the world and makes "Otherness" impossible as a way of being and doing; (2) the

**Table 11.1** Addressing issues in systems and structures

| | Systems and structures | | |
|---|---|---|---|
| Barriers | Issue | Agenda | Processes and dispositions |
| Abyssal thinking | Divides the world and makes "otherness" impossible as a way of being | Decolonize the whole system – policies, curriculum, administrative structures, funding mechanisms; addresses institutional racism | Radical change – minds, discourses, and systems as the battleground; critical interculturality using post-abyssal thinking and decolonizing processes as the weapons; commitment to withdrawing allegiance to hegemonies and abyssal thinking; pedagogy of **solidarity**; Ethical relation: Inter-faith, inter-cultural, inter-disciplinary, inter-agency, inter-... |
| Hegemony of European version of education | Suits students from mainstream backgrounds; individualistic; disadvantages/ perpetrates violence on others | | |
| Othering discourses | Often hidden under rhetoric of liberalism, inclusion, care, and responsibility – hard to think or be otherwise; renders otherness unintelligible to mainstream | | |
| Hegemony of English language | Represents the world using a language system developed through colonialism | | |

*Note*: Copyright 2016 by Martin, Pirbhai-Illich and Pete

hegemony of westernized education – which suits students from mainstream backgrounds, and fails/traumatizes students from marginalized communities; (3) othering discourses – which are often hidden under a rhetoric of liberalism, inclusion, care, and responsibility making it both hard to imagine otherwise and rendering Otherness unintelligible to the mainstream; and (4) the hegemony of the English language – which represents the world using a symbolic system developed through colonialism. Our agenda here is both simple and complex. It is simply to decolonize the whole system – policies, curriculum, administrative structures, and funding mechanisms. It is complex because of the enormity of the task, the processes that are involved, and the risks that are inherent for marginalized peoples in any call for them to work with the very people who subjugated them in the first place. In this

**Table 11.2**   Addressing issues in practices

| | Practices | | |
|---|---|---|---|
| Barriers | Issue | Agenda | Processes and dispositions |
| Whiteness<br><br>White privilege<br><br>Epistemic blindness | Not seen as racial category; assumed normalcy; racist Invisible to whites; creates inequalities; individualistic Own way of being is considered to be the only way of being; denial or minimization of difference | Awareness raising; make visible the histories of peoples who have been subjugated over centuries; ethical accountability; relational responsibility; expand notions of culture beyond race and ethnicity; awareness of dispositions towards difference | Anti-racist; commitment to work on decolonizing "self"; hyper self-reflexivity; humility; learning from the other as a gift; letting go of old investments and investing in new ways of being; expanding repertoires |

*Note*: Copyright 2016 by Martin, Pirbhai-Illich and Pete

radical agenda, the minds, discourses, and systems are the ground on which the decolonizing project will be enacted, where critical intercultural dialogue using post-abyssal thinking will be the tools. As we have already pointed out, this is not a project that can be achieved by any one group – it must involve the voices and experiences of the diaspora, the colonized, Indigenous peoples, and European colonizers/settler colonizers. For those from mainstream groups who might be initially involved, the work requires them to commit to withdrawing allegiance to hegemonies and abyssal thinking, to developing an ethical relational responsibility (Wilson 2001; Swanson 2009) with the Other, and to work as allies with them in solidarity.

The concept of solidarity has been used in many ways with many connotations, so we set out here what we understand by the term. Gaztambide-Fernández (2012) explores the concept of solidarity, showing it to stem in part from Freire (2000) who described it as an inextricable relation between the oppressor and the oppressed. The relation is at the heart of what we propose as critical interculturality. Solidarity can be shown at a human, social, political, or civic level (Gaztambide-Fernández 2012), and it is associated with a moral obligation, a sense of mutual responsibility, and an ethic of reciprocity. The danger of social, political, civic (and we would add global) solidarity is that "it always operates in tension with [the] logics of domination" (Gaztambide-Fernández 2012, p. 47). Any form of solidarity therefore needs to break with the past, to be non-normative and non-hierarchical, to hinge not on similarities but on radical differences, on "relationships of incommensurable interdependency" (Gaztambide-Fernández 2012, p. 46), to have an orientation not of *doing to* but of *being with*, and it needs to be clear about who has a moral obligation to whom. This might be an ethical, relational foundation for a post-abyssal decolonizing project.

At the micro-level – that of working with pre-service and in-service teachers in teacher education – we identified (a) whiteness, (b) white privilege, and (c) the epistemic blindness that flows from that as the key themes. Our agenda therefore also focuses on decolonizing the spaces and places within which teacher education is enacted – that is, on decolonizing the mind (Thiong'o 1986). Whiteness and white privilege are either invisible to the mainstream, denied, or resisted by them. Associated with this is the racism that is also denied. People from dominant groups have a lot to lose and, as DiAngelo (2011) points out, they often develop defensive discourses of victimization that enable them to avoid the discomfort of owning up to their responsibility for, and complicity in, "the racial power and privilege they wield" (p. 64). Raising awareness of whiteness has to be the starting point (see, e.g., Andreotti's (2016) HEADS UP tool, pp. 107–109) from which to then disrupt the colonial socialized teacher ontology by moving away from questions such as *what or how will you teach?* to questions of "Who is the self that teaches? How does that quality of my selfhood form – or deform – the way I relate to my students, my subject, my colleagues, my world?" (Sapp 2013, p. 200). This awareness raising has to go hand in hand with making visible the histories of peoples who have been subjugated over the centuries, with notions of culture that are expanded beyond race and ethnicity, and with an understanding of the colonial world system. Expanded notions of culture, the concept of multiple identities, and culture as something that is fluid and constantly in the making are not new, but these are still rooted in the colonial world system with an idée fixe (Bhabha 1994). Gaztambide-Fernández (2012) rejects the idea of multiple cultures and identities and instead proposes that there are multiple ways, multiple spaces, and places in which cultures are made, and this can only happen through encounters with difference.

The spaces of teacher education are precisely those where difference is encountered. The types of relationships that are created in these spaces need to be based on an understanding that people's cultural identities are made in and through relationships. To break with abyssal ways of relating requires a break from thinking it is possible to know the other "since the other is, according to Levinas, 'infinitely unknowable'" (Gaztambide-Fernández 2012, p. 52). This is a further area where we depart from CRP, where one of the tenets is based on teachers getting to know about the cultures of diverse groups they are working with so as to positively utilize their funds of knowledge (Gay 2002, 2013). Aside from the practicalities, this is based on the assumption that it is possible to know the Other despite all one's subjectivities. We propose that, alongside developing awareness of whiteness, it would be productive to develop awareness of one's dispositions towards difference and how these relate to one's subjectivities. Andreotti (2013) identifies four dispositions: the first is a refusal to engage with difference; the other three are different dispositions towards engaging with difference that are objectivist, relativist, and plural (p. 13). She uses the idea of dispositions (plural) because its meaning is contingent. A disposition is an inclination towards, a tendency, and an emotional outlook; in the plural it suggests that a person can have several dispositions towards the same thing, but that the prevailing one may vary according to the circumstances. They differ from "competencies" approach to interculturality

> in that they do not bring with them guaranteed behavioural patterns. . . . we carry all of these dispositions (and many others) with us at any time. Thus, when we face a concrete encounter with difference . . . we tend to manifest a combination of dispositions. (Andreotti 2013, p. 13)

We find the use of metaphor and dispositions helpful, as they are not offered "as progressive stages but rather as different positions, all of which might be appropriate in particular contexts[,] [i]n order to genuinely enlarge possibilities for learning" (Andreotti 2013, p. 13). This is not about developing them or even *a* way of relating, but of increasing repertoires for responding to difference.

We would like to conclude by considering the work that needs to be done by those towards whom these ways forward are intended – the pre-service and in-service teachers, the education policy-makers, the teacher educators, the librarians, administrators, and managers, who are from mainstream backgrounds or who have been socialized into mainstream ways of being and doing education. This work requires a commitment: a commitment to discomfort, a commitment to questioning oneself and one's identity, a commitment to engagement with difficult truths and alternative histories, a commitment to developing ethical relations with the Other, a commitment to being taught in unexpected ways in unexpected situations by unexpected people, a commitment to seeing learning from the Other as a gift, a commitment to critical and hyper self-reflexivity, a commitment to letting go of investments that support unearned privileges, and a commitment to investing in new ways of being and doing. For the privileged, a suspension of the ego that has developed over centuries (as the trauma experienced by subjugated peoples has been felt over the centuries) and a disposition of humility in relation to the learning relationships is essential when thinking about how to change the colonial self and to develop a new way of relating with the Other. For the subjugated, these commitments may be the beginning of a new relationship in which the trust, destroyed through colonialism, might gradually re-emerge. For both, this is a journey into the unknown and currently unimaginable, but,

> What unimagined and unimaginable outcomes might become available if we were willing to risk the possibility that we simply do not know where we are going? (Gaztambide-Fernández 2012, p. 55)

## References

Andreotti, V. (2011). *Actionable postcolonial theory in education*. London, UK: Palgrave Macmillan.

Andreotti, V. (2013, Spring). Taking minds to other places. *Primary Geography*, 2(80), 12–13.

Andreotti, V. (2016). The educational challenges of imagining the world differently. *Canadian Journal of Development Studies/Revue Canadienne D'études Du Développement*, 37(1), 101–112.

Battiste, M. (2013). *Decolonizing education: Nourishing the learning spirit*. Saskatoon, SK, CAN: Purich Publishing.

Bennett, J. M., & Bennett, M. J. (2004). An integrative approach to global and domestic diversity. In D. Landis, J. M. Bennett, & M. J. Bennett (Eds.), *Handbook of intercultural training* (3rd ed., pp. 147–165,). Thousand Oaks, CA: SAGE.

Bennett, M. J. (1993). Towards ethnorelativism: A developmental model of intercultural sensitivity. In R. M. Paige (Ed.), *Education for the intercultural experience* (2nd ed., pp. 1–51). Yarmouth, ME: Intercultural Press.

Bhabha, H. K. (1994). *The location of culture* (2nd ed.). London, UK: Routledge.
Byram, M. (1997). *Teaching and assessing intercultural communicative competence.* Clevedon, UK: Multilingual Matters.
Byram, M., & Parmenter, L. (Eds.). (2012). *The common European framework of reference: The globalisation of language education policy.* Bristol, UK: Multilingual Matters.
Cote-Meek, S. (2014). *Colonized Classrooms: Racism, trauma and resistance in post-secondary education.* Black Point, NS, CAN: Fernwood Publishing.
Dascal, M. (2009). Colonizing and decolonizing minds. In I. Kuçuradi (Ed.), *Papers of the 2007 World Philosophy Day* (pp. 308–332). Ankara, TU: Philosophical Society of Turkey.
De Sousa Santos, B. (2007, June 29). Beyond abyssal thinking: From global lines to ecologies of knowledges. *Eurozine*, (pp. 1–33). Retrieved from http://www.eurozine.com/articles/.
Deardorff, D. K. (2006). Assessing intercultural competence in study abroad students. In M. Byram & A. Feng (Eds.), *Living and studying abroad: Research and practice* (pp. 232–256). Clevedon, UK: Multilingual Matters.
Dervin, F., & Layne, A. (2013). A guide to interculturality for international and exchange students: An example of hospitality? *Journal of Multicultural Discourses, 8*(1), 1–19.
DiAngelo, R. (2011). White fragility. *International Journal of Critical Pedagogy, 3*(3), 54–70.
Dussel, E. D. (2012). Transmodernity and interculturality: An interpretation from the perspective of philosophy of liberation. *Transmodernity: Journal of Peripheral Cultural Production of the Luso-Hispanic World, 1*(3), 28–59.
Fanon, F. (1967). *Black skin, white masks (original French ed., 1952).* New York, NY: Grove Press.
Freire, P. (2000). *Pedagogy of the oppressed* 30th Anniversary ed., M. Bergman Ramos, Trans.. New York, NY: Continuum. (Original work published 1968).
Gay, G. (2002). Preparing for culturally responsive teaching. *Journal of Teacher Education, 53*(2), 106–116.
Gay, G. (2013). Teaching to and through cultural diversity. *Curriculum Inquiry, 43*(1), 48–70.
Gaztambide-Fernández, R. A. (2012). Decolonization and the pedagogy of solidarity. *Decolonization: Indigeneity, Education & Society, 1*(1), 41–67.
Gillborn, D. (2010). Reform, racism and the centrality of whiteness: Assessment, ability and the 'new eugenics'. *Irish Educational Studies, 29*(3), 231–252.
Gilligan, C. (1982). *In a different voice: Psychological theory and women's development.* Cambridge, MA: Harvard University Press.
Gorski, P. C. (2008). Good intentions are not enough: A decolonizing intercultural education. *Intercultural Education, 19*(6), 515–525.

Grosfoguel, R. (2011). Decolonizing post-colonial studies and paradigms of political-economy: Transmodernity, decolonial thinking, and global coloniality. *Transmodernity: Journal of Peripheral Cultural Production of the Luso-Hispanic World*, *1*(1), 1–37.

Hammer, M. R., Bennett, M. J., & Wiseman, R. (2003). Measuring intercultural sensitivity: The intercultural development inventory. *International Journal of Intercultural Relations*, *27*(4), 421–443.

Held, V. (2005). *The ethics of care: Personal, political, and global*. New York, NY: Oxford University Press.

Howard, G. R. (2007). Dispositions for good teaching. *Journal of Educational Controversy*, *2*(2), 1–6.

James, M. (2008). *Interculturalism: Theory and policy*. London, UK: The Baring Foundation.

Kabir, A. H. (2011). A new discourse of "international understanding": Nothing but "Americanism". *Critical Literacy: Theories and Practices*, *5*(1), 38–50.

Ladson-Billings, G. (1992). Culturally relevant teaching: The key to making multicultural education work. In C. A. Grant (Ed.), *Research and multicultural education* (pp. 106–121). London, UK: The Falmer Press.

Ladson-Billings, G. (1995). But that's just good teaching! The case for culturally relevant pedagogy. *Theory Into Practice*, *34*(3), 159–165.

Lampert, M., & Ball, D. L. (1998). *Teaching, multimedia, and mathematics*. New York: Teachers College Press.

Lund, D. E., & Carr, P. R. (2013). Disrupting denial and white privilege in teacher education. In P. C. Gorski, K. Zenkov, N. Osei-Kofi, & J. Sapp (Eds.), *Cultivating social justice teachers: How teacher educators have helped students overcome cognitive bottlenecks and learn critical social justice concepts* (pp. 108–125). Sterling, VA: Stylus.

Martin, F. (2008). Ethnogeography: Towards liberatory geography education. *Children's Geographies*, *6*(4), 437–450.

McIntosh, P. (1988). *White privilege and male privilege: A personal account of coming to see correspondences through work in women's studies*. Working Paper No. 189 Wellesley, MA: Center for Research on Women, Wellesley College. Retrieved from http://eric.ed.gov/?id=ED335262.

Moen, T. (2006). Reflections on the narrative research approach. *International Journal of Qualitative Methods*, *5*(4), 56–69.

Noddings, N. (2003). *Happiness and education*. Cambridge, UK: Cambridge University Press.

Osberg, D. (2008). The logic of emergence: An alternative conceptual space for theorizing critical education. *Journal of the Canadian Association for Curriculum Studies*, *6*(1), 133–162.

Pirbhai-Illich, F., Austin, T., Paugh, P., & Farriño, Y. (2011). Responding to "innocent" racism: Educating teachers in politically reflexive and dialogic engagement in local communities. *Journal of Urban Learning, Teaching and Research (JULTR)*, 7, 27–40.

Preston, J. (2013). *Whiteness in academia: Counter-stories of betrayal and resistance*. Newcastle upon Tyne, UK: Cambridge Scholars Publishing.

Richert, A. (1991). Case methods and teacher education: Using cases to teach teacher reflection. In B. R. Tabachnich & K. Zeichner (Eds.), *Issues and practices in inquiry-oriented teacher education* (pp. 130–150). London: Falmer.

Sapp, J. (2013). "You're going to hell!" When critical multicultural queer affirmation meets Christian homophobia. In P. C. Gorski, K. Zenkov, N. Osei-Kofi, & J. Sapp (Eds.), *Cultivating social justice teachers: How teacher educators have helped students overcome cognitive bottlenecks and learn critical social justice concepts* (pp. 184–203). Sterling, VA: Stylus.

Swanson, D. M. (2009). Where have all the fishes gone? Living Ubuntu as an ethics of research and pedagogical engagement. In D. M. Caracciolo & A. M. Mungai (Eds.), *In the spirit of Ubuntu: Stories of teaching and research* (pp. 3–22). Rotterdam, The Netherlands: Sense Publishers.

Thiong'o, N. W. (1986). *Decolonizing the mind: The politics of language in African literature*. Nairobi, KE: East African Educational Publishers.

Wilson, S. (2001). What is indigenous research methodology?. *Canadian Journal of Native Education*, 25(2), 175–179.

**Fran Martin** University of Exeter, works in Initial Teacher Education. Her research interests are global education and intercultural learning. From 2009 to 2013 she worked with researchers in The Gambia and India on a project titled: "Global Partnerships as Sites for Mutual Learning". She is currently researching with colleagues in Canada and China.

**Dr. Fatima Pirbhai-Illich** is an associate professor and chair of the Language and Literacy Education Department in the Faculty of Education at the University of Regina, Saskatchewan. Fatima has taught initial and in-service teachers in various parts of the world. Her community-based interest and research focuses on critical multicultural literacy education for marginalized and disenfranchised youth.

**Dr. Shauneen Pete** is a Nehiyaw (Cree) woman from Little Pine First Nation, Saskatchewan. She is associate professor, Faculty of Education (University of Regina). She served as Vice-President (Academic) and Interim President at First Nations University of Canada. She is a teacher educator and served as the Executive Lead: Indigenization at her university.

# INDEX

© The Author(s) 2017
F. Pirbhai-Illich et al. (eds.), *Culturally Responsive Pedagogy*,
DOI 10.1007/978-3-319-46328-5

Printed by Printforce, the Netherlands